AN ANNOTATED CHECK-LIST
OF THE
BIRDS OF ILLINOIS

by

H. David Bohlen

Illinois State Museum
Popular Science Series, Vol. IX

Illinois State Museum
Springfield, Illinois
1978

ISSN 0360-0297   ISBN 0-89792-071-6
Printed by authority of the State of Illinois
(P.O. 6979—2M—8-78)

This Check-list is dedicated to

William V. O'Brien

who has spent over half a century
watching and studying the birds of Illinois.

4-07

19 ᵛ⦿ 12

15

POPULAR SCIENCE SERIES

TABLE OF CONTENTS

PREFACE

Ludlow Griscom (1922) had four rules for becoming a good field ornithologist, the first and most important of which was to "learn by heart the published information on the birds in your locality." Intended for those interested in studying birds in Illinois, this check-list is an attempt to bring together in concise form the known distributional information on all species of birds which have been found in the state to date. Not since "A Distributional Check List of the Birds of Illinois" by Harry R. Smith and Paul W. Parmalee (*Illinois State Museum Popular Science Series*, Vol. IV, 1955) has a comprehensive record of the birds of Illinois been published. The present check-list (*Illinois State Museum Popular Science Series*, Vol. IX) includes new information derived from reports since that time and from further study of previous records. This report is mainly qualitative; for a more detailed work on bird populations in Illinois, see Graber and Graber (1963).

The status of bird populations as determined here represents the species in Illinois at the present time, providing a reference point with which a comparison can be made should the status change. It is hoped that the student of birds will use this check-list not only to determine when, where, and what birds are present but also to make comparisons so that he can help clarify or rectify the status of the avifauna of Illinois. It is hoped also that this check-list might encourage regional studies (particularly by counties) and that these studies be quantified by some means.

In this era of rapid environmental change, there must be baseline studies of bird populations so that critical reductions of certain species can be detected early. Several current trends are decimating bird populations either directly or indirectly by elimination of the birds themselves or destruction of their habitats. If the avian diversity which Illinoians have enjoyed in the past is to continue, these practices must be halted or altered: (1) continued growth of human populations; (2) continued expansion of industrial and urban areas; (3) continued employment of intensive agricultural practices (the plowing-up-to-the-ditch variety); (4) continued logging of the remaining bottomland; (5) stream channelization; (6) continued unchecked growth of pet populations, especially cats and dogs; and (7) continued use of remaining "wild" areas for so-called recreational purposes. It is sad, but we are still beating back the wilderness when we have already beaten it to death many times over.

H. David Bohlen
January 1978

ACKNOWLEDGMENTS

I wish to thank the other members of the Illinois Ornithological Records Committee (see *Illinois Audubon Bulletin* No. 171:15) for their contributions of records, examination of specimens, and proof-reading: Vernon M. Kleen, Springfield; Charles T. Clark, Des Plaines; and Lawrence G. Balch, Chicago. Others with whom I was in constant touch on records were: William O'Brien, Robert Randall, and Pat Ward of Jacksonville; Richard Sandburg and Richard Palmer of Decatur; Jim Funk of Liberty; Gerald Rosenband of Chicago; and Richard Anderson of St. Louis.

I am grateful to the following for the use of the collections under their supervision: William Southern, Northern Illinois University; Dale Birkenholz, Illinois State University; William George, Southern Illinois University, Peter C. Petersen, Putnam Museum, Davenport, Iowa; and Donald Hoffmeister, University of Illinois. I appreciate the information and identification of selected specimens provided by Allan R. Phillips, Delaware Museum of Natural History; George Watson, National Museum of Natural History; and John Bull, American Museum of Natural History.

To Richard and Jean Graber I owe a special thanks for their many suggestions and advice on the manuscript and for the use of their data on specimens and records.

I am particularly indebted to members of the staff of the Illinois State Museum: Director R. Bruce McMillan and fellow zoologists, John R. Paul and Everett D. Cashatt, for their suggestions; Former Director Milton D. Thompson who proposed the project; Orvetta Robinson and Ronald Sauberli for editing, proofreading, and helping put the check-list together; Robert Larson for the drawings on the cover; Steve Mercer who designed the cover; Paul Deigl who designed the maps; Diane Lenger and Gladys Rockwell who typed much of the manuscript; and especially Dennis Guernsey for his rapid and precise production of the final camera-ready copy.

I am grateful to particular members of the Illinois Department of Conservation who kindly supplied data on waterfowl and game birds and to personnel of the Illinois State Library who so courteously assisted me in searching out old records.

Last but not least, I want to thank Judy, my wife, for typing and proofreading and my daughters, Nicole and Shannon, for their help and understanding for the many times I was not there because I was out "birdin'."

INTRODUCTION

The map of Illinois (page 2) has been divided into three sections—north, central, and south—after Gault (1922) and Smith and Parmalee (1955) so that a more definitive regional status could be applied to each species. The lines separating these three regions, drawn along county boundaries, follow isothermal lines as much as possible. The boundaries are largely artificial; for example, there is a great difference in the birdlife of Pope and Calhoun counties. Even though both counties are considered to be in the southern region, it should be expected that wintering birds, such as the Rufous-sided Towhee, would be much more numerous in Pope than in Calhoun. There is also a great variance between the birds in the eastern and the western parts of the state. Lake Michigan has a noticeable effect on birdlife which is very discernible as one goes through the check-list.

The status of birds is described here by the following terms:

Permanent Resident — birds that are present all year in approximately the same locality. This includes very few species since most migrate to some degree. (Bobwhite)

Migrants — birds that pass through the state enroute to their wintering grounds or breeding area. (Black-throated Green Warbler)

Winter Resident — birds that are present only during the winter and usually proceed north with the coming of spring. (Dark-eyed Junco)

Summer Resident — birds that nest in the state. (Great-crested Flycatcher)

Nonbreeding Summer Resident — birds that are present in the summer months but do not breed, probably young birds or unmated birds. (Semipalmated Sandpiper)

Postbreeding Wanderers — birds that drift (principally but not entirely northward) after breeding. (Little Blue Heron)

Vagrant — birds that are out of their normal range. (Lark Bunting)

Stragglers — birds that normally occur but stay later than the majority of the population. (Orange-crowned Warbler—in December)

Probable Escapes or Escapes — birds that have been released or have gotten away from confinement. (European Goldfinch)

Introduced — birds that have been released into the state by man, usually for the purpose of hunting. (Ring-necked Pheasant)

1

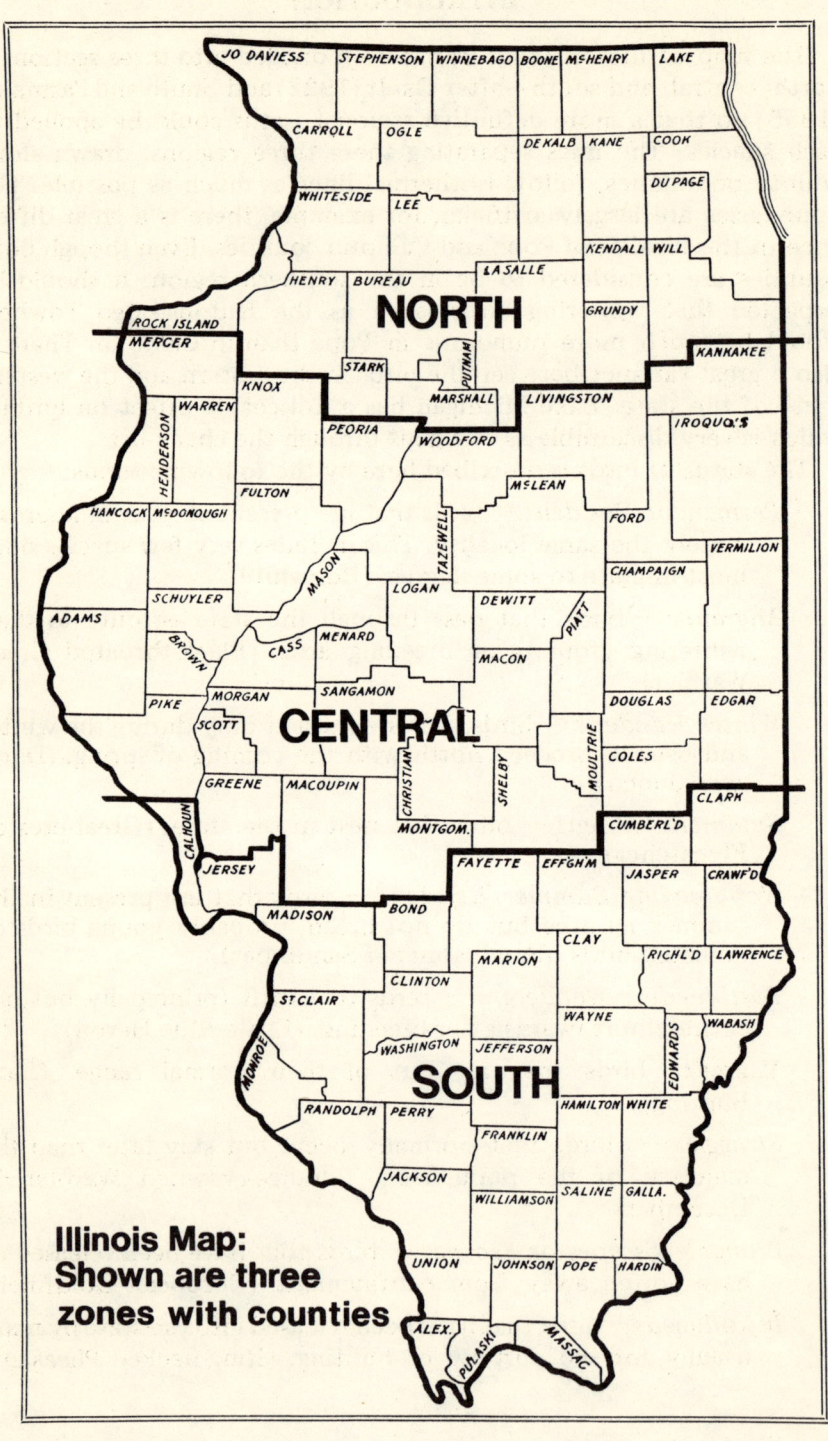

**Illinois Map:
Shown are three
zones with counties**

Extirpated — birds that were once present in the state but can no longer be found and are not likely to occur again except as vagrants. (Swallow-tailed Kite)

Extinct — birds that were once present but have been totally exterminated. (Passenger Pigeon)

Hypothetical — birds that were reported for the state but were not properly documented (see **Documentation**). (Gray Jay)

The numerical status of a species is separated arbitrarily into seven categories:

Abundant — occurs in great numbers at the right season and habitat; many can be seen in one day. Usually applied to birds with large populations that occur in dominant habitats or several different habitats. (Red-winged Blackbird)

Common — occurs in considerable numbers at the right season and habitat; several can be seen in a day. (Red-headed Woodpecker)

Fairly Common — occurs in numbers but to a lesser degree than common; if looked for, one or two can be seen in a day at the right season and habitat. (Greater Yellowlegs)

Uncommon — occurs in small numbers and may be limited by habitat; even if looked for at right season and habitat, might be missed in a day. (King Rail)

Occasional — occurs a few times a year; hard to find, probably limited by habitat or season. (White-fronted Goose)

Rare — occurs once or twice a year, some years not at all, probably on the edge of its range or in small local populations; could apply to some regular vagrants. (Piping Plover)

Very Rare — occurs only a few times ever in the state; usually applies to a vagrant. (Townsend's Solitaire)

All birds do not neatly pigeonhole into these categories, and occasionally two species marked as *common* might have very different population sizes. Other terms used are:

Irregular — occurring at unpredictable times. (Red Crossbill)

Cyclic — occurring at intervals of predictable times. (Snowy Owl)

Local — occurring but confined to certain areas, probably because of habitat. (Lark Sparrow)

If the species had a former status which has now obviously changed, this is noted in brackets.

It should be understood that the status of the bird is given as it applies to the bird *in its habitat*. For example, the Willow Flycatcher is a common summer resident only in its habitat of willow thickets and shrub areas and may have a rare status elsewhere or probably not be present at all.

Documentation is the corroborating evidence that the species has occurred in the state. The most reliable evidence is a specimen (listed as "specimen(s)" if more than one is known for the state). There is specimen documentation for 349 species of Illinois birds. For each, a representative specimen is listed giving location, date, and institution where kept; this shows proof of its existence in the state and indicates where some of the Illinois collections are located. Only specimens examined by the author or by reliable sources are included. Sometimes in the past, specimens were taken but were either discarded, lost, or placed in private collections that have not been located.

The documentation section is presented so that anyone researching a certain species in Illinois can immediately see the present evidence available. If a species is listed only as an accepted sight record, it may be desirable to collect the bird. All birds found dead should be given to museums or universities since representatives of numerous species and subspecies are lacking in state collections and a great deal of information can be derived from such specimens. Of course, date, place, and name of collector should accompany the specimen.

Photographic evidence is an additional means of documentation. Nineteen bird records in the state are based on photographs. Many photographs are taken of rare or unusual birds but are never published. Oftentimes when rare birds occur, no one thinks to photograph them, thus losing valuable evidence. Photography is the best method of verifying the presence of an endangered species, such as the Whooping Crane or Kirtland's Warbler. Certain species cannot be identified in a photograph, however. In such instances, a specimen should be taken. The Illinois State Museum has a photographic file of birds; anyone possessing photographs of rare or unusual birds from Illinois is urged to send a copy for the Museum files along with complete data on date, place, and collector(s).

Banding is a documentation of sorts. However, a bander should obtain photographs or consider collecting when rare or unusual birds are trapped. At the very least, a complete detailed description of the bird should be made.

In this check-list, 15 species have been accepted on the basis of a detailed written description of a sight record. The most difficult part of compiling a check-list is dealing with the reliability of records. Consequently, no sight records were accepted for inclusion in this state list unless two or more observers saw and thoroughly documented the sighting. However, if the bird had been documented in the state, one observer's records are accepted, based on the known competence of the observer and the details of the record. It is preferable that sight records be published in some ornithologically oriented journal, for example, the *Illinois Audubon Bulletin*. If not published, these written descriptions should be on file at the Illinois State Museum. It is understood that everyone cannot have a collector's permit or be a photographer, but anyone can take detailed notes in the field; those who are not willing to support their findings with documentation should not try to publish their records as it adds confusion to the state list and to the status of the bird in question.

Under **remarks**, a very brief statement of habitat or other pertinent information is given. A few locality records of recent origin are listed—that is, post-Smith and Parmalee (1955). In this check-list, the records essentially stop at the end of 1976, although a few significant 1977 records are included. These records should support the status as given above, show concentrations (sometimes these "high counts" show concentrations of observers rather than birds), late and early dates of arrivals and departures, stragglers, and nesting records. For the species that have occurred only a few times, all records for the state may be listed. Some species, because of interest or rarity, have a tremendous amount written about them in Illinois. Other species, frequently the most common, have very little written about them. Many species can be documented only from such sources as Christmas and spring bird counts, while summer residents often have no sources at all. It should be remembered that the Christmas and spring bird counts are collective projects, and the records for all practical purposes are anonymous.

Mainly, the records come from *American Birds* (AB), formerly called *Audubon Field Notes* (AFN), and *Illinois Audubon Bulletin*, formerly called *The Audubon Bulletin* (IAB). The person who made the record in these publications is listed. When the information was obtained from personal communications or unpublished notes, the locality record is followed only by a reference to the observer.

Subspecies, hybrids, and color morphs are included only when these are identifiable in the field or have an influence on the identification of another species.

The dates that each species is normally present are given. These dates are not meant to be all encompassing; since Illinois is approximately 385 miles long, the dates differ somewhat in the three sections of the state. However, they provide an indication of when the bulk of the populations is present. Migrational dates may not include certain regions. For example, the Loggerhead Shrike is generally present from late March to early October in the north and central but is a permanent resident in the south; so the section on status must be read to determine if the dates apply.

5

ILLINOIS PLACE NAMES
USED IN TEXT

1. Barrington
2. Beverly
3. Carbondale
4. Carlyle Lake
5. Channahon
6. Chautauqua NWR
7. Crab Orchard NWR
8. Crane Lake
9. DeKalb
10. East St. Louis
11. Evanston
12. Fults Marsh
13. Goose Lake Prairie
14. Hamilton (Pool 19)
15. Havana
16. Heron Pond
17. Horseshoe Lake
18. Illinois Beach State Park
19. Lake Calumet

20. Lake Charleston
21. Lake Decatur
22. Lake Springfield
23. Mark Twain NWR (Calhoun Division)
24. Mason State Forest
25. McGraw Wildlife Area
26. Morton Arboretum
27. Olney
28. Peoria
29. Pere Marquette State Park
30. Quincy
31. Rend Lake
32. Rockford
33. Sangchris State Park
34. Skokie Lagoons
35. Thomson
36. Union County Refuge
37. Urbana
38. Wilmette

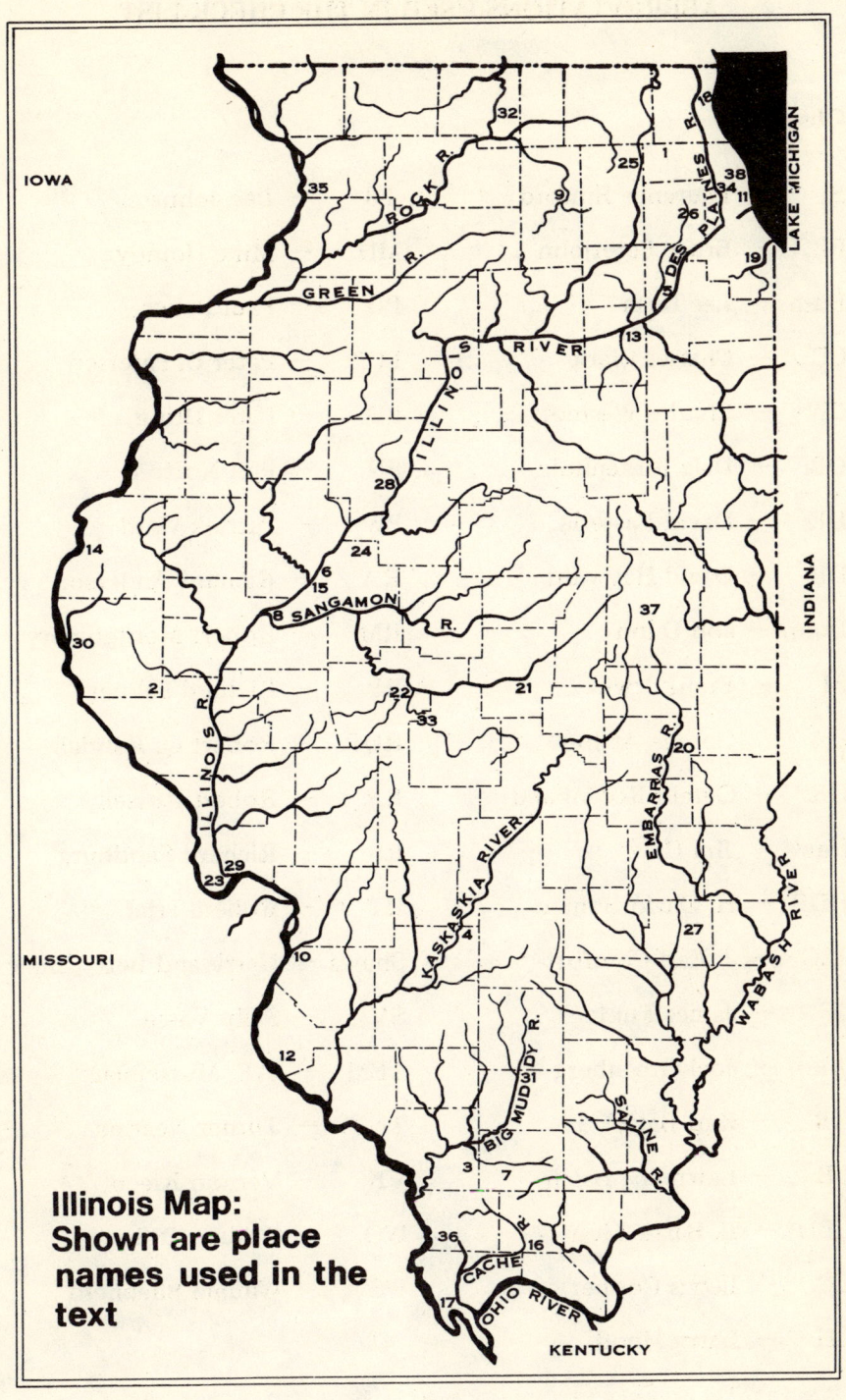

Illinois Map:
Shown are place
names used in the
text

ABBREVIATIONS USED IN THE CHECK-LIST

Observers:

Bi	— Laurence Binford	LJ	— Lee Johnson
BP	— Bruce Peterjohn	MH	— Mike Homoya
Bush	— Lee Bush	PB	— Paul Bauer
CC	— Charles Clark	PCP	— Peter C. Petersen
CW	— Charles Westcott	PD	— Peter Dring
DBi	— Dale Birkenholz	PN	— Phil Norton
DE	— David Easterla	PW	— Patrick Ward
DH	— David Hayward	RA	— Richard Anderson
Dunn	— Jon Dunn	RM	— Robert Montgomery
FI	— Frank Irwin	RP	— Richard Palmer
GA	— George Arthur	RQR	— Robert Q. Randall
GR	— Gerald Rosenband	RR	— Robert Russell
Haw	— Jim Haw	RS	— Richard Sandburg
HDB	— H. David Bohlen	RT	— Robert Trial
JEC	— J. Earl Comfort	Shaws	— Harry and Betty Shaw
JF	— James Funk	SV	— Sally Vasse
JG	— Joel Greenberg	TEM	— T.E. Musselman
KB	— Karl Bartel	TN	— Turner Nearing
LB	— Lawrence Balch	VK	— Vernon Kleen
LBH	— L. Barrie Hunt	WO	— William O'Brien
LC	— Lewis Cooper	WS	— William Shepherd
LH	— Larry Hood		

Other abbreviations:

AB	—	*American Birds*
Ad	—	Adult
AFN	—	*Audubon Field Notes*
AOU	—	American Ornithological Union
BBS	—	Breeding Bird Survey
CAS	—	Chicago Academy of Science
CBC	—	Christmas Bird Count
Co	—	County
COS	—	Chicago Ornithological Society
FMNH	—	Field Museum of Natural History of Chicago
IAB	—	*Illinois Audubon Bulletin*
IAS	—	Illinois Audubon Society
IDOC	—	Illinois Department of Conservation
Im	—	Immature
INHS	—	Illinois Natural History Survey at Urbana
ISM	—	Illinois State Museum at Springfield
ISU	—	Illinois State University at Normal
NIU	—	Northern Illinois University at DeKalb
NMNH	—	National Museum of Natural History at Washington, D.C.
NWR	—	National Wildlife Refuge
PM	—	Putnam Museum at Davenport, Iowa
SBC	—	Spring Bird Count
SIU	—	Southern Illinois University at Carbondale
S & P	—	Smith and Parmalee, 1955
St Pk	—	State Park
UI	—	University of Illinois at Champaign-Urbana
UMMZ	—	University of Michigan Museum of Zoology at Ann Arbor, Michigan
WU	—	Washington University at St. Louis, Missouri

HISTORY OF THE ILLINOIS LIST

The first phase of ornithology is the listing of species present in a given area. Illinois was blessed with some very fine early ornithologists. Some like Robert Ridgway reached the highest prominence in ornithological circles. Robert Kennicott, Illinois' first ornithologist, in his "Catalogue of Animals Observed in Cook County" (1855), listed 187 species of birds. At the same time (1855), Henry Pratten in his "Catalogue of the Birds of Illinois" recorded 184 species. Their combined lists totaled 233 species in the state. In 1859-60, R.H. Holder had 247 species in his "Birds of Illinois" (1861). Robert Ridgway listed 311 species in his "Catalogue of the Birds Ascertained to Occur in Illinois" (1874); he added to this number in "A Revised Catalogue of the Birds Ascertained to Occur in Illinois" (1881), making a total of 341 species. This led J.A. Allen (1881) to state in his review of Ridgway's list: "Illinois takes the lead among the states in respect to number of species of birds . . . ." Ridgway also compiled the next list, this time a two-volume book, "The Ornithology of Illinois" (Vol. I, 1889; Vol. II, 1895), in which he covered 349 species. Ridgway obtained most of his northern Illinois material from E.W. Nelson who wrote "Birds of Northeastern Illinois" in 1876. Nelson's work was enlarged upon by Frank M. Woodruff in "The Birds of the Chicago Region" in 1907. Another important summary on Illinois birds appeared in 1909, "The Birds of Illinois and Wisconsin," by Charles B. Cory.

The next three check-lists appeared in *The Audubon Bulletin* (now the *Illinois Audubon Bulletin*). The first was a nominal list of 258 species (IAB, Spring 1916). The two that followed were much alike, one containing 346 species (IAB, Spring 1917), and the other 347 species (IAB, Winter 1917-18). These check-lists laid the ground work for the 1922 presentation published by the Illinois Audubon Society. Entitled a "Check List of the Birds of Illinois," it was written by Benjamin T. Gault, contained 354 species, and first defined the three portions of the state. Two more works on Chicago area birds were produced: "Birds of the Chicago Region" by Edward R. Ford, Colin C. Sanborn, and C. Blair Coursen was written in 1934; then Ford updated the Chicago list in a work of the same title in 1956.

Little had been done on the birds of southern Illinois until Esther Bennett wrote "Check List of Birds of Southern Illinois" in 1952. This was updated by William G. George in 1968. In 1955 the Illinois Audubon Society and the Illinois State Museum jointly published "A Distributional Check List of the Birds of Illinois" by Harry R. Smith and Paul W. Parmalee, describing 383 species. The present list, a revision of Smith and Parmalee, treats 416 species; of these, 33 were

11

relegated to hypothetical status. With some having recently been designated subspecies, the total accepted species that have occurred in Illinois is now 383, including 4 extinct, 5 extirpated, and 9 introduced species. Since Smith and Parmalee (1955), 362 species have been observed in the state.

The species given in the present list (as well as common and scientific names) are those accepted by the "A.O.U. Check-List of North American Birds," 5th edition, (1957), plus changes made by the 32nd Supplement (A.O.U., 1973) and the 33rd Supplement (A.O.U., 1976). The species order for "Shorebirds" is taken from Bull (1974).

ANNOTATED LIST

GAVIIFORMES: Loons.

Common Loon *(Gavia immer)*

Early April — Mid-May
Mid-October — Early December

Status: Common migrant on Lake Michigan. Uncommon migrant in remainder of state. Rare winter resident. [Formerly rare breeding species in north.]
Documentation: Specimen(s) — ♂, near Blue Island, Cook Co, Apr 12, 1961 (NIU 003).
Remarks: Found on large bodies of water. Creation of several large lakes has produced more resting places during migration. Birds seen from late spring into June are in winter plumage, suggesting nonbreeding individuals. Set of eggs collected at Deer Lake, 3 miles from Hickory (now Antioch), Lake Co, May 1892 (Woodruff, 1907). No recent evidence of nesting. *Records:* 4, Crab Orchard NWR (CBC), Dec 30, 1957 (AFN12:176); 1, Lake Decatur, Dec 28, 1958 (AFN13:187); 1, Joliet, Jan 2, 1960 (AFN14:203); 1, Baker Lake, Cook Co, June 1, 1964 (CC-AFN18:511); 1, Gorham, Jackson Co, May 6, 1972 (G. Cooper-AB26:766); 6, McLean Co (SBC), May 4, 1974; 1, Effingham, June 3, 1974 (P. Clark-AB28:909); 1, Sangchris St Pk, June 8, 1974 (RP); 1 summered, Vermilion Co, 1975 (M. Campbell-AB29:979). *High counts:* 46, Crab Orchard NWR, Nov 4, 1959 (Bush-AFN14:39); 67, Lake Springfield, Nov 12, 1972 (HDB); 30, Chicago, Nov 2, 1974 (RR).

Arctic Loon *(Gavia arctica)*

Early November — Early December

Status: Very rare fall vagrant.
Documentation: Photographic — 1, Lake Springfield, Nov 3, 1974 (HDB, 1975b).
Remarks: 4 acceptable records. Probably regular in small numbers in fall but must be well observed at close range to be identified correctly. Found primarily along West Coast of U.S. during migration and winter. *Records:* 1 photographed, Lake Decatur, Dec 3, 1974 (RS, TN); 1 observed, Taylorville Lake, Nov 2, 1970 (HDB) but no documentation obtained; 2 undocumented records near Rockford with dates May 8-15, and Nov 2 - Dec 5 with no years listed (Nature Study Society of Rockford, 1917-18).

Red-throated Loon *(Gavia stellata)*

Late February — Early May
Late October — Mid-November

Status: Occasional migrant on Lake Michigan. Rare migrant in remainder of state.
Documentation: Specimen(s) — ♂, Waukegan, Apr 14, 1928 (UMNZ 92036).
Remarks: Found on large lakes and rivers. Probably migrates along the Great Lakes to and from the Coasts. *Records:* 1, southeastern Cook Co (CBC), Dec 29, 1955 (AFN10:166); 1, Mark Twain NWR, Oct 24 & 27,

1970 (SV-AB25:65); 1, Lock 13, Mississippi River, Whiteside Co, Nov 6, 1970 (Shaws, Greaves-IAB157:28); 1, Chautauqua NWR, May 1, 1971 (HDB); 1, Chicago, Nov 7, 1971 (LB, GR-AB26:71); 3, Evergreen Lake, McLean Co, Apr 16, 1974, (DBi); 1, Illinois Beach St Pk, Nov 18, 1974 (GR-AB29:64); 1, Evanston, Nov 24, 1974 (LB-AB29:64).

PODICIPEDIFORMES: Grebes.

Red-necked Grebe *(Podiceps grisegena)*

Late March — Late April
Late October — Late November

Status: Occasional migrant on Lake Michigan. Rare migrant in remainder of state.
Documentation: Specimen(s) — Im ♂, Champaign Co, Feb 21, 1904 (UI-Eiseman, 1957).
Remarks: Usually found on large lakes but can occur on ponds and sloughs. Occurs singly or in small numbers. Listed by Kennicott (1855) as breeding in Cook Co. *Records:* 1, Chicago, Feb 15-16, 1959 (Fetter-AFN13:296); 1, Stump Lake, Jersey Co, Oct 14, 1967 (PW, RQR); 3, Lake Glendale, Pope Co, Oct 28, 1967 (V. Shaw-AFN22:48); 1, Evanston, Dec 6, 1969 (CC); 2 photographed, Crab Orchard NWR, Mar 20 - Apr 2, 1971 (G. Cooper, VK-AB24:585); 1, Wilmette, Oct 28, 1971 (LB, GR-AB26:71); 3, Illinois Beach St Pk and Glencoe, Nov 14, 1971 (LB, GR-AB26:71); 1, Chicago, Mar 26, 1972 (CC, LB-AB26:610); 1, Chicago, Apr 10, 1972 (B. Tweit-AB26:766); 2, Evanston, Nov 24, 1974 (LB-AB29:64); Im, Lake Springfield, Dec 19, 1974 (HDB).

Horned Grebe *(Podiceps auritus)*

Early March — Late April
Early October — Early December

Status: Fairly common migrant. Rare winter resident. Very rare summer resident. [Formerly nested in northeastern Illinois (Nelson, 1876).]
Documentation: Specimen(s) — ♀, backwaters of Illinois River, near La Grange, Brown Co, Nov 15, 1972 (ISM 605353).
Remarks: Found on lakes, ponds, and other bodies of water. Seems to prefer deep water lakes. No reports of recent nesting. *Summer records:* 3, northern Illinois marshes, summer 1958, (Graber and Graber, 1963); 1 in breeding plumage, small impoundment near Prairie Du Rocher, Randolph Co, June 13, 1971 (HDB). *Other records:* 2, Chicago (CBC), Dec 27, 1958 (AFN13:186); 1, Belmont Harbor, Chicago, Jan 24, 1972 (LB-AB26:610); 1 wintered, Lake Decatur, 1972-73 (HDB); 1, Wabash Co, Feb 22, 1974 (P. Roush-AB28:649); 7, Cook Co (SBC), May 10, 1975. *High counts:* 3,000, lower Lake Michigan, Nov 11-13, 1955 (KB-AFN10:37); 34, Lake Charleston, Mar 5, 1970 (M. Conlin); 21, Lake Decatur, Oct 27, 1974 (RP-AB29:64); 55, Rend Lake, Nov 30, 1975 (BP).

Eared Grebe *(Podiceps nigricollis)*

Late March — Mid-May
Late September — Late November

Status: Rare migrant.
Documentation: Specimen — 1, Chicago, Nov 3, 1888 (CAS — Ford, Sandborn and Coursen, 1934).
Remarks: Found on lakes and ponds. From 1 to several of this western species observed in the state every year. More fall records than spring records. *Records:* 2, Decatur, Aug 7, 1955 (RS-AFN10:27); 1, Crab Orchard NWR, Dec 27, 1956 (AFN11:167); 1, Chicago, Apr 18, 1965 (CC-AFN19:481); 1 photographed, Chicago, May 14, 1966 (LB); 1, Wolf Lake, Chicago, Nov 27, 1971 (LB, CC, GR, and B. Tweit-IAB162:20); 1, Jacksonville, Oct 28, 1973 (PW-AB28:59); 1, Chicago, Mar 20, 1974 (GR-AB28:645); 1 in changing plumage, Jacksonville, May 11, 1975 (PW, and several observers); 1, Decatur, Nov 29 - Dec 4, 1975 (RS).

Western Grebe *(Aechmophorus occidentalis)*

Early April — Early May
Mid-October — Late November

Status: Rare migrant.
Documentation: Specimen — 1, Swan Lake, Putnam Co, about Dec 24, 1921 (Gregory, 1923).
Remarks: A western species recently found nearly every year. Usually occurs on large lakes. *Records:* 1, Glencoe, Apr 7, 1955 (Bi-AFN9:334); 4, Wilmette, Cook Co, Nov 12, 1960 (RR-AFN15:44); 1, Mark Twain NWR, Nov 8-9, 1969 (SV, PB-AFN24:54); 1 photographed (on file ISM), Crab Orchard NWR, Nov 23, 1970 (G. Cooper, VK-AB25:65); 1, Chicago, Oct 27 - Nov 1, 1972 (LB-AB27:67); 1, Mark Twain NWR, Sep 6 - Oct 13, 1973 (SV-AB28:59); 1, Whiteside Co, May 2-4, 1974 (R. Parsons-AB28:807); 2, Rend Lake, Nov 15, 1975 (BP, M. Morrison).

Pied-billed Grebe *(Podilymbus podiceps)*

Early March — Mid-May
Early September — Mid-November

Status: Common migrant. Fairly common summer resident in north. Uncommon summer resident in central. Rare summer resident in south. Uncommon winter resident in central and south; occasional winter resident in north.
Documentation: Specimen(s) — ♀, 10 miles east of Springfield, Sep 17, 1971 (ISM 604874).
Remarks: Found on lakes, ponds, and sloughs. Recent breeding records from Monroe Co, 1963 (M. Fleig); Cook Co, 1976 (LB); Kane Co, 1972 (RM-AB26:865); Mason Co and Jackson Co, 1973 (AB27:875). *High counts:* 400, Mark Twain NWR, last half of Oct, 1963 (SV); 94, Lake Charleston, Oct 8, 1969 (M. Conlin); 112, Powderhorn Marsh, Chicago, Sep 26, 1972 (LB); 20, Crab Orchard NWR (CBC), Dec 28, 1974 (RS); 560, Lake Springfield, Oct 1, 1975 (HDB); 51, Cook Co (SBC), May 8, 1976.

15

PELECANIFORMES: Pelicans, Cormorants and allies.

White Pelican *(Pelecanus erythrorhynchos)*

Late April — Early June
Late August — Early November

Status: Occasional migrant along Mississippi and Illinois rivers. Rare migrant in the remainder of the state. Rare (nonbreeding) summer resident.
Documentation: Specimen(s) — ♀, Crab Orchard Lake, Williamson Co, Oct 14, 1955 (SIU A-353).
Remarks: Found in rather shallow water and on sandbars and mudflats. More fall records than spring records. *Records:* 1, Dixon, Lee Co, Dec 1, 1958 (LJ-AFN13:296); 1 photographed, near Cerro Gordo, Piatt Co, Oct 19, 1959 (TN); 20, Ft. Kaskaskia, June 14, 1963 (M. Flieg); 1, Lake Calumet, Aug 21-27, 1965 (CC-AFN20:53); 1, Crane Lake, Mason Co, June 29, 1969 (RQR, PW); 60, Mark Twain NWR, June 9-10, 1971 (SV-AB25:868); 7, Jacksonville, Oct 6-15, 1971 (E. Leonhard-AB26:71); 1, Horseshoe Lake, Alexander Co, Nov 1, 1974 (D. Kennedy-AB29:64); 1, 8 miles east of Urbana, Dec 23, 1974 (John Findley); 16, Lake Baldwin, Randolph Co, June 11, 1975 (AB29:979); 1, Waukegan, Nov 15, 1975 (RS, HDB). *High count:* 100, near Quincy, spring 1967 (TEM-AFN21:513).

Brown Pelican *(Pelecanus occidentalis)*

Status: Very rare vagrant.
Documentation: Specimen — Ad ♂, Fayette Co, June 19, 1916 (E.F. Steinhauer Coll-ISM 605934).
Remarks: 5 records. No recent records; less likely to occur because of decline along Gulf Coast and elsewhere. *Records:* 1 observed, Lima Lake, near Warsaw, Oct 1873 (Ridgway, 1880); 1 shot near Lacon, Marshall Co, May 27, 1903 (Gault, 1910); 1 observed, near Quincy, 1913 (TEM); 3 observed south of Quincy, Apr 24, 1948 (TEM, 1950). *Note:* 1 photographed, west of Montpelier, Iowa, on the Mississippi River, May 10, 1969, by E. Deters (Petersen, 1972).

Double-crested Cormorant *(Phalacrocorax auritus)*

Early April — Mid-May
Early September — Late November

Status: Uncommon migrant along Mississippi and Illinois rivers. Rare summer resident along the upper Mississippi River. Occasional migrant in the remainder of the state. [Formerly common migrant and uncommon summer resident along Illinois River.]
Documentation: Specimen(s) — ♂, Crab Orchard NWR, Nov 27, 1955 (SIU A-11).
Remarks: Prefers large lakes and rivers and sits on snags near water. A very significant decline noted on the Illinois River since the 1950's. For example, 12,000 passed Havana, Oct 7, 1940 (Mills, Starrett, and Bellrose, 1966). Still a few pairs nesting west of Thomson and south of Savanna, Carroll Co (Shaws).

Records: 1, Crab Orchard NWR, Dec. 29, 1960 (AFN15:212); 1, Chillicothe (CBC), Jan 2, 1966 (AFN20:262); 2, Crane Lake, Cass Co, Dec 2, 1972 (WO); 2 Im, Lake Renwick, Will Co, June 8, 1973 (LB, GR-AB27:875). *High counts:* 66, Horseshoe Lake, Alexander Co, Apr 7, 1971 (Haw-AB25:750); 80, Mark Twain NWR, Oct 24, 1971 (SV-AB26:71); 130, Lock 13, Whiteside Co, Oct 7, 1972 (Wickstrom-IAB164:41); 142, Illinois River Valley, Oct 20, 1975 (IDOC).

Olivaceous Cormorant *(Phalacrocorax olivaceus)*

Status: Very rare vagrant.
Documentation: Specimen — 1, along Ohio River near Cairo, July 10, 1878 (ISU 12).
Remarks: Only 1 record. Native to west Gulf Coast. This specimen received by Charles K. Worthen in spring of 1879 (Ridgway, 1880).

Anhinga *(Anhinga Anhinga)*

April — October

Status: Very rare vagrant in central and south.
Documentation: Sight record with acceptable details — 1, presumably ♂, Stephen A. Forbes St Pk, Marion Co, Oct 10, 1968 (Matthews, 1969).
Remarks: Recorded by Ridgway (1881) as "summer sojourner in extreme southern part of the state." 2 sight records in southern Illinois, Apr 1928 or 1930 (Cahn, 1930). 1 at Ridge Lake, Fox Ridge St Pk, Coles Co, Apr or May 1942 (S & P, 1955, p. 10). Another (or same bird?) near Lake Springfield, May 23, 1942 (S & P, 1955, p. 10).

[Magnificent Frigate-bird *(Fregata magnificens)*]

Status: Hypothetical.
Remarks: 1 killed, near Burlington, Iowa; disagreement as to whether it was on the Illinois or Iowa side and whether it was killed in the spring of 1904 (Coale, 1910) or August 1903 (Bartsch, 1922). Photograph of the specimen in possession of the Audubon Naturalist Society of the Central Atlantic States (Briggs, 1969). Also an undocumented sight record near Rockford, mid-Sep 1961 (Prentice-AFN16:36).

CICONIIFORMES: Herons, Bitterns, Ibises and allies.

Great Blue Heron *(Ardea herodias)*

Early March — Late November

Status: Common migrant and locally common summer resident along major rivers of state. Uncommon migrant in remainder of state. Uncommon winter resident in south. Occasional winter resident in central and rare winter resident in north.
Documentation: Specimen(s) — ♂, near Irving, Montgomery Co, May 15, 1972 (ISM 605298).
Remarks: Found near lakes and rivers. Several heronries located mostly in the western and southern parts of the state. Late summer population increased

by postbreeding wanderers. *Records:* 2, Morton Arboretum, Dec 27, 1959 (AFN14:204); 1, Rockford, Jan 1, 1960 (AFN14:204); 14, Crane Lake (CBC), Dec 14, 1974 (AB29:411); 37, Union County Refuge (CBC), Dec 29, 1974 (AB29:418). *High counts:* 86, Chautauqua NWR, Dec 20, 1958 (AFN13:186); 80, McGinnis Slough, Cook Co, Aug 30, 1969 (CC); 40, Lake Co (SBC), May 4, 1974; 94, Cook Co (SBC), May 10, 1975. *Note:* Ridgway (1895) claims to have seen a Wurdeman's Heron (an intergradation between the Ward's Great Blue Heron and the Great White Heron) Sep 11-22 (no year given), in the Wabash River near Mt. Carmel, Wabash Co.

Green Heron *(Butorides striatus)*

Mid-April — Mid-October

Status: Common migrant and summer resident. Very rare winter resident.
Documentation: Specimen(s) — ♀, Genoa Twp, DeKalb Co, June 2, 1966 (NIU 2299).
Remarks: Found along creeks and around ponds. *Winter records:* 1, Decatur (CBC), Dec 28, 1958 (AFN13:187); Im collected, Geneseo, Henry Co, Nov 19, 1970 (PM); 1, Georgetown (CBC), Dec 29, 1971 (AB26:373). *High counts:* 37, Will Co (SBC), May 5, 1973; 50, near Big Muddy River, Jackson Co, Aug 29, 1974 (VK, CC, HDB); 94, Cook Co (SBC), May 10, 1975.

Little Blue Heron *(Florida caerulea)*

Mid-April —Early September

Status: Common migrant and summer resident in south. Uncommon migrant and postbreeding wanderer in central. Occasional migrant and postbreeding wanderer in north.
Documentation: Specimen(s) — ♀, Miller City road, Alexander Co, Apr 26, 1969 (SIU uncatalogued).
Remarks: Found around shallow pools and sloughs. Small number of birds (usually adults) arrive in central and north in spring for which status is unclear; may be over-migrants. *Records:* 1, Lake Calumet, Cook Co, May 20, 1962 (CC, R. Grow-AFN16:418); 1, McGraw Wildlife area, June 25, 1970 (Dillon, 1971); 1, Jackson Park, Chicago, Apr 30, 1972 (LB-AB26:766); 2, Northbrook, Cook Co, Aug 13 - Sep 10, 1972 (LB-IAB164:40); 1, Barrington, July 21, 1974 (CC-AB28:909); 1, Lee Co, Aug 4, 1974 (Shaws-AB29:65); Ad, Mason Co, Apr 19, 1975 (RP, HDB). *Nesting:* 100± pairs, E. St. Louis, 1972 (SV-AB26:865). *High counts:* 10, Saganashkee Slough, Cook Co, Aug 1, 1964 (CC); 35, Stump Lake, Jersey Co, Aug 1, 1971 (HDB); 300, St. Clair Co (SBC), May 5, 1973; 20, Mason Co, Aug 3, 1974 (HDB); 200, near Big Muddy River, Jackson Co, Aug 29, 1974 (CC, VK, HDB).

Cattle Egret *(Bubulcus ibis)*

Mid-April —Mid-October

Status: Fairly common but irregular migrant. Uncommon local summer resident.

Documentation: Specimen — Ad ♀, southeast of Urbana, Champaign Co, May 30, 1974 (INHS AR-ca-1).

Remarks: Found in wet areas and pastures. Eurasian species. Believed to have come to New World from Africa, then to U.S. via South America. Is expanding its range and will probably increase in numbers in the future. *First Illinois record:* 1, Saganashkee Slough, Cook Co, Aug 10, 1952 (R. Pringle, CC-AFN6:284). *Nesting records:* 8 nests, Lake Renwick, Will Co (LB-AB26:766); some nesting in E. St. Louis heronries (RA). *Other records:* 1, Rockford, Apr 22, 1962 (LJ, D. Seal-AFN16:418); 1 photographed, east of Oswego, Kendall Co, May 6, 1962 (M. Grossman — on file ISM); 1, Beverly, Adams Co, May 13, 1967 (JF-AFN21:577); 1, Pere Marquette St Pk, Oct 7, 1972 (SV-AB27:67); 1, near Snicarte, Mason Co, Nov 1, 1973 (WO); 1, near Hamilton, Hancock Co, Nov 23, 1974 (RS, HDB); 1, Carlyle Lake, Dec 7, 1975 (C. Marbut). *High counts:* 300, Illinois levees below St. Louis, Sep 12, 1970 (K. Arhos-AB25:65); 260, near E. St. Louis, Sep 3, 1973 (HDB, VK-AB28:59); 76, St. Clair Co (SBC), May 4, 1974.

[Reddish Egret *(Dichromanassa rufescens)*]

Status: Hypothetical.

Remarks: Nelson (1877) reported this southern species to be "quite common" in vicinity of Cairo during last week of August 1875; but no specimens were taken. Could have confused it with Little Blue Heron. Only other record is 1 seen near the Chain of Rocks Bridge, St. Clair Co, July 29, 1949 (S & P, 1955, p. 11). No specimen, photograph, or description was secured from this sighting.

Great Egret *(Casmerodius albus)*

Early April — Late October

Status: Common migrant and summer resident along the Illinois and Mississippi rivers and a few other areas where nesting colonies are present. Uncommon migrant and postbreeding wanderer in the remainder of the state.

Documentation: Specimen(s) — ♂, Yates City, Knox Co, May 31, 1970 (ISM 604522).

Remarks: Found along lakes, rivers, and sloughs. Several breeding colonies in western part of the state. Nesting colony at Lake Renwick, Will Co. Concentrations in late summer and fall. *Records:* 1, Princeton, Dec 28, 1956 (W.D. Boyle-AFN11:170); 1, McGinnis Slough, Cook Co, Nov 1, 1959 (P.R. Snider-AFN14:39); 1, Quincy, wintered 1960-61 (TEM-AFN15:533); 6, Mark Twain NWR, Nov 27, 1963 (SV); 6, Waukegan, Aug 13, 1967 (RR); 1 photographed, Union Co, Dec 19, 1971 (VK-AB 26:378). *High counts:* 300, Chautauqua NWR, Aug 18, 1961 (Norman-AFN15:471); 300, Mark Twain NWR, mid-Sep 1963 (SV); 92 adults and 154 Im, E. St. Louis, summer 1973 (L. Wrischnik-IAB166:26); 75, St. Clair Co (SBC), May 4, 1974.

Snowy Egret *(Egretta thula)*

Late April — Late August

Status: Rare migrant and postbreeding wanderer. Rare local summer resident.

Documentation: Specimen(s) — 1, Mt. Carmel, Wabash Co, Aug 13, 1875 (USNM 85463).
Remarks: Found near ponds and sloughs. Birds appearing in spring in north and central may be over-migrants. 4 nests found in an E. St. Louis heronry in 1969 (RA). *Records:* 1, Lock 13 near Fulton, Whiteside Co, Apr 15-17, 1968 (Grabers, Shaws-AFN22:532); 1, Lake Calumet, Cook Co, May 16, 1971 (LB-AB25:751); 1, Meredosia, Morgan Co, Aug 22, 1971 (JF-AB26:71); 2, Frank Holten St Pk, Madison Co, mid-July 1972 (SV-AB26:865); 3, Horseshoe Lake, Alexander Co, Aug 12, 1972 (VK-AB26:865); 1, Whiteside Co, and 1, Monroe Co (SBC), May 5, 1973; 10, Miller City, Alexander Co, Aug 11, 1974 (DH-AB29:65); 1, Mason Co, May 11, 1975 (RQR and several observers).

Louisiana Heron *(Hydranassa tricolor)*

Status: Very rare vagrant.
Documentation: Photographic — 1, near Ware, Union Co, Apr 28, 1974 (R. Madding, ISM).
Remarks: 6 records. A southern heron. Probably an over-migrant. *Other records:* 1, Jackson Park, Chicago, May 22, 1939 (Ford, 1956, p. 13); 1, Illinois levees, south of St. Louis, June 2-6, 1968 (RA-AFN22:532); 1, St. Clair Co, May 23, 1974 (D. Jones-AB28:807); 1, E. St. Louis, Apr 24-25, 1976 (J. Eades and photographed by B. Adams-on file ISM); 1, Waukegan, June 27 - July 4, 1976 (E.L. Coffin, W. Grundy); 1, Lake Springfield, Oct 4-5, 1976 (HDB).

Black-crowned Night Heron *(Nycticorax nyciticorax)*

Early April — Late October

Status: Fairly common migrant and uncommon summer resident. Rare winter resident.
Documentation: Specimen(s) — Im ♀, 1 mile south of DeKalb, DeKalb Co, Sep 29, 1961 (NIU 015).
Remarks: Found in swampy areas. Nesting colonies slowly being wiped out by so-called "progress." *Summer records:* Colony of 50-75 nests, St. Clair Co, Aug 5, 1958 (SV); 5 nests, Lake Decatur, July 17, 1959 (TN-IAB115:7); 71 Ad and 120 Im, E. St. Louis, July 11, 1971 (IAB160:18). *Winter records:* 4, Channahon, Grundy Co, Dec 31, 1955 (AFN10:163); 5, Chicago, Dec 26, 1970 (AB25:351); 2, Little Calumet River, Cook Co, Jan 23, 1972 (CC-AB26:610). *High counts:* 20, Barrington, mid-Aug 1965 (RR); 100, Lake Renwick, Will Co, Apr 12, 1969 (CC); 50, Fults Marsh, Monroe Co, Aug 1971 (RA, PB-AB25:863); 187, St. Clair Co (SBC), May 5, 1973; 114, Will Co (SBC), May 4, 1974.

Yellow-crowned Night Heron *(Nyctanassa violacea)*

Mid-April — Late August

Status: Fairly common migrant and summer resident in south. Uncommon migrant and summer resident in central. Occasional migrant and summer resident in north.

Documentation: Specimen(s) — Ad ♂, Busey Pasture, Urbana, Champaign Co, Apr 29, 1951 (UI 4425).

Remarks: Found in swampy areas. Number may increase in late summer due to postbreeding dispersal northward. Seems to be a recent northward extension of the breeding range. *Records:* 2, Rockton, Winnebago Co, June 2, 1956 (Mrs. F. Mezger-AFN10:337); 3 pairs summered, New Boston, Mercer Co, 1959 (RT-AFN13:433); 1, Palos area, Cook Co, Mar 31, 1963 (LB); 1, Long John Slough, Cook Co, Oct 1, 1967 (CC); 2 Ad with 2 young, 2 miles south Willow Springs, Cook Co, June 22, 1968 (PD); 2 pairs nested, Skokie Lagoons, Cook Co, 1972 (LB-AB26:766); 1, Jackson Co, Mar 29, 1975 (RP-AB29:697). *High counts:* 14, Oakwood Bottoms, Jackson Co, June 7, 1973 (RS, HDB); 8, Cook Co (SBC), May 10, 1975.

Least Bittern *(Ixobrychus exilis)*

Early May — Late September

Status: Uncommon migrant and summer resident.

Documentation: Specimen(s) — ♀, east of Springfield, Sangamon Co, Oct 1, 1973 (ISM 605767).

Remarks: A secretive species found primarily in cattail marshes. May be more common in north in Lake and Cook counties than status suggests. *Records:* 2 nests, Plano, Kendall Co, June 12, 1960 (H. Walley-IAB120:3); nest, Powderhorn Marsh, Cook Co, June 27, 1965 (LB); nest, Saganashkee Slough, Cook Co, Aug 1, 1966 (PD); 2 nests, Mermet Lake, Massac Co, summer 1973 (DH-AB27:778). *Other records:* 1, Chicago, Apr 7, 1974 (W. Krawiec-AB28:807); 1, near Havana, Mason Co, July 6, 1974 (RS, RP). *Color morph:* The dark form, Cory's Least Bittern, collected along the fox River at Cary, McHenry Co, May 23, 1914 (Eifrig, 1915).

American Bittern *(Botaurus lentiginosus)*

Mid-April — Mid-May
Early September — Late October

Status: Uncommon migrant and rare summer resident. Rare winter resident.

Documentation: Specimen(s) — 1, 3 miles southwest of Hull, Pike Co, Apr 19, 1956 (ISM 603803).

Remarks: Found in marshes and swamps. Seems to be on decline. *Records:* 1, Rockford, Mar 28, 1959 (LJ-AFN13:373); 1, Sand Ridge Nature Center, Cook Co, Dec 30, 1967 (AFN22:273); 1, Ashmore, Coles Co, Dec 30, 1970 (LBH-AB25:585); 1, Champaign, Dec 25, 1973 (R. Cooper-IAB169:10); Im, north of Cuba, Fulton Co, July 6, 1974, (RS, RP, HDB). *High counts:* 10, Jackson Co (SBC), May 5, 1973; 5, Lake Co (SBC), May 10, 1975; 12, Cook Co (SBC), May 8, 1976.

Wood Stork *(Mycteria americana)*

Late May — Late September

Status: Very rare vagrant or postbreeding wanderer. [Formerly more regular.]

Documentation: Specimen(s) — Ad ♂, Horseshoe Lake (listed as Cantine, IL) Madison Co, Aug 24, 1880 (WU Hurter Coll 26).

Remarks: Found around swampy pools, lakes, and river bottoms. Many old records; definitely not as numerous now, probably due to poor breeding success in southern states. Recently discovered specimens in the E.F. Steinhauer collection (ISM) taken in Fayette Co, July 28, 1898. *Recent records:* 23 first-year birds, Fults Marsh, Monroe Co, Aug 8, 1963 (Walley George-IAB29:18); 1, Quincy, late May 1967 (TEM-AFN21:513); 2, late Sep 1967 (TEM-AFN22:48).

Glossy Ibis *(Plegadis falcinellus)*

Mid-April — Early October

Status: Rare vagrant.
Documentation: Specimen — ♂, 7 miles from St. Louis, Madison Co (listed as Marion Co) Illinois, Feb 27, 1880 (Hurter, Bull. Nutt. Ornith. Club, 6:124; supposedly in the Hurter Coll. at WU—now listed as missing, RA).
Remarks: Found at shallow lakes and sloughs. *Records:* 1, Decatur, May 2, 1956 (Chaniot, W. Mannering-AFN10:337); 1, Barrington, Oct 20-21, 1962 (RR-AFN17:36); 1, Mark Twain NWR, Oct 1, 1964 (SV-AFN19:45); 1, Lake Calumet, May 10, 1969 (CC-AFN23:596); 1 captured and photographed, Cuba, Fulton Co, Sep 13, 1970 (R. Pointer-AB25:66); 1, E. St. Louis, July 22-25, 1971 (JEC-AB25:863); Ad, Sangchris St Pk, Sangamon Co, Sep 9, 1971 (HDB); 1 photographed (on file ISM), south of Chillicothe, Peoria Co, Apr 14, 1972 (Ralph Scott); 1 photographed, near Pecatonica, Winnebago Co, May 23, 1975 (F. Brechlin, J. Armstrong); Ad, near Havana, May 21, 1976 (P. Gibson, RS).

White-faced Ibis *(Plegadis chihi)*

Status: Very rare vagrant.
Documentation: Sight record with acceptable details — 1, Powderhorn Marsh, Cook Co, May 30, 1965 (LB-IAB135:11).
Remarks: 3 records. A western species which is easily confused with the Glossy Ibis. *Other records:* 2, near Peoria, April 24; 1 stayed until May 1, 1967 (Princen); 1, near Gorham, Jackson Co, May 6, 1972 (M.J. McNerney and others).

White Ibis *(Eudocimus albus)*

Early May — Early August

Status: Very rare vagrant, possibly a postbreeding wanderer in south and central.
Documentation: Specimen(s) — 1, Swan Lake, Green Co, Aug 1917 (S & P, 1955, p. 12).
Remarks: Southern species. Occurs in swampy or marshy areas. Flock of 7-8 seen near Mt. Carmel, Wabash Co, May 1878 (Ridgway, 1895); 2 mounted specimens (no date) in collections at Quincy taken from a flock of 4 (Widmann, 1907). *Recent records:* Im, Moredock Lake, Monroe Co, July 4 - July 20, 1963 (JEC-IAB129:18); 1, Fults Marsh, Monroe Co, July 15 - Aug 3, 1963 (RA-IAB129:18); Ad, Monroe Co levees, May 2-3, 1964 (Wally George-IAB130:19); Im, Gilbert Lake, Jersey Co, Aug 6, 1977 (HDB).

Roseate Spoonbill *(Ajaia ajaja)*

Status: Extirpated. [Formerly very rare summer resident in central and south.]
Documentation: Specimen — skeleton found in archaeological site in Calhoun Co (Parmalee & Perino, 1970).
Remarks: No records since Apr 28, 1887, when O.C. Poling supposedly obtained specimen from Adams Co (TEM). Only other mention is vague statement by Ridgway (1880) of some specimens taken (no date) by a Mr. A. Wolle below St. Louis.

[American Flamingo *(Phoenicopterus ruber)*]

Status: Hypothetical. Probable escapes.
Remarks: Has little place in the avifauna of Illinois since any reported are probably zoo escapes. *Records:* 1, Havana, Aug 8, 1959, then at Banner, Fulton Co, Sep 28, 1959, then 10 miles from Banner, Oct 3, 1959 (TEM-AFN14:39); 1, Chicago Sanitary Dist. settling pond, July 28, 1966 (PD).

ANSERIFORMES: Swans, Geese and Ducks.

Mute Swan *(Cygnus olor)*

Status: Recently introduced; now uncommon local permanent resident and very rare migrant. Some probably escapes from captivity.
Documentation: Photographic — 4 young with parent, Fulton Co, 1972 (on file ISM).
Remarks: 23 swans released in Fulton Co in 1971, and 10 released at Sangchris St Pk, Sangamon Co, and Baldwin Reservoir, Randolph Co in 1972 by IDOC. Migrants in Illinois probably from the Michigan population. *Record before introduction:* 4, McHenry Co, Dec 26, 1964 (AFN19:234).

Whistling Swan *(Olor columbianus)*

Early November — Mid-April

Status: Occasional migrant in north. Rare migrant in central and south. Rare winter resident.
Documentation: Specimen(s) — Ad, Orland Park, Cook Co, Apr 1931 (FMNH 67674).
Remarks: More often seen in fall. Majority migrate east and west across northern part of state instead of north and south; A few use the Illinois and Mississippi rivers. *Records:* 6, Shirland, Mar 27, 1959 (LJ-AFN13:374); Im wintered, Lake Decatur, Dec 29, 1970 - last of Mar 1971 (HDB); 1, Horseshoe Lake, Alexander Co, Nov 6, 1971 (L. Wegman-AB26:376); 2 wintered, Mark Twain NWR, Dec 26, 1971 - Feb 29, 1972 (SV-AB26:610). *High counts:* 55, flying along Lake Michigan, Nov 14, 1972 (LB, CC, GR-AB27:67); 40, Lock 13, near Fulton, Whiteside Co, Nov 11, 1974 (Shaws-AB29:65); 28, Des Plaines River, Apr 4-5, 1975 (J. Neal-AB29:859).

Trumpeter Swan *(Olor buccinator)*

Status: Extirpated. [Formerly a migrant and summer resident.]

Documentation: Specimen(s) — (skeletal) approximately 375 bones identified from an archaeological site at Cahokia, St. Clair Co (Parmalee, 1958).

Remarks: No longer found in Illinois. May occur in future if flocks in northwest build up sufficient populations. The Long Expedition reported a flightless swan at mouth of Kaskaskia, June 5, 1810 (Schorger, 1964). An occasional swan was reported to nest at Lima Lake, 18 miles north of Quincy, in the "early days" (TEM, 1921). A specimen was reported (with no date) in the University of Illinois Collection by F. Smith who obtained it in Anna, Union Co, 1880. Reported from Shawneetown, Gallatin Co, Mar 19, 1885, and Paris, Edgar Co, Mar 31, 1885 (Cook, 1888).

Canada Goose *(Branta canadensis)*

Late September — Late April

Status: Common migrant. An abundant winter resident in south. Locally uncommon winter resident in central and north. Occasional summer resident. Introduced in some areas of the state.

Documentation: Specimen(s) — Ad ♂, Crab Orchard NWR, Jan 29, 1955 (SIU A-19).

Remarks: Found on lakes, overflow areas, and fields. Often seen flying overhead during migration. *Nesting records:* Ad and young, Crabtree Lake, Barrington, early July 1961 (RR-AFN15:471); pair nested, Wolf Lake, Cook Co, summer 1967 (McHenry IAS-IAB144:16). *High counts:* 87,000, Crab Orchard NWR, Nov 26, 1956 (Bush-AFN11:29); 400 (small race), Mark Twain NWR, Oct 20, 1963 (RA); 90,000, Crab Orchard NWR area, Dec 30, 1972 (AB27:368); 63,000, Union Co Refuge, Dec 31, 1972 (AB27:376); 160, Fulton Co (SBC — probably resident birds), May 4, 1974; 16,885, Illinois River Valley, Nov 17, 1975 (IDOC).

Subspecies: Giant race, *B. c. maxima*, has been propagated and introduced into different areas of the state (e.g., Fulton Co). Common subspecies in southern Illinois in winter is *B. c. interior*. Small geese are probably *B. c. hutchinsii* (there are some specimens of this form). Many more specimens of all sizes are needed to determine exactly what forms are present.

Brant *(Branta bernicla)*

Status: Very rare migrant.

Documentation: Specimen — first-year ♂, Gilbert Lake, Jersey Co, Nov 9, 1964 (Principia College-AFN19:45).

Remarks: A few old records of this coastal species are undocumented except for the Im captured at Lacon, Marshall Co, Nov 9, 1921 (Gault, 1922). *Recent records:* 1 photographed, Crab Orchard NWR, Dec 19 & 31, 1963 (RM and Rice, 1967); Im, Jacksonville, Oct 14-24, 1964 (E. Leonhard, WO-IAB133:3); 1 photographed, breeding plumage, Illinois levee below St. Louis, May 4, 5, 6, 1968 (RA, PB, J. Ruschill-AFN22:532); Ad, Union Co Refuge, Oct 15, 1976 (D. Thornburg).

Subspecies: Black Brant *(B. b. nigricans)* is hypothetical in the state. A bird described as this West Coast species but listed as "Brant" observed by Dreuth at Lincoln Park, Chicago, Oct. 9, 1932 (Clark and Nice, 1950).

White-fronted Goose *(Anser albifrons)*

Late February — Early May
Mid-October — Mid-November

Status: Occasional migrant. Rare winter resident in south.
Documentation: Specimen(s) — Ad ♂, Chicago, Mar 1876 (USNM 84701).
Remarks: Prefers mudflats, shallow water areas, and grain fields. More frequently seen in spring; fluctuates from year to year in numbers. *Records:* 43, Mark Twain NWR, Nov 25, 1963 (SV); 132, Mark Twain NWR, Mar 29, 1965 (SV & Hanselman); 2, Mark Twain NWR, May 31, 1970 (SV); 6, east of Moweaqua, Shelby Co, Mar 20, 1971 (HDB); 10, Stump Lake, Jersey Co, Feb 26, 1972 (PW); 3, Union Co Refuge, winter 1971-72 (VK-AB26:611); 4, Crab Orchard NWR, Oct 8, 1973 (MH-AB28:59); 70, Sangchris St Pk, Apr 6, 1974 (VK, HDB); 1, Mason Co, May 5, 1974 (WO, HDB); 60, Chautauqua NWR, Oct 12, 1974 (RS, HDB); 1 photographed, near Chautauqua NWR, Oct 29, 1974 (R. Hall).

[Bar-headed Goose *(Anser indicus)*]

Status: Hypothetical. Probable escape.
Remarks: Siberian species. Observed at Crab Orchard NWR, Dec 22, 1961 (Bush-AFN16:209). Since most waterfowl species can be purchased, this exotic was probably an escape.

Snow Goose *(Chen caerulescens)*

Mid-February — Early May
Mid-October — Early December

Status: Fairly common migrant, especially along the Illinois and Mississippi rivers where at times it is abundant. Uncommon winter resident in central and south. Rare winter resident in north.
Documentation: Specimen(s) — white phase Ad, Swan Lake, Henry, Marshall Co, Nov 20, 1947 (FMNH 17010).
Remarks: Found in lakes, sloughs, and grain stubble fields. *Records:* 7 blue and 1 white, Lake Calumet, May 12, 1956 (CC, Levy-AFN10:337); 1 blue, Fulton Co (SBC), May 6, 1972; 4 white, DuPage Co (SBC), May 5, 1973; 2 blue, Williamson Co (SBC), May 5, 1973; 4 white, Randolph Co (SBC), May 4, 1974. *High counts:* 3,100, Crab Orchard NWR, Nov 18, 1955 (Bush-AFN10:28); 8,000, Chautauqua NWR, Oct 28, 1959 (Norman-AFN14:39); 10,000, Mark Twain NWR, Feb 1, 1966 (SV); 15,000, Mason Co, Dec 15, 1973 (JF, HDB); 21,995, Mississippi Valley, Nov 17, 1975 (IDOC). *Color morphs:* This species includes color phases formerly known as Blue Goose and Snow Goose, now considered conspecific. In Illinois, Blue phase outnumbers White phase by a considerable margin, and intergrades between the two are not uncommon.

Ross' Goose *(Chen rossii)*

Status: Very rare vagrant.
Documentation: Specimen — Ad, Horseshoe Lake, Alexander Co, Nov 26, 1956 (Coll. of Glen Smart, Campbell, Mo).
Remarks: 1 record. An Ad (specimen above) and juvenile of this western species, Horseshoe Lake, Alexander Co, fall of 1956 (Smart, 1960).

[Black-bellied Whistling Duck *(Dendrocygna autumnalis)*]

Status: Hypothetical.
Remarks: South-Texas species. 1 reported shot along Illinois River near LaSalle, LaSalle Co, Sep 15, 1930 (Moyer, 1931); no specimen or description available.

Fulvous Whistling Duck *(Dendrocygna bicolor)*

Status: Very rare vagrant.
Documentation: Sight record with acceptable details — 1, at junction of Big Muddy River and Route 3, Jackson Co, Aug 24-31, 1974 (R. Madding — on file ISM).
Remarks: 2 records. Southwestern species. *Other records:* 1, taken off Navy Pier, Chicago, Dec 7, 1919 (Moyer, 1931) but may have been an escape. 1, reported killed by Evers, Adams Co, 1915 (Musselman in S & P, 1955, p. 14) was actually taken in Missouri, Apr 29, 1909 (Widmann, 1909).

Mallard *(Anas platyrhynchos)*

Early September — Early April

Status: Abundant migrant. Fairly common summer resident locally in central and north. Uncommon summer resident in south. Common winter resident.
Documentation: Specimen(s) — ♂, Sangchris St Pk, Christian Co, Dec 12, 1970 (ISM 604818).
Remarks: Found along major river systems, lakes, ponds, and grain fields. Domestic Mallards cause problems in estimating actual numbers in certain areas. *High counts:* 100,000, Crab Orchard NWR, Nov 27 & 28, 1955 (Bush-AFN10:38); 300,000, Chautauqua NWR, Dec 2, 1958 (Norman-AFN13:296); 45,000, Illinois River near Morris, Jan 24, 1971 (LB); 1,080, Chicago North Shore (CBC), Dec 26, 1971 (AB26:370); 50,000, Pere Marquette St Pk (CBC), Dec 23, 1972 (AB27:373); 12,247, Crane Lake—Sangamon (CBC), Dec 15, 1973 (AB28:380); 418, Cook Co (SBC), May 10, 1975; 836,665, Illinois River Valley, Nov 17, 1975 (IDOC).

Black Duck *(Anas rubripes)*

Early September — Mid-April

Status: Fairly common migrant and winter resident. Rare summer resident.
Documentation: Specimen(s) — ♂, Gillespie Lake, Macoupin Co, Dec 6, 1972 (ISM 605410).
Remarks: Occurs on lakes and ponds, usually with Mallards. *Summer records:* 2 broods, Barrington, June 13, 1965 (CC-AFN19:551); nest, Powderhorn Marsh, Chicago, May 29, 1965 (CC); 1, Chautauqua NWR, June 26, 1971 (HDB); 3, Rend Lake, Franklin Co, July 10, 1971 (VK, F. Reuter-AB25:863); 2, Lake Co, summer 1973 (LB-AB27:875). *High counts:* 15,000, Channahon, Grundy Co (CBC), Dec 31, 1955 (AFN10:163); 952, Lake Decatur (CBC), Dec 26, 1955 (AFN10:164); 3,289, Crab Orchard NWR (CBC), Dec 27, 1956 (AFN11:167); 1,600, Chautauqua NWR (CBC), Dec 20, 1958 (AFN13:186); 1,000, Morris-Wilmington (CBC), Dec 27, 1964 (AFN19:234); 1,000, Springfield (CBC), Dec 27, 1964 (AFN19:237); 27,555, Illinois River Valley, Dec 8 & 9, 1975 (IDOC).

Gadwall *(Anas strepera)*

Early March — Mid-May
Early October — Early December

Status: Fairly common migrant. Fairly common winter resident in south. Uncommon winter resident in central and north. Rare summer (nonbreeding) resident in north and central.

Documentation: Specimen(s) — ♀, Carrier Mills, Saline Co, Oct 28, 1955 (SIU A-37).

Remarks: Found on ponds, lakes, and overflow areas. Several species of ducks, but this one in particular, are utilizing sewage lagoons for resting and feeding. These lagoons usually do not freeze in winter, allowing birds to stay farther north than normal. *Summer records:* Pair, Long John Slough, near Chicago, in 1967 (CC, PD-AFN21:577); pair, near Havana, June 1, 1974 (HDB); ♀, Lake Calumet, June 30, 1974 (CC-AB28:909). *Other records:* 9, Will Co (SBC), May 4, 1974. *High counts:* 75, Pere Marquette St Pk (CBC), Dec 26, 1965 (AFN20:265); 88, Horseshoe Lake, Alexander Co, Jan 8, 1972 (VK, DH-AB26:611); 100, Mark Twain NWR, Mar 28, 1972 (HDB); 3,065, Mississippi River Valley, Oct 27, 1975 (IDOC).

Pintail *(Anas acuta)*

Mid-February —Mid-April
Early August — Early December

Status: Common migrant. Uncommon winter resident in central and south. Occasional winter resident in north. Rare summer resident in north and central.

Documentation: Specimen(s) — ♂, Sanganois Conservation Area, Mason Co, Nov 7, 1967 (ISM 603941).

Remarks: Found on ponds, lakes, and overflow areas. *Nesting records:* ♀ with 6 young, Whiteside Co, June 17, 1959 (Shaws-IAB115:7); pair nested, Woodstock, June 19-21, 1967 (McHenry IAS-IAB144:17); 4 young, Goose Lake Prairie, Grundy Co, summer 1973 (DBi-AB27:875); nest with 10 eggs, Goose Lake Prairie, May 14, 1974 (Verner, 1975). *Other records:* 20, Marshall Co (SBC), May 4, 1974. *High counts:* 116,000, Illinois, Oct 17, 1956 (INHS-AFN11:29); 131, Crab Orchard NWR (CBC), Dec 27, 1956 (AFN11:167); 1,548, Pere Marquette St Pk (CBC), Dec 26, 1965 (AFN20:265); 175, Sangchris St Pk, Christian Co, Dec 26, 1970 (HDB); 101,630, Mississippi River Valley, Nov 11, 1975 (IDOC).

[Bahama Duck *(Anas bahamensis)*]

Status: Hypothetical. Probable escape.

Remarks: Specimen — Steward Lake, Mason Co, Nov 2, 1968 (ISM 606696). Since the bird was not sexed, it was not possible to determine the subspecies, which could have determined whether or not it was a wild bird (letter, Emmet R. Blake, Oct 26, 1970).

Green-winged Teal *(Anas crecca)*

Early March — Early May
Late July — Early December

Status: Fairly common migrant. Uncommon winter resident in south and occasional winter resident in north and central. Rare summer resident in north and central.
Documentation: Specimen(s) — ♂, Chautauqua NWR, Mason Co, Sep 4, 1971 (ISM 605636).
Remarks: Found in shallow water areas and mudflats. *Summer records:* ♀ with 8 young, Chicago, July 31, 1966 (CC-AFN20:574); young in groups of 10 and 11, Goose Lake Prairie, summer, 1973 (DBi-AB27:875); ♀ with 6 young, near Havana, Mason Co, Aug 10, 1974 (HDB); *Winter records:* 25, Chicago North Shore (CBC), Dec 27, 1975 (AB30:428). *High counts:* 600, Mark Twain NWR, Oct 1963 (SV); 2,500, Chautauqua NWR, Oct 18, 1975 (Bellrose); 10,965, Illinois River Valley, Nov 17, 1975 (IDOC).

Blue-winged Teal *(Anas discors)*

Mid-March — Late October

Status: Common migrant. A fairly common summer resident in north, uncommon summer resident in central, and occasional summer resident in south. Rare winter resident.
Documentation: Specimen(s) — ♂, Chautauqua NWR, Mason Co, Sep 4, 1971 (ISM 604847).
Remarks: Found on shallow ponds, sloughs, and overflow areas. *Winter records:* 1, Rockford, Dec 30, 1956 (AFN11:170); 1, Peoria (CBC), Dec 23, 1967 (AFN22:272); 1, Chicago area, Dec 30, 1967 (AFN22:267); 10 Pere Marquette St Pk (CBC), Dec 20, 1969 (AFN24:313); 1, Crane Lake (CBC), Dec 18, 1971 (AB26:372). *High counts:* 2,000, Mark Twain NWR, mid-Sep 1963 (SV); 100, Illinois Beach St Pk, Apr 20, 1966 (J. Probst); 236, Monroe Co (SBC), May 5, 1973; 1,200, Mason Co, Apr 20, 1974 (HDB); 5,000, Chautauqua NWR, Aug 30, 1975 (HDB); 21,420, Illinois River Valley, Sep 12, 1975 (IDOC).

Cinnamon Teal *(Anas cyanoptera)*

Late March — Mid-April

Status: Rare vagrant.
Documentation: Photographic — ♂, Quiver Creek, Mason Co, Apr 7, 1971 (Howard Ermeling; bird captured by Robert Crompton-photo on file ISM).
Remarks: Mostly observed in spring, but may be due to resemblance of fall plumaged Blue-winged Teals. Usually migrates farther west. *Recent records:* ♂, Tazewell Co, Mar 21, 1959 (Kanapel, Starrett-AFN13:374); ♂, 3 miles north of Sparland, Marshall Co, Mar 18, 1967 (Princen, 1968); ♂, near Thomson, Apr 9-17, 1968 (Grabers, Shaws-AFN22:532); ♂, Horseshoe Lake, Alexander Co, Mar 23, 1970 (HDB).
Hybrid: A hybrid, Cinnamon x Blue-winged Teal, photographed at Aledo, Mercer Co, Apr 15, 1975 (Bill Betrand-photo on file ISM).

European Wigeon *(Anas penelope)*

Late March — Late April
Mid-September — Late October

Status: Very rare vagrant in north and central.
Documentation: Specimen(s) — Ad ♂, Nippersink Lake, Lake Co, Apr 1, 1904 (Deane, 1905).
Remarks: There are at least 13 old records, some without details, of this Old World species (see Hasbrouck, 1944a, for an interesting account of this species in North America). Majority of the records are for spring. Occurs in same habitat as American Wigeon. *Recent records:* ♂, east of Sterling, Whiteside Co, Apr 14, 1958 (Keegan-IAB108:16); ♂, Illinois River near Chillicothe, Peoria Co, Jan 25, 1968 (Princen, 1969); 1 with no details, Lock 13 near Fulton, Whiteside Co, Apr 18, 1970 (Wickstrom-IAB155:26).

American Wigeon *(Anas americana)*

Late February — Early May
Mid-September — Early December

Status: Common migrant. Uncommon winter resident in south and central. Occasional winter resident in north. Rare summer (nonbreeding) resident.
Documentation: Specimen(s) — ♀, DeKalb, DeKalb Co, Apr 5, 1963 (NIU 306).
Remarks: Found on ponds, lakes, and overflow areas. *Records:* 1, Baker Lake, Cook Co, July 21, 1963 (CC); 4, Barrington (CBC), Dec 17, 1973 (AB28:376); 1, near Havana, Mason Co, June 1-23, 1974 (HDB); 2, Lake Calumet, July 20, 1975 (AB29:979). *High counts:* 46,400, in Illinois, Oct 17, 1956 (INHS-AFN11:29); 400, Palos Park, Cook Co, Nov 7, 1965 (J. Probst); 500, Pere Marquette St Pk, Dec 26, 1965 (AFN20:265); 37,960, Illinois River Valley, Nov 17, 1975 (IDOC).

Northern Shoveler *(Anas clypeata)*

Mid-March — Mid-May
Late August — Late November

Status: Common migrant. Rare summer resident in north and central. Uncommon winter resident in south. Occasional winter resident in north and central.
Documentation: Specimen(s) — ♀, Lake Calumet, Cook Co, Sep 1957 (PM 1959-138).
Remarks: Found on shallow lakes, ponds, and overflow areas. *Summer records:* ♀ with 6 young, Cook Co, July 21, 1968 (PD); ♂, Powderhorn Lake, Cook Co, July 15, 1972 (CC-AB26:865); 3 broods, north of Cuba, Fulton Co, June 30, 1973 (HDB); 4, near Havana, June 15, 1974 (HDB). *Other records:* 5, Calumet City (CBC), Dec 14, 1974 (AB29:408). *High counts:* 70, Pere Marquette St Pk (CBC), Dec 26, 1965 (AFN20:265); 43, Union County Refuge (CBC), Dec 31, 1972 (AB27:376); 65, McLean Co (SBC), May 5, 1973; 1,000, Mason Co, Mar 16, 1974 (HDB); 2,190, Mississippi River Valley, Nov 24, 1975 (IDOC).

Wood Duck *(Aix sponsa)*

Early March — Mid-November

Status: Common migrant and summer resident. Occasional winter resident in north and central. Uncommon winter resident in south.
Documentation: Specimen(s) — ♀, Fulton Co (across river from Havana), Oct 17, 1970 (ISM 604804).
Remarks: Found along wooded creeks and ponds. Most numerous duck breeding in the state. *Winter records:* 1, Robert Allerton Park (CBC), Jan 1, 1957 (AFN11:170); 80, Mermet Lake Area (CBC), Dec 21, 1965 (AFN20:263); 2, Chicago Lake Front, Dec 22, 1966 (AFN21:252); 3, Barrington, Dec 28, 1966 (AFN21:250). *High counts:* 504 captured and banded, Gilbert Lake, Jersey Co, summer, 1963 (SV); 200, Milan, Rock Island Co, Aug 1, 1966 (J. Frink); 296, Lake Charleston, Coles Co, Oct 19, 1969 (M. Conlin); 73, Will Co (SBC), May 4, 1974; 2,140, Illinois River Valley, Oct 20, 1975 (IDOC).

Redhead *(Aythya americana)*

Mid-February — Late April
Early October — Early December

Status: Fairly common migrant. Uncommon winter resident in central and south. Occasional winter resident in north. Rare summer resident.
Documentation: Specimen(s) — ♂, near LaGrange, Brown Co, Nov 3, 1972 (ISM 605390).
Remarks: Found on ponds and lakes. *Summer records:* 1, Chicago, July 20, 1968 (CC-IAB148:18); 1, Grand Tower, Jackson Co, June 1, 1973 (DH-AB27:875); 1, Goose Lake Prairie, June 13, 1973 (DBi-AB27:875); 3 ♂, and 1 ♀, near Havana, June 15, 1974 (HDB); pair, Lake Calumet, June 9, 1974 (CC-AB28:909); pair, plus 10 young, marsh east of Lake Calumet July 6, 1975 (CC); 2 family groups, Lake Co, summer 1975 (GR). *High counts:* 430, Shelbyville Lake, Mar 20, 1971 (HDB); 500, Wolf Lake, Chicago, Mar 25, 1972 (LB-AB26:611); 500, Mason Co, Mar 3, 1973 (HDB); 8,000, Keokuk Pool, Mississippi River, Mar 1974 (GA-AB28:646); 4,100, Mississippi River Valley, Nov 17, 1975 (IDOC).

Ring-necked Duck *(Aythya collaris)*

Early March — Late April
Mid-October — Late November

Status: Uncommon migrant. Uncommon winter resident. Rare (nonbreeding) summer resident.
Documentation: Specimen(s) — ♂, 7 miles north of Ohio, Lee Co, Mar 17, 1961 (NIU 036).
Remarks: Found on ponds and lakes. *Summer records:* ♀, Urbana, June 6, 1963 (PN); two pairs, Grand Tower, Jackson Co, June 9, 1973 (DH-AB27:875); 1, Lake Co, summered, 1973 (LB-AB27:875); ♂, Powderhorn Lake, Cook Co, June 30, 1974 (CC-AB28:909). *High counts:* 2,500, Mark Twain NWR, Nov 27, 1963 (SV); 127, Crab Orchard NWR (CBC), Dec 18, 1971 (AB26:371); 184, Pere Marquette St Pk (CBC), Dec 26, 1971 (AB26:376);

1,285, McGinnis Slough, Cook Co, Apr 9, 1972 (LB); 159, Lake Co (SBC), May 6, 1972; 200, Palos Park, Cook Co, Nov 5, 1972 (LB); 40,000, Keokuk Pool, Mississippi River, Mar 1974 (GA-AB28:646); 18,145, Mississippi River Valley, November 17, 1975 (IDOC).

Canvasback *(Aythya valisineria)*

Mid-February — Mid-April
Late October — Mid-December

Status: Fairly common migrant (often abundant along Illinois and Mississippi rivers). Uncommon local winter resident in south and central. Rare winter resident in north. Very rare summer resident.
Documentation: Specimen(s) — ♂, Lake Lou Yeager, Montgomery Co, Dec 7, 1975 (ISM 606279).
Remarks: Found on large rivers and lakes. *Summer records:* ♀ and three young, Powderhorn Lake, Cook Co, July 5, 1965 (CC-AFN19:551); ♂, near Grand Tower, Jackson Co, July 3, 1973 (DH-AB27:875). *Other records:* 1, Lake Co (SBC), May 6, 1972; 2, McHenry Co (SBC), May 5, 1973; 1, Cass Co (SBC), May 4, 1974; 1, Mason Co, May 31, 1975 (HDB). *High counts:* 2,500, Rockford, Mar 29, 1959 (LJ-AFN13:374); 400, Chautauqua NWR, wintered 1959-60 (AFN14:312); 948,500, Keokuk Pool between Hamilton and Nauvoo, Hancock Co, Nov 5, 1969 (Wilds, 1972-73); 600, Mississippi River, near Grafton, Jan 11, 1972 (HDB); 50,000, Keokuk Pool, Mid-Nov 1973 (GA-AB28:59); 80,000, Keokuk Pool, Mar 1974 (GA-AB28:646); 251, Crab Orchard NWR (CBC), Dec 28, 1974 (AB29:411); 100, Lawrence Co, Mar 8-15, 1975 (D. Jones).

Greater Scaup *(Aythya marila)*

Mid-October — Late March
Status: Common migrant and fairly common winter resident along Lake Michigan. Rare migrant and winter resident in the remainder of state.
Documenation: Specimen(s) — ♂, Mississippi River, Keokuk Pool, Hancock Co, Nov 1972 (ISM 605603).
Remarks: Status is unclear due to confusion with Lesser Scaup. The two species often fly in mixed flocks on Lake Michigan and are by far the most numerous migrant on the lake (LB). Usually found on large lakes and rivers.
Records: Pair, Barrington, Aug 7, 1966 (Horwitz-AFN20:574); 1, Chicago, July 20, 1968 (CC-IAB148:18); 3, Cook Co (SBC), May 6, 1972; 2, Lake Co (SBC), May 4, 1974; ♂, Waukegan, June 29, 1975 (CC-AB29:979). *High counts:* 1,700, Chicago Harbor, Mar 21, 1971 (LB); 1,080, Chicago Lake front (CBC), Dec 28, 1971 (AB26:370).

Lesser Scaup *(Aythya affinis)*

Late September — Mid-May

Status: Abundant Migrant. Uncommon winter resident. Rare summer resident.
Documentation: Specimen(s) — ♀, Springfield, Apr 1, 1973 (ISM 605607).

Remarks: Found on ponds, lakes, and overflow areas. *Summer records:* Pair nested, Hackney's Sandbar in the Mississippi River, near Quincy, summer, 1968 (TEM-AFN22:612); 2 ♀, Mark Twain NWR, July 18, 1973 (SV-AB27:875); 12, near Havana, June 23, 1974 (HDB). *High counts:* 14,000, Crab Orchard NWR, Mar 16, 1955 (Bush-AFN9:334); 4,500, Wilmette, Nov 5, 1960 (RR-AFN9:334); 140, Hancock Co (SBC), May 4, 1974; 152,360, Mississippi River Valley, Nov 17, 1975 (IDOC).

Tufted Duck *(Aythya fuligula)*

Status: Very rare vagrant in north.
Documentation: Sight record with acceptable details — Ad ♂, Chicago Harbor, Dec 3, 1972 - Apr 10, 1973 (CC — on file ISM).
Remarks: 3 records. Eurasian species, believed to migrant south with Greater Scaup. *Other records:* ♂, Chicago, Dec 23-27, 1973 (CC-AB28:646); Im ♂ (with shorter tuft), Lake Calumet, Mar 17, 1974 (CC-AB28:646).

Common Goldeneye *(Bucephala clangula)*

Late October — Mid-April

Status: Common migrant and winter resident. Very rare (nonbreeding) summer resident.
Documentation: Specimen(s) — ♀, near Hamilton, Hancock Co, Nov 7, 1968 (ISM 604208).
Remarks: Found on the deeper lakes and rivers. *Records:* Ad ♂, Lake Calumet, July 5, 1965 (CC); ♀, Lake Calumet, May 16, 1971 (LB-AB25:751); ♂, Fox River, near Dundee, Cook Co, May 28, 1971 (RM-AB25:751); 5, Lake Co (SBC), May 6, 1972; ♀ (cripple), Cash River, Alexander Co, June 22, 1973 (VK, D. Kennedy-AB27:875); pair, Waukegan, June 29, 1975 (CC-AB29:970). *High counts:* 2,217, Chicago, Dec 26, 1955 (AFN10:163); 221, Decatur (CBC), Dec 27, 1956 (AFN11:168); 350, Rockford, Jan 17, 1959 (Prentice-AFN13:296); 500, Mark Twain NWR, Dec 1, 1963 (SV); 820, Chicago (CBC), Dec 21, 1965 (AFN20:261); 1,500, Wilmette, Nov 11, 1971 (LB); 10,840, Mississippi River Valley, Dec 8 & 9, 1975 (IDOC).

Barrow's Goldeneye *(Bucephala islandica)*

Mid-November — Mid-April

Status: Rare migrant and winter resident.
Documentation: Specimen(s) — ♂, Illinois River near Chillicothe, Peoria Co, Nov 1964 (Mounted specimen—Jack Rinehart, private collection, partial skeleton in ISM 684872).
Remarks: Found on deep lakes and rivers. Hens of two species of Goldeneye very difficult to separate. Reports of experienced observers only are acceptable. There are two old specimens from Illinois (see Hasbrouck, 1944b). *Recent records:* 2 ♂, and 1 ♀, killed (from a flock of 7) Quincy, Nov 15, 1955 (TEM-AFN10:28); ♂, Belmont Harbor, Chicago, Dec 15-31, 1956 (Nork, King, Bi-AFN11:268); ♂, Crab Orchard NWR, Mar 11, 1957 (Bush-AFN11:269); first year ♂, Wilmette, Apr 12, 1963 (RR-IAB159:17); ♂, Mark Twain NWR, Dec 13, 1963 (SV); ♂, Crab Orchard NWR, Mar 10, 1967 (George, 1968, p. 5); ♂, Nauvoo, Hancock Co, Mar 14, 1968 (Franks-AFN22:444); ♂, Lake Calumet, Feb 20, 1971 (LB, CC, JF, GR-AB25:585); ♂, Mississippi River near Grafton, Jan 20, 1973 (VK, WO, HDB).

Bufflehead *(Bucephala albeola)*

Late February — Late April
Late October — Early December

Status: Fairly common migrant and occasional winter resident.
Documentation: Specimen(s) — ♂, Mississippi River, Keokuk Pool, Hancock Co, Nov 1972 (ISM 605413).
Remarks: Found on ponds, especially in spring; at other times prefers lakes. *Records:* ♀, Waukegan, Aug 10, 1968 (CC-AFN23:64); 1, McGinnis Slough, Cook Co, May 23, 1970 (CC-AFN24:614); 1, Goose Lake Prairie, June 2, 1972 (CC-AB28:909); 8, Cook Co (SBC), May 5, 1973; 8, McHenry Co (SBC), May 4, 1974. *High counts:* 75, Mark Twain NWR, Nov 22, 1969 (SV-AFN24:54); 40, Chicago, Nov 11, 1971 (LB-IAB162:20); 150, Chautauqua NWR, Nov 22, 1975 (RS, RP, HDB); 1,305, Mississippi River Valley, Dec 1, 1975 (IDOC).

Oldsquaw *(Clangula hyemalis)*

Early November — Mid-April

Status: Common migrant and winter resident on Lake Michigan. Rare migrant and winter resident in the remainder of state.
Documentation: Specimen(s) — ♂, Wilmette, Cook Co, Mar 26, 1972 (ISM 605342).
Remarks: Found on large lakes. *Records:* 2, Crab Orchard NWR, Oct 31, 1959 (Bush-AFN14:39); ♂ collected, Cairo, Dec 11, 1961 (SIU); 1, Lake Decatur, Dec 22-24, 1961 (RS, TN-AFN16:333); ♂, Mattoon, Jan 2, 1965 (HDB); 1, Waukegan, May 24, 1970 (CC-AFN24:614); 1, Crab Orchard NWR, Dec 28, 1970 (DH-AB25:352); 3, Lake Shelbyville, Oct 16, 1973 (WO, RS, HDB); 1, Lake Decatur, Oct 1, 1974 (RS). *High counts:* 1,000, Waukegan (CBC), Jan 1, 1962 (AFN16:213); 875, Wilmette, Nov 4, 1970 (LB); 1,200, Glencoe, Apr 4, 1971 (RR-AB25:585).

Harlequin Duck *(Histrionicus histrionicus)*

Mid-October — Late March

Status: Rare migrant and winter resident on Lake Michigan. Very rare winter resident in the remainder of state.
Documentation: Specimen — 7 miles from St. Louis (Madison Co, Illinois), Oct 29, 1880 (Hurter Coll. WU—reported as missing by Bennet, Mar 17-18, 1933).
Remarks: Found near rocky shores on large lakes. Recently has occurred yearly on Lake Michigan. *Records:* 3, Chicago, between Dec 8-18, 1955 (Eiseman, Campbell-AFN9:261); ♂, Lake Decatur, from Dec 30, 1955 to Mar 28, 1956 (RS; photographed, TN-copy ISM); ♀, Wilmette, Nov 1, 1961 (RR-AFN16:36); 1, Waukegan, Jan 1, 1963 (RR-AFN17:206); 1, Chicago, Feb and Mar 1964 (F. Brecklin-AFN18:359); 1, Chicago, Dec 30, 1964 (RR-AFN9:231); Im ♂, Evanston, Oct 28 - late Nov 1968 (RR-AFN23:64); 1, Evanston, Nov 22, 1969 (CC-AFN24:54); ♀, Lock and Dam 13 on Mississippi River, Whiteside Co, Nov 13, 1971 (LB, GR-AB26:71); ♂, Montrose Harbor, Chicago, Nov 27, 1971 (LB, CC-AB26:71); 1, Chicago, Oct 15, 1972

(LB, CC-AB27:67); 1, Chicago, Oct 22, 1972 (LB, GR-AB27:67); 1, Chicago, Dec 23, 1972 (GR, W. Krawiec-AB27:367); 1, Chicago, Sep 22, 1973 and Oct 28 - Nov 3, 1973 (LB, CC-AB28:59); 1, Evanston, Oct 13, 1974 (LB-AB29:65); 1, Evanston, May 9, 1975 (GR-AB29:859).

Common Eider *(Somateria mollissima)*

Early December — Mid-April

Status: Very rare vagrant on Lake Michigan.
Documentation: Specimen — Im, near Chicago, Dec 1874 (Nelson, 1876).
Remarks: Only 4 records of this coastal species. *Records: ♂, S. m. dresseri,* Lincoln Park, Chicago, Apr 12, 1943 (Clark & Nice, 1950); 1, Belmont Harbor, Cook Co, Dec 7, 1945 (Ford, 1956); ♂, Chicago, Feb 1, 1960 (Fetter, Lane-AFN14:312).

King Eider *(Somateria spectabilis)*

Late November — Mid-March

Status: Very rare winter resident.
Documentation: Specimen(s) — Im ♂, Outer Basin of Mississippi River, near New Boston, Mercer Co, Nov 18, 1950 (PM 1950-32).
Remarks: Sea duck. Usually found on large lakes and rivers. *Recent records:* Im ♂, Calumet Park, Mar 3, 1968 (Bi, JG, CC-AFN22:444); ♀ photographed (on file (ISM), Lake Decatur, from Feb 13 - Mar 26, 1971 (TN, HDB); Im ♂ and 2 ♀ were shot (specimens in private collections), Rend Lake, Jefferson Co, Nov 1973 (Harvy Pitt); 1 dead, Chicago, Nov 24, 1974 (LB-AB29:65); 1, Wilmette, Dec 14-23, 1974 (GR, LB-AB29:697).

White-winged Scoter *(Melanitta deglandi)*

Mid-October — Mid-April

Status: Uncommon migrant and occasional winter resident on Lake Michigan. Rare migrant and winter resident in the remainder of state.
Documentation: Specimen(s) — ♀, 4 miles south of Warsaw, Hancock Co, Nov 25, 1955 (ISM 683832).
Remarks: Most numerous of the scoters in Illinois. Found on large lakes and rivers. *Records:* 1, Lake Mauvesterre, Jacksonville, Apr 26, 1969 (WO); 1, Lake Decatur, Dec 27, 1969 (RS, FI-AFN24:309); 1, Crab Orchard NWR, late Jan - Feb 16, 1971 (DH, F. Reuter-AB25:585); ♂, Clifton Terrace, Mississippi River, Feb 13, 1972 (HDB); 1, Thomson, Oct 29, 1972 (Shaws-IAB164:41); 1, Pierce Lake, Winnebago Co, Nov 18, 1972 (Dunn-AB27:68); 1, Champaign, Dec 8-10, 1973 (D. Friedman-AB29:697). *High counts:* 520, Glencoe, Dec 29, 1955 (Bi-AFN10:254); 1,000, Wilmette, Feb 24, 1963 (RR); 1,000, Wilmette, Mar 12 &17, 1972 (RR, LB-AB26:611).

Surf Scoter *(Melanitta perspicillata)*

Early March — Mid-April
Early October — Early December

Status: Uncommon migrant and rare winter resident on Lake Michigan. Rare migrant in the remainder of state.
Documentation: Specimen(s) — Im, Horseshoe Lake, Madison Co, Oct 29, 1976 (SIU Cooperative Wildlife Research Laboratory).

Remarks: Found on larger bodies of water. Practically all seen in fall are females and Im. *Records:* 1, Crab Orchard NWR, Oct 30, 1957 (Bush-AFN12:35); ♀, Peoria, Nov 10, 1966 (IAB140:6); 40, Chicago, Nov 4, 1967 (CC-AFN22:48); ♀, Lincoln Park, Chicago, Dec 15, 1968 (CC); Im, Lake Charleston, Nov 5, 1969 (M. Conlin, LBH-AFN24:54); 7, Chicago, Oct 17, 1971 (LB-IAB162:20); ♀, Alton Dam, Madison Co, Mar 8, 1972 (RA, PB-AB26:611); 3, Tazewell Co, Apr 13, 1974 (R. Bjorklund-AB28:808); 1, Wilmette, May 11, 1974 (LB-AB28:808); 6, Lake Decatur, Oct 14, 1974 (RS); 1 photographed, Whiteside Co, May 10, 1975 (EF); 1, Chicago, Dec 27, 1975 (RR-AB30:428).

Black Scoter *(Melanitta nigra)*

Mid-March — Late March
Early October — Early December

Status: Uncommon migrant and rare winter resident on Lake Michigan. Rare migrant in remainder of state.
Documentation: Specimen(s) — Im ♂, Crab Orchard NWR, Oct 23, 1958 (SIU A-722).
Remarks: Found on large lakes. *Records:* 1, Mark Twain NWR, Nov 24, 1963 (RA); 1, Wilmette, June 16, 1964 (RR-AFN18:511); 40, Chicago, Nov 4, 1967 (CC-AFN22:48); 1 collected, Charleston Lake, Dec 5, 1970 (LBH-AB24:585); 1, Waukegan, Sep 8, 1971 (RR-AB26:71); 1, Alton Dam, Madison Co, Mar 25, 1972 (DE-AB26:611); 25, Chicago, Oct 13, 1974 (LB-AB29:65); 14, Pool 19, Mississippi River, Hancock Co, Oct 27, 1974 (GA-AB29:65); ♀, Rend Lake, Nov 4, 1974 (Harvy Pitt); ♀, Chautauqua NWR, Nov 29, 1974 (HDB); 1, Peoria, Mar 24-25, 1975 (R. Scott). *High count:* 111, Wilmette, Oct 25, 1976 (LB, GR).

Ruddy Duck *(Oxyura jamaicensis)*

Early March — Early May
Late September — Late November

Status: Common migrant. Uncommon summer resident and occasional winter resident in north. Rare summer resident and occasional winter resident in central and south.
Documentation: Specimen(s) — ♀, Keokuk Pool, Mississippi River, Hancock Co, Nov 1969 (ISM 604814).
Remarks: Found on lakes, ponds, and overflow areas. *Summer records:* 2 pairs nested, Lake Calumet, summer, 1955 (KB-AFN9:381); downy young, Chicago, Sep 18, 1959 (Fetter-AFN14:39); 10 pair, McGinnis Slough, June 1, 1964 (CC); pair, Jacksonville, July 19, 1972 (WO); 2 broods, Grand Tower, Jackson Co, July 18, 1973 (DH-AB27:875); 10 ♂ and 5 ♀, Lake Co, summer, 1973 (LB-AB27:875). *Other records:* 17, Channahon (CBC), Dec 29, 1956 (AFN11:167); 4, Chicago, Dec 27, 1969 (AFN24:307); 118, Cook Co (SBC), May 5, 1973. *High count:* 7,000, Alton area, Madison Co, Apr 15, 1964 (SV-AFN18:455); 20,000, Chautauqua NWR, Apr 16, 1964 (Bellrose-AFN18:455).

Hooded Merganser *(Lophodytes cucullatus)*

Late October — Early April

Status: Uncommon migrant. Occasional winter resident in north. Uncommon winter resident in central and south. Rare summer resident throughout state.

Documentation: Specimen(s) — ♂, 6 miles southwest of Hull, Pike Co, Dec 12, 1953 (ISM 603663).
Remarks: Found on wooded lakes and rivers; also occurs on open lakes especially during migration. *Summer records:* ♂ collected, Crab Orchard NWR, June 30, 1966 (SIU); ♀ with a brood of 5, Mark Twain NWR, June 12 and 18, 1970 (SV-IAB156:21); ♀, Powderhorn Marsh, Cook Co, May 27, 1972 (LB, CC-AB26:766); ♀, Springfield, May 12, 1973 (HDB); Im, Grand Tower, June 20, 1973 (VK, DH-AB27:875); young, Massac Co, June 1, 1974 (VK-AB28:808). *High counts:* 400, Crab Orchard NWR, Nov 30, 1960 (Bush-AFN15:45); 185, Mark Twain NWR, Nov 25, 1963 (S.J. Hanselmann); 100, Springfield (CBC), Dec 26, 1965 (AFN20:267).

Common Merganser *(Mergus merganser)*

Mid-November — Early April

Status: Common migrant and winter resident. Very rare summer (nonbreeding) resident.
Documentation: Specimen(s) — ♀, Keokuk Pool, Mississippi River, Hancock Co, Nov 1969 (ISM 604639).
Remarks: Found on open water, usually large lakes and rivers. Much less numerous on Lake Michigan due to the disappearance of certain fish. *Summer records:* ♂, Hampton, Lock 14, Rock Island Co, June 12 - July 10, 1955 (PCP-IAB98:15); pair, Lake Calumet, June 26 - Aug 2, 1970 (CC-AFN24:690). *High counts:* 2,634, Chicago (CBC), Dec 27, 1958 (AFN13:186); 1,390, Crab Orchard NWR, Nov 30, 1960 (Bush-AFN15:45); 750, Pere Marquette St Pk (CBC), Dec 26, 1966 (AFN21:257); 835, Crane Lake, Mason Co (CBC), Jan 2, 1971 (JF, HDB).

Red-breasted Merganser *(Mergus serrator)*

Early March — Early May
Early November — Early December

Status: Common migrant (at times abundant along Lake Michigan). Uncommon winter resident in north. Occasional winter resident in central and south. Much more common spring migrant than fall migrant in central and south. Very rare summer (nonbreeding) resident.
Documentation: Specimen(s) — ♀, Lake Decatur, Dec 23, 1973 (ISM 606226).
Remarks: Found on large bodies of water. *Summer records:* ♂, Lake Calumet, July 11 and Aug 2, 1970 (CC-AFN24:690); ♀, Wolf Lake, Cook Co, Aug 8, 1970 (CC-AFN24:690); 2 ♀, Sangchris St Pk from June 8 - July 4, 1974 (RP, HDB). *Other records:* 45, Cook Co (SBC), May 4, 1974. *High counts:* 686, Chicago (CBC), Dec 29, 1956 (AFN11:167); 1,000, Wilmette, Nov 12, 1960 (RR-AFN15:45); 1,200, Evanston, Apr 11, 1968 (RR-AFN22:532); 2,300, Illinois Beach St Pk, Nov 14, 1971 (LB); 700, Wolf Lake, Cook Co, Mar 25, 1972 (LB, GR-AB26:611); 1,400, Chicago, Apr 21, 1975 (LB-AB29:859); 175, Rend Lake, Nov 23, 1975 (BP).

FALCONIFORMES: Vultures, Eagles and Hawks.

Turkey Vulture *(Cathartes aura)*

Early March — Late October

Status: Common migrant and summer resident in south. Uncommon migrant and summer resident in north and central. Occasional winter resident as far north in eastern Illinois as Vermilion Co; very rare winter resident in western Illinois.

Documentation: Specimen(s) — Ad, Henry, Marshall Co, Apr 21, 1906 (FMNH 21339).

Remarks: Found in hilly areas and bluff areas along rivers. *Summer record:* 2 nests, Lake County, summer, 1975 (RR). *Winter records:* 3, Urbana, Dec 26, 1955 (AFN10:166); 1, western Mercer Co, Jan 2, 1961 (Greer-AFN15:215); 1, Morton Arboretum, Jan 18, 1964 (CC-AFN18:359); 1, near Georgetown (CBC), Dec 29, 1970 (AB25:354); 7, near Marshall, Clark Co (CBC), Dec 28, 1970 (AB25:355). *High counts:* 23, Quincy, Oct 2, 1964 (TEM); 62, Johnson Co (SBC), May 6, 1972; 41, Clark Co (SBC), May 5, 1973; 75, Jersey Co (SBC), May 4, 1974.

Black Vulture *(Coragyps atratus)*

Status: Uncommon permanent resident in south. Very rare vagrant in central and north.

Documentation: Photographic — Ad, northeast corner of Union Co, June 4, 1972 (VK — on file ISM).

Remarks: Found in swampy areas and bluffs of extreme southern Illinois. Migrational status of this species is unclear; some of the population may leave the breeding grounds during winter. *Old record for north:* 1 found dead, near Highland Park, Lake Co, Nov 18, 1909 (Coale, 1912). *Records:* 1, Adams Co, Mar 26, 1961 (TEM-AFN15:414); 1, Fort Chartres, July 28, 1962 (RA, IAB129:18); 1, Mermet Lake, Massac Co, Dec 21, 1965 (AFN20:263); 1 young banded, Union Co, Aug 12, 1971 (VK-AB25:863); 30, Heron Pond Nature Preserve, Johnson Co, Mar 6, 1974 (VK, HDB); 4, Pope Co (SBC), May 4, 1974.

[White-tailed Kite *(Elanus leucurus)*]

Status: Hypothetical

Remarks: Ridgway (1889) states: "As to the occurrence of this species in Illinois, we have little information, the only record being that of the writer's previous lists, based on a pair observed near the river at Mt. Carmel during the summer of 1863 or 1864." There are several records from Rantoul for winter and spring of 1917, but these seem quite unbelievable and must have been a misidentification (Ekblaw, 1917). No specimens or other documentation from Illinois. Now spreading in California and Texas and vagrants could well be found in Illinois.

Swallow-tailed Kite *(Elanoides forficatus)*

Status: Extirpated. Now a very rare vagrant. [Formerly a fairly common migrant and summer resident throughout state, probably more numerous in south.]

Documentation: Specimen(s) — 3 Ad, Highland Park, Lake Co, Apr 1905; 1 in collection of James S. White (Ford, 1956).

Remarks: Can occur as vagrant from southern populations. *Old records:* Ridgway saw hundreds at one time performing their graceful aerial evolutions near Olney, Richland Co, in 1871 (George, 1968, p. 7). 1, about 5 miles southeast of Clinton, DeWitt Co, in early June 1906 (Hull, 1913); 1, listed for Rockford and vicinity, May 5, 1917, without details (Nature Study Society of Rockford, 1917-18). *Recent record:* 1, Lodge Park, Piatt Co, May 20, 1974 (Clemens & Kulesza, 1973-74).

Mississippi Kite *(Ictinia mississippiensis)*

Early April — Early September

Status: Uncommon migrant and local summer resident along the Mississippi River in south. Very rare vagrant in central and north. [Formerly common in south.]

Documentation: Specimen — ♂, Falling Spring (now part of E. St. Louis), St. Clair Co, July 26, 1885 (WU, Hurter Coll 57).

Remarks: Found in swamps and open areas near Mississippi River. Very few recent records until June 1962, along a Mississippi levee between Fults and Kidd in Monroe Co. Nest discovered there in mid-Aug 1962 (RA). *Other records:* 1, Pere Marquette St Pk, Jersey Co, Sep 22, 1956 (D. Jones, JEC-AFN11:29); Ad, Evanston, Aug 18 and 24, 1968 (RR); nest photographed, Kaskaskia St Pk, Randolph Co, summer, 1972 (RA-AB26:865); 1, Monroe Co (SBC), May 6, 1972; 1, Jackson Co (SBC), May 5, 1973; 1, Chicago, May 12, 1974 (W. Krawiec-AB28:808); 1, 10 miles south of Jacksonville, Morgan Co, May 23, 1976 (P. Gibson, RS). *High count:* 19, Union Co, June 3, 1974 (VK).

Goshawk *(Accipiter gentilis)*

Late November — Early March

Status: Occasional winter resident in north and rare in central and south (except in invasion years, then uncommon in north and central and occasional in south).

Documentation: Specimen(s) — Ad ♀, near Lake Carlyle, Fayette Co, Nov 25, 1972 (ISM 605412).

Remarks: Woodland species. Seems to prefer coniferous woods. In the winter of 1972-73, the largest invasion on record took place. 243 records (some probably the same birds) totaled between Sep 30, 1972 and Apr 8, 1973. Other invasion years, 1870-71, 1896-97, 1907-08, and 1916-17 (Burr & Current, 1974). *Invasion records:* 8, Illinois Beach St Pk, Nov 11, 1972 (LB, CC-AB27:68); 18 banded, Max McGraw Wildlife Area at Dundee during the winter of 1972-73 (AB27:68); Ad, Chautauqua NWR, Oct 21 - Nov 24, 1972 (HDB); Ad, north of Sparta, Randolph Co, Dec 1, 1972 (VK-AB27:68); 2, Boone Co (SBC), May 5, 1973. *The following winter an echo invasion occurred:* 3, Max McGraw Wildlife Area, Sep 25, 1973 (Stan Dahlke-AB28:60); Ad, Mason Co, Nov 10-23, 1973 (HDB). *Other records:* 1, Decatur, Feb 1 & 12, 1956 (Chaniot-AFN10:254); 1, Pere Marquette St Pk, Dec 26, 1965 (RA-AFN20:265); 1, S. Cook Co, Nov 12, 1974 (LB-AB29:65).

Sharp-shinned Hawk *(Accipiter striatus)*

Late March — Mid-May
Mid-September — Late October

Status: Fairly common migrant and uncommon winter resident. [Formerly rare summer resident in north.]

Documentation: Specimen(s) — Ad ♀, near Genoa, DeKalb Co, Apr 9, 1969 (NIU 2787).

Remarks: Found in woodland and along woodland edges. During migration can be seen flying with other hawks. *High counts:* 24, Chicago, Apr. 29, 1959 (Fetter, Lane-AFN13:374); 39, Lake Forest, Lake Co, Sep 24, 1964 (J. Probst); 70, Illinois Beach St Pk, Oct 10, 1966 (R. Gustafson, J. Probst); 40, Illinois Beach St Pk, Oct 22, 1968 (RR, K. Eckert); 7, Mason Co, Sep 22, 1973 (VK, RS, HDB); 35, Illinois Beach St Pk, Oct 14, 1973 (LB-AB28:60).

Cooper's Hawk *(Accipiter cooperii)*

Mid-September — Late April

Status: Uncommon migrant and winter resident. Rare summer resident in north and central and occasional summer resident in the south.
Documentation: Specimen(s) — Ad ♂, near Cave-in-Rock, Hardin Co, June 27, 1954 (ISM 603664).
Remarks: A woodland or semiwoodland species. Seems to be declining. Far outnumbered by Sharp-shinned Hawks. *Summer records:* Nest, McHenry Co, Apr 30, 1963 (Carroll); nest, Lee Co, May 20, 1964 (Mades); nest, Lake Co, summer, 1965 (RR-IAB138:15); nest, Pomona, Jackson Co, Apr 1971 (William George-AB25:751); Ad, Williams Hill, Pope Co, July 27, 1971 (HDB); 1, near Decatur, May 27, 1974 (RP). *Other records:* 3, Tazewell Co, Sep 16, 1972 (Burr & Ogle, 1973).

Red-tailed Hawk *(Buteo jamaicensis)*

Status: Common migrant and winter resident. Fairly common summer resident.
Documentation: Specimen(s) — Im ♂, north of Browning, Schuyler Co, Jan 23, 1971 (ISM 604686).
Remarks: A species of semiopen areas and woodlots. Usually small flights occur during migration. *High counts:* 37, Port Byron, Rock Island Co, Sep 20, 1958 (RT-AFN13:35); 69, Rockford (CBC), Dec 26, 1960 (AFN15:214); 56, Pere Marquette St Pk (CBC), Dec 26, 1965 (AFN20:265); 71, Barrington (CBC), Dec 29, 1971 (AFN26:368); 55, Beverly (CBC), Dec 22, 1973 (AB28:377).
Subspecies: This species is quite variable in plumage and many recognizable forms are found in the state. The common subspecies is *B. j. borealis.* The other subspecies are uncommon to rare. *Records: B. j. kriderii* (occurs in light phase): Ad, near Channahon, Grundy Co, Dec 19, 1964 (CC); 1, near Beardstown, Cass Co, Dec 4, 1971 (HDB). *B. j. harlani* (occurs in dark and light phase; until the recent 32nd Supplement to the A.O.U. Check-list, this form was considered a full species): 1, Urbana, Dec 30, 1961 (Graber-AFN16:213); 1, Alexander Co, Apr 3, 1971 (VK-AB25:586). *B. j. calurus* (occurs in dark phase): 1, Elmhurst, Cook Co, Dec 19, 1971 (CC, LB-AB26:611). All 3 of these subspecies have specimen documentation.

Red-shouldered Hawk *(Buteo lineatus)*

Status: Common permanent resident in south. Occasional migrant; summer and winter resident in central and north. [Formerly fairly common migrant; summer and winter resident in central and north.]

39

Documentation: Specimen(s) — Ad ♂, 6 miles southwest of Hull, Pike Co, Nov 3, 1953 (ISM 603658).

Remarks: Woodland species. Very evident population decline in recent years in central and north. Has become sporadic in north and central and could occur any time of the year, but most often during migration. *Summer records:* Nest, Mason State Forest, 1972 (Bjorklund); nest, Winnebago Co, summer, 1975 (R. Knisley-AB29:979). *Other records:* 5, Wilmette, June 1, 1972 (RR-AB26:767); 2, Illinois Beach St Pk, Nov 11, 1972 (CC-AB27:68); 1, Decatur, Aug 3, 1974 (RP-AB29:65); 10, Crab Orchard NWR (CBC), Dec 29, 1973 (AB28:380); 1, Vermilion Co, Sep 22, 1974 (M. Campbell-AB29:65). *High counts:* 24, Port Byron, Rock Island Co, Sep 20, 1958 (RT-AFN13:35); 18, Olney (CBC), Dec 27, 1958 (AFN13:185); 18, Rockford (CBC), Dec 21, 1958 (AFN13:189); 15, Union Co (CBC), Jan 2, 1976 (AB30:437).

Broad-winged Hawk *(Buteo platypterus)*

Early April — Mid-May
Mid-September — Late October

Status: Common migrant. Uncommon summer resident in heavily wooded areas of the state.

Documentation: Specimen(s) — ♀, south side Crab Orchard Lake, Williamson Co, Mar 14, 1972 (SIU A-2344).

Remarks: Woodland species. Highly migratory. Usually follows rivers and bluff areas. At times fly high and can pass unnoticed. *Summer records:* Nest, Grafton, summer, 1964 (SV-AFN18:511); nest, Cook Co, May 10, 1966 (PD). *Most winter records highly doubtful:* Ad, Barrington, Dec 28, 1966 (Burger, Oldenberg-AFN21:250); 1, Crab Orchard, Dec 18, 1971 (Bush, Gelman-AB26:371). *High counts:* 400, Bushnell, McDonough Co, Sep 22, 1957 (LH-AFN12:35); 500, Quincy, Apr 18, 1966 (TEM-AFN20:514); 300, Rockford, Sep 11, 1969 (WS-AFN24:54); 8,000, East Peoria, Sep 16, 1974 (V. Humphreys-IAB172:28); 40, Skokie Lagoons, Apr 20, 1975 (LB); 2,000, Palos Park, Cook Co, Sep 23, 1975 (PD); 1,000, Bureau Co, Apr 26, 1976 (J. Hampson-AB30:848).

Color Morph: Dark phase, Springfield, Oct 5, 1971 (HDB).

Swainson's Hawk *(Buteo swainsoni)*

Late March — Mid-October

Status: Rare migrant. Rare local summer resident in north. [Formerly rare summer resident in central.]

Documentation: Specimen(s) — ♀, 4 miles south Kaneville, Kane Co, Apr 24, 1965 (NIU 995).

Remarks: Found in open areas with scattering of large trees. *Summer records:* 2 nests (later both destroyed), Boone Co, May 3, and Winnebago Co, May 11, 1958 (Seal-IAB108:6); 5 nests, northern Kane Co, spring, 1973 (J. Keir-AB27:781). *Other records:* 1, McGraw Wildlife Area, July 23, 1968 (Dillon, 1971); 1, Barrington, Oct 10, 1971 (CC-AB26:71); 1, Peoria Co, and 1, Whiteside Co (SBC), May 6, 1972; 1, Boone Co, 1, Kane Co, and 1, Kendall Co (SBC), May 5, 1973; 1, west of Decatur, May 4, 1974 (RS); Im, Mason Co, Apr 26, 1975 (HDB).

Rough-legged Hawk *(Buteo lagopus)*

Mid-October — Mid-April

Status: Common migrant and winter resident in north. Fairly common migrant and winter resident in central and south.

Documentation: Specimen(s) — light phase ♀, Rt. 74 on Knox Co and Peoria Co line, Dec 30, 1974 (ISM 606230).

Remarks: Found in open areas. Definite year-to-year fluctuations in numbers. From a 2-year census (1964-66), in DeKalb Co, of 441 birds observed, 31% were dark phase, 17% were intermediate phase, and 52% were light phase (Schnell, 1967). *Records:* Im, Lake Calumet, May 20, 1972 (LB-AB26:767); 1, Knox Co (SBC), May 10, 1975. *High counts:* 70, DeKalb (CBC), Jan 3, 1965 (AFN19:233); 73, DeKalb (CBC), Dec 27, 1970 (AB25:353); 22, Beverly (CBC), Dec 27, 1976 (AB31:679).

Ferruginous Hawk *(Buteo regalis)*

Mid-September — Mid-April

Status: Rare migrant and winter resident.

Documentation: Specimen(s) — ♀, Cook Co, Apr 21, 1939 (Gregory, 1948).

Remarks: Found in open hilly country. Most records come from western side of the state. *Records:* 2, Quincy, Sep 8, 1957 (TEM, Hartford-AFN12:35); 1, Quincy, Dec 21, 1958 (TEM-AFN13:297); 1, Quincy, Oct 8, 1961 (TEM-AFN16:36); Ad, Wood River, Jan 20, 1963 (RA-AFN17:328); 1, Morton Arboretum, Dec 26, 1964 (PD-AFN19:234); Im, Maquon, Knox Co, Apr 28, 1971 (HDB); Ad, Joliet, Dec 24, 1972 (Bi, CC-AB26:611); Im, Cuba, Fulton Co, Apr 1, 1972 (LB, HDB); Im, Chautauqua NWR, Nov 20, 1975 (RS).

[Gray Hawk *(Buteo nitidus)*]

Status: Hypothetical.

Remarks: This record is based on Ridgway's statement (1889): "A specimen of this tropical species was seen by the writer on Fox Prairie, in Richland Co, on the 19th of August, 1871." There are no specimens or other Illinois records, and the above statement is hardly enough evidence to add this species of the extreme southwestern U.S. to the state list.

Golden Eagle *(Aquila chrysaetos)*

Mid-October — Late March

Status: Rare migrant and winter resident. More numerous along the Mississippi River and the southwestern portion of the state.

Documentation: Specimen(s) — Im, Clark Co, Dec 11, 1968 (ISM 606459).

Remarks: Found in large trees along rivers, in open areas, and especially on waterfowl refuges in southern Illinois. This species has recently occurred yearly in the state. *Records:* 1, Rockford, Feb 7, 1958 (Prentice-AFN13:297); 2, Crab Orchard NWR, Jan 25, 1967 (Bush-AFN11:269); 1, Lisle, DuPage Co, Mar 28, 1968 (Campbell-AFN22:444); 1, Illinois Beach St Pk, May 10, 1972 (GR, RR-AB26:767); 1, Pere Marquette St Pk, Dec 23, 1972 (VK-AB27:373); 4 Im, Union Co, Dec 31, 1972 (VK, G. Cooper, MH-AB27:376); Im, Union Co Refuge, Apr 19, 1975 (BP-AB29:860); Im, Crane Lake, Mason Co, Dec 20, 1975 (JF, HDB).

Bald Eagle *(Haliaeetus leucocephalus)*

Late September — Early April

Status: Fairly common migrant and winter resident along the Illinois and Mississippi rivers and in southern Illinois on wildlife refuges. Rare migrant and winter resident in remainder of state. [Formerly nested.]
Documentation: Specimen(s) — Ad, Cordova, Rock Island Co, Dec 21, 1963 (PM 352.7).
Remarks: Usually found perched in large trees, on ice feeding, or soaring high overhead. Last known nesting, Horseshoe Lake, Alexander Co, in 1943 (Bellrose, 1944); two nests attended by pairs of Ad in the spring of 1974 at Crab Orchard NWR and Union County Refuge, but later deserted (VK). *Records:* 1, Grafton, Sep 11, 1965 (SV-AFN20:53); Im, Illinois Beach St Pk, May 30, 1971 (HDB); Ad, Crab Orchard NWR, May 6, 1972 (Bush-AB26:767). *High counts:* Eagle survey along Mississippi and Illinois rivers totaled 1,181, Feb 1972 (EF-AB26:611); 964, Feb 1973 (EF-AB27:623); and 825, Feb 8, 1975 (EF-IAB171:13).

Marsh Hawk *(Circus cyaneus)*

Late August — Early May

Status: Common migrant and winter resident. Occasional summer resident.
Documentation: Specimen(s) — Ad, Willow Springs, Cook Co, Dec 8, 1929 (FMNH 97544).
Remarks: Usually found over fallow fields. *Summer records:* 3, Rend Lake, Franklin Co, July 26, 1972 (VK-AB26:865); 2 nests, Goose Lake Prairie, summer, 1973 (DBi-AB27:875); ♀, Mason Co, and ♀, Fulton Co, June 30, 1973 (HDB). *Records:* 7, Lee Co (SBC), May 5, 1973; 3, Macon Co (SBC), May 4, 1974. *High counts:* 25, Decatur (CBC), Dec 23, 1961 (AFN16:210); 59, near Olney (CBC), Dec 26, 1961 (AFN16:208); 26, Lake Forest, Lake Co, Apr 6, 1965 (J. Probst); 250, Illinois Beach St Pk, Oct 10, 1966 (R. Gustafson, J. Probst); 30, along Lake Michigan, Oct 3, 1970 (CC); 71, between Evanston and Zion, Oct 14; 1973 (LB-AB28:60); 93, Illinois Beach St Pk, Oct 10, 1975 (LB, GR).

Osprey *(Pandion haliaetus)*

Early April — Late May
Early September — Late October

Status: Uncommon migrant. [Formerly summer resident.]
Documentation: Specimen(s) — ♀, Jacksonville, Morgan Co, Oct 4, 1972 (ISM 605533).
Remarks: Usually observed singly or in pairs along rivers and lakes. Seems to be more numerous in fall. Last known breeding record, Crab Orchard NWR, 1952 (Bennett, 1957). There are a few unverified winter records. *Records:* 6, Quincy, Aug 30, 1964 (TEM); 1, Mark Twain NWR, June 12, 1970 (SV-AFN24:690); 3, Lake Mattoon, Shelby Co, Sep 19-20, 1970 (J. Seets & W. Anderson-IAB156:23); 4, Tazewell Co, Sep 16, 1972 (Burr & Ogle, 1973); 1, Jackson Co, July 19, 1975 (BP-AB29:980).

Gyrfalcon *(Falco rusticolus)*

Early October — February

Status: Very rare migrant and winter resident in the north and central.
Documentation: Specimen — Im ♀, gray phase, south of Galena, Jo Daviess Co, Nov 3, 1971 (INHS-Burr and Current, 1975).
Remarks: Large arctic falcon. May be more numerous than previously expected. *Records:* 1 white phase, Arlington Heights, Cook Co, Dec 20 & 27, 1953 (Lukasik-IAB89:8); 1 no details, Chatsworth, Livingston Co, Feb 1964; Im ♀ gray phase photographed (on file — INHS), Spring Bluff Forest Preserve, Lake Co, Oct 4, 1966; 1 no details, Illinois Beach St Pk, Lake Co, Dec 28, 1966 (R. Gustafson-IAB140:6); 1 no details, Spring Bluff Forest Preserve, Lake Co, Oct 8, 1972; 1st-year ♀ gray phase photographed (on file — INHS), southeast of Esmond, DeKalb Co, Jan 7, 1973; Im ♂ gray phase photographed (on file — INHS), east of Roscoe, Winnebago Co, Oct 12, 1973; 1 no details, southwest of Polo, Ogle Co, Dec 1973; 1 gray phase Tazewell Co, Dec 31, 1976 (R. Jackson). *Note:* All from Burr & Current, 1975, unless otherwise noted.

Prairie Falcon *(Falco mexicanus)*

February — Early May
September — Mid-November

Status: Very rare vagrant.
Documentation: Specimen(s) — 1, near Emden, Logan Co, Feb 1937. (In possession of O.S. Biggs, San Jose, Ill.-Bellrose, 1939).
Remarks: Found in open areas. Due to population decrease, appearance in future more unlikely. 9 records, but some unsubstantiated. *Records:* 2 specimens, Rock Island Co: 1, date unknown; 1 collected, Oct 1857 (Bellrose, 1939); 1, Mt. Carmel, Wabash Co, Sep 1871 and 1, near Bridgeport, Lawrence Co, Sep 1871 (Ridgway, 1889); 1 collected, Warsaw, Mar 3, 1889 (Bellrose, 1939); 1 observed, Calumet region, May 4, 1930 (Ford, 1956, p. 29); 1 killed, near Morris, Grundy Co, Jan 26, 1933 (Cooke, 1941). *Recent record:* 1 no details, near Quincy, Nov 14, 1959 (TEM-AFN14:40).

Peregrine Falcon *(Falco peregrinus)*

Early April — Mid-May
Early September — Early November

Status: Occasional migrant along Lake Michigan and rare migrant in remainder of state. [Formerly fairly common migrant and rare summer resident.]
Documentation: Specimen(s) — Im ♂, near Murphysboro, Jackson Co, Oct 5, 1959 (SIU A-862).
Remarks: Occurs mainly along large rivers and lakes. *Summer records:* Last known nesting, Jackson Co, in 1950 and 1951 (George, 1968); 1, Union Co, July 17, 1955 (Brewer-AFN9:381). *Other records:* 1, Waukegan, May 30, 1966 (CC-AFN20:514); 1, Pere Marquette St Pk, Dec 30, 1967 (Bromet-AFN22:272); 8, Chicago, between Sep 16 and October 30, 1971 (LB, CC-AB26:71); 1, Carroll Co, Sep 19, 1971 (H. Shaw-AB26:71); Ad, Morgan Co, May 13, 1973 (P. Gibson, RQR, T. Crabtree-AB27:779); 2, Chautauqua NWR, Sep 29, 1973 (RS, HDB); 1, Chicago, May 31, 1975 (LB). *High count:* 47, Evanston, Oct 1, 1977 (LB, GR).

Merlin *(Falco columbarius)*

Mid-April — Mid-May
Early September — Late October

Status: Rare but fairly regular migrant. Very rare winter resident. [Formerly nested in north? (Kennicott, 1855).]
Documentation: Specimen — ♀, 2 miles east of Carbondale, Jackson Co, Oct 14, 1958 (SIU A-622).
Remarks: Found in forest areas and semiopen areas. Observed mostly while migrating. *Records;* 1, Illinois Beach St Pk, July 31, 1966 (Palmquist-(AFN20:574); ♀, Waukegan, Aug 12, 1967 (CC-AFN21:578); 1, Shelby County Forest, May 29, 1970 (HDB); 1, McGraw Wildlife Area, Mar 23, 1971 (Dillon, 1973); ♀, Evanston, Apr 28, 1971 (LB); 1, Urbana, Dec 16, 1972 (R & J Graber-AB27:376); 4, Illinois Beach St Pk, Oct 14, 1973 (LB-AB28:60); Ad photographed, Mason Co, Jan 10, 1976 (B. Adams). *High count:* 6, Illinois Beach St Pk, Oct 14, 1974 (LB-AB29:66).

American Kestrel *(Falco sparverius)*

Status: A common permanent resident throughout state.
Documentation: Specimen(s) — ♀, 8 miles east of Jerseyville, Jersey Co, Dec 1, 1972 (ISM 605411).
Remarks: Found in open areas; mainly perches on telephone wires and in tops of trees. Migration occurs but is not as detectable as in other species of Falcons. Spring migration often conspicuous along Lake Michigan beginning in late February (LB). Seems to be population decline in some sections of state, especially north and central. *High counts:* 13, Morris-Wilmington (CBC), Dec 23, 1972 (AB27:373); 21, Forest Glen (CBC), Dec 26, 1972 (AB27:370); 33, Olney (CBC), Dec 27, 1972 (AB27:366); 33, Crab Orchard NWR (CBC), Dec 30, 1972 (AB27:368); 11, Will Co (SBC), May 4, 1974; 28, Cook Co (SBC), May 8, 1976.

GALLIFORMES: Grouse, Quail, Pheasants and allies.

Ruffed Grouse *(Bonasa umbellus)*

Status: Introduced. Rare permanent resident in Pope Co and Alexander Co. [Formerly uncommon permanent resident.]
Documentation: Specimen(s) — extirpated population: ♂, Warsaw, Jan 17, 1892 (FMNH 16350); introduced population: 1, Alexander Co, fall, 1973 (IDOC).
Remarks: Original population in Illinois extirpated. Still a possibility of vagrants coming into Illinois from Wisconsin. 31 (mostly gray phase), introduced into Pope Co from Ohio, fall, 1967. A drumming count in 1973 showed 15 ♂ present. 42 (red phase), released in Alexander Co, from Indiana, in 1972 (Jack Calhoun, IDOC).

[Willow Ptarmigan *(Lagopus lagopus)*]

Status: Hypothetical.
Remarks: Kennicott (1855) stated: "Sometimes found in the timber along Lake Michigan." No other records or statements concerning this extremely unlikely species for Illinois.

Greater Prairie Chicken *(Tympanuchus cupido)*

Status: Rare and local permanent resident in south. [Formerly common permanent resident in prairie areas of state.]
Documentation: Specimen(s) — ♂, Chicago, 1898 (ISM 606460).
Remarks: Remnant population of approximately 500. Counties still having population (in order of abundance): Jasper, Marion, Effingham, Wayne, Clay, and Washington (Westemeier). Last one seen in north: Green River Preserve, Lee Co, Apr 12, 1959 (Shaws). *Record:* 151, Jasper Co (SBC), May 5, 1973.

Sharp-tailed Grouse *(Pedioecetes phasianellus)*

Status: Extirpated. [Formerly fairly common permanent resident in north.]
Documentation: Specimen(s) — Ad ♂, Rock Island Co, June 29, 1901 (PM 308).
Remarks: Kennicott (1855) stated that it was known to nest in Cook Co. Supposed to have been abundant in northern Illinois south to Chicago between 1840 and 1845 (Ford, 1956). 1, Geneva, Kane Co, collected prior to 1894 (Ford, 1956). Recently released into Fulton Co from South Dakota, but population did not survive (Jack Calhoun).

Bobwhite *(Colinus virginianus)*

Status: Common permanent resident in central and south. Fairly common permanent resident in western portion of north. Occasional permanent resident in eastern portion of north.
Documentation: Specimen(s) — ♂, 7 miles south of Springfield, May 22, 1973 (ISM 605669).
Remarks: Found in open woodland, edge of woods, hedges, and cultivated areas. *Records:* 1, Barrington, Dec 29, 1965 (AFN20:260); 1, Chicago area, Dec 31, 1966 (AFN21:252); 269, western Mercer Co, Jan 1, 1967 (AFN21:260); 188, Bureau Co (SBC), May 4, 1974; 140 (Route 51 BBS) Madison Co and Clinton Co, June 29, 1975 (N.P. Lane, U.S. Fish & Wildlife Service, 1976, p. 636).

Ring-necked Pheasant *(Phasianus colchicus)*

Status: Introduced. Now common permanent resident in north and in Grand Prairie of east-central Illinois. Uncommon to rare permanent resident in south and remaining portions of central.
Documentation: Specimen(s) — ♂, south of Springfield, Apr 3, 1973 (ISM 605558).
Remarks: Found in intensively cultivated areas but does require cover. Introduced in 1890 near Macomb (Jim Moak, IDOC). Many areas in southern Illinois where it does not occur. *High counts:* 300, southwest of Chicago, mid-Feb 1972 (LB, CC-AB26:611); 195, Livingston Co (SBC), May 6, 1972; 56, DeKalb, Dec 17, 1972 (AB27:369); 268, Will Co (SBC), May 4, 1974; 127, (Route 34 BBS) Iroquois Co and Vermilion Co, June 19, 1975 (R. Gruenewald, U.S. Fish & Wildlife Service, 1976, p. 636).

Gray Partridge *(Perdix perdix)*

Status: Introduced. Now uncommon permanent resident in north.
Documentation: Specimen(s) — ♂, 2 miles west of Cloverdale, DuPage Co, Mar 15, 1973 (NIU 3631).
Remarks: Introduced from 1906-27. Highest concentration, Lee Co (Farris, 1970). *Records:* 8, Boone Co (SBC), May 6, 1972; 17, Lee Co (SBC), May 5, 1973; 14, Whiteside Co (SBC), May 4, 1974.

Turkey *(Meleagris gallopavo)*

Status: Introduced. Now uncommon permanent resident in south. [Formerly a common permanent resident. Later extirpated.]
Documentation: Specimen(s) — ♂, north end of Possum Trot Trail, Alexander Co, Sep 17, 1970 (ISM 604592).
Remarks: Original Illinois population extirpated. Last reports in 1935 (S & P, p. 23). Restocked beginning in 1960; can now be found in most of the Shawnee National Forest (Jack Calhoun). Small population in Whiteside Co (LB, CC). A total of 55 killed during 1974 hunting season in Union Co, Jackson Co, Pope Co, and Alexander Co. *Other records:* 3, Union Co (SBC), May 5, 1973; 3, Jackson Co (SBC), May 5, 1973; 3, Jackson Co (SBC), May 4, 1974.

GRUIFORMES: Cranes, Rails, Gallinules and allies.

Whooping Crane *(Grus americana)*

Status: Very rare migrant. [Formerly fairly common migrant and summer resident (Nelson, 1876).]
Documentation: Specimen(s) — ♂, Champaign Co, Mar 27, 1871 (Hahn, 1963).
Remarks: After 70-year absence, Ad photographed (ISM), near Hull, Pike Co; observed Oct 16 - Nov 5, 1958 (Mills & Bellrose, 1959). Ad reported, 2 miles south of Wisconsin line near Geneva, Wis., Apr 19, 1964 (Groth-IAB130:24).

Sandhill Crane *(Grus canadensis)*

Mid-March — Early May
Early October — Early November

Status: Uncommon migrant in north. Rare migrant in central and south. Majority migrate northwest/southeast across northern part of state. [Formerly summer resident (Ridgway, 1895).]
Documentation: Specimen — Ad, Fayette Co, Apr 10, 1894 (Steinhauer Coll. ISM 605960).
Remarks: Usually observed flying high during migration when moving to and from Jasper Pulaski Preserve in Indiana. Uses a well-defined corridor across northeastern part of state. Last known nest, Champaign Co, 1872 (Gault, 1922, p. 42). *Records:* 1, Crab Orchard NWR, Oct 24, 1959 (Bush-AFN14:40); 1 near Jacksonville (wintered), Dec 8, 1971 - Mar 1972 (Leonhard); 3, McHenry

Co (SBC), May 5, 1973; 1, Bloomington, early Mar 1974 (DBi-AB28:647); 10, Lawrence Co, Mar 17, 1975 (D. Jones); 15, DesPlaines, Cook Co, Sep 21, 1975 (CC). *High counts:* 650, Chicago area, Mar 28, 1963 (RR-AFN17:408); 2,000, Chicago area, Mar 14 - Apr 8, 1966 (PD-IAB138:7); 450, Chicago Lake Front, Nov 6, 1971 (LB, CC, PW); 250, Stockton, Jo Daviess Co, Oct 4, 1973 (Fiske-AB28:60); 100, Kane Co, Mar 10, 1974, and 100, Will Co, Mar 11-14, 1974 (LB-AB28:647).

[Limpkin *(Aramus guarauna)*]

Status: Hypothetical.
Remarks: I.E. Hess supposedly collected this species near Philo, Champaign Co, in 1896, and claimed to have the wings of the bird (Cory, 1909, p. 380). Apparently no one else saw the specimen; it seems very unlikely this species of the Florida Everglades would be found as far north as Illinois.

King Rail *(Rallus elegans)*

Mid-April — Late October

Status: Uncommon migrant and locally uncommon summer resident. Very rare winter resident.
Documentation: Specimen(s) — ♂, 2 miles north of Creal Springs, Williamson Co, Feb 26, 1957 (SIU A-140).
Remarks: Found in cattail marshes. Population apparently declining. Very few fall records. *Winter records:* Cripple, Rock Island, Dec 26, 1960 (IAB117:15); 1, Chillicothe, Peoria Co, Jan 2, 1967 (Princen-AFN21:253). *Other records:* 1, Sangchris St Pk, Apr 6, 1974 (HDB). *High count:* 6, Decatur, Apr 19, 1973 (RP).

[Clapper Rail *(Rallus longirostris)*]

Status: Hypothetical.
Remarks: This coastal species listed from near Rockford, Aug 5, 1916, without further comment (Nature Study Society of Rockford, 1917-18).

Virginia Rail *(Rallus limicola)*

Early April — Mid-May
Late August — Late October

Status: Fairly common migrant. Fairly common summer resident in north. Rare summer resident in central and south. Very rare winter resident.
Documentation: Specimen(s) — ♀, 2 miles north of Springfield, May 19, 1973 (ISM 605658).
Remarks: Found in marshes and along lake edges. *Winter records:* 1, Rockford, Dec 23, 1961 (Johnson, LJ-AFN16:333); 1, Chicago area, Dec 31, 1966 (AFN21:252); Ad collected, E. Moline, Rock Island Co, Dec 16, 1967 (PM); 1, Sand Ridge Nature Center, Cook Co, Dec 30, 1967 (AFN22:273); 1, Quiver Creek, Mason Co, Feb 10, 1973 (VK, HDB); 1, Horseshoe Lake (CBC), Jan 3, 1976 (BP, VK). *Summer records:* 4 young with Ad, Jasper Co, June 25, 1968 (Westemeier); 4, Oakwood Bottoms, Jackson Co, July 9, 1973 (DH-AB27:876). *High counts:* 12, McHenry Co (SBC), May 4, 1974; 14, Cook Co (SBC), May 8, 1976.

Sora *(Porzana carolina)*

Early April — Late October

Status: Common migrant. A fairly common summer resident in north. Occasional summer resident in central and south.
Documentation: Specimen(s) — Im ♂, Peoria, Peoria Co, Aug 31, 1971 (ISM 605091).
Remarks: Most numerous rail in the state. Occurs in wet grassy fields, marshes, and hayfields. There are old winter records, but none recently. *Summer records:* Nest, Mason Co, July 21, 1973 (HDB); 1, Vermilion Co, July 1, 1975 (M. Campbell). *Other records:* 1, Sangchris St Pk, Mar 31, 1973 (HDB); 1, Mason Co, Oct 18, 1975 (HDB). *High counts:* 32, Lake Co (SBC), May 6, 1972; 24, Lee Co (SBC), May 5, 1973; 60, Cook Co (SBC), May 8, 1976; 25, Chautauqua NWR, Aug 29, 1976 (RS).

Yellow Rail *(Coturnicops noveboracensis)*

Mid-April — Early May
Mid-September — Late October

Status: Rare migrant. [Formerly rare summer resident in north.]
Documentation: Specimen(s) — ♀, east of Springfield, Oct 24, 1971 (ISM 604905).
Remarks: Found in wet grassy areas. In fall may be found in hayfields. Very secretive; probably more numerous than realized. *Nesting record:* Winnebago, May 17 (no year given) by J.W. Tolman (Butler, 1897). *Records:* 1, Champaign, Apr 24, 1958 (Packard, 1958); 1, Waukegan, May 10, 1959 (Lehman-AFN13:375); 1, Gilbert Lake, Jersey Co, Sep 11, 1965 (JEC, SV-AFN20:54); 1, Chicago, May 2, 1971 (CC, LB); 1, west of Jacksonville, Morgan Co, May 7, 1972 (PW, RQR); 1, Sangchris St Pk, Apr 2, 1974 (HDB); 3 in clover field, Liberty, Adams Co, Sep 24, 1974 (JF-AB29:66); 3 Im, along Lake Michigan, Oct 2 - Mid-Oct 1975 (LB).

Black Rail *(Laterallus jamaicensis)*

Mid-April — Late May
Mid-September — Mid-October

Status: Rare migrant. Rare summer resident in central and north.
Documentation: Specimen(s) — 1, Chicago, July 4, 1925 (CAS-Ford, 1956).
Remarks: Most difficult of the rails to flush; stays in wet grasses, rushes, and sedges. *Summer records:*   2 young banded (last nesting evidence), Adams Co, Aug 22, 1932, and an Im observed, July 25, 1936 (TEM, 1937); 1 (possibly 2) heard and seen, near Snicarte, Mason Co, June 20-21 & 25, 1975 (RS, HDB). *Other records:* 1, Rockford, Apr 8 & 13, 1959 (Prentise-AFN13:375); 1 found dead (hit window), Chicago, early Sep 1964 (C.O. Palmquist); 1 photographed, Jackson Park, Chicago, May 7-13, 1972 (LB-AB26:767); 1, Waukegan, May 21, 1972 (LB-AB26:767); 1 caught, banded, and photographed, in weedy field at Beverly, Adams Co, May 28, 1973 (JF-AB27:779); 1, near Havana, May 21, 1976 (RS, P. Gibson).

Purple Gallinule *(Porphyrula martinica)*

Late April — Early June

Status: Very rare spring vagrant. Very rare summer resident in south.
Documentation: Specimen(s) — Ad ♀, Hudson, McLean Co, Apr 13, 1964 (ISU 180).
Remarks: Usually appears in spring as over-migrant and can occur out of habitat. Found in marshy or swampy areas, especially those with lotus. *Summer records:* Nested, Lake Mermet, Massac Co, 1963 (Waldbauer & Hays, 1964); nested (8 eggs found), Lake Mermet, June 19, 1973 (MH, M. Swayne-AB27:876); 1 with Common Gallinules, Moredock Lake, Monroe Co, June 8, 1963 (Wally George, DE-AFN17:464). In the spring of 1973, a dispersal flight must have occurred. *Records:* 1 photographed, Morton, Tazewell Co, Apr 17, 1973 (B. Stroud-IAB166:25); 1 photographed, Springfield, Apr 24-28, 1973 (Martin-AB27:779); 1, Nelson, Lee Co, May 5, 1973 (Keegan, Paulson-AB27:779); 1, Eggers Woods, Chicago, May 6, 1973 (LB-AB27:779). *Other records:* 1, LaRue Swamp, Union Co, May 9, 1974 (R. Madding-AB28:808); 1 collected, Piper City, Ford Co, early Apr 1975 (Adam Weber-Specimen ISM 606253); 1, Lincolnwood, May 2-3, 1976 (D. Brenner).

Common Gallinule *(Gallinula chloropus)*

Late April — Early September

Status: Uncommon migrant and locally common summer resident in north. Occasional migrant and summer resident in central and south.
Documentation: Specimen(s) — Im, near Roxana, Madison Co, Sep 24, 1971 (ISM 605059)
Remarks: Found in marshy areas and lakes. Local during summer; certain areas that appear to be proper habitat have no gallinules. *Summer records:* Nest, Grand Marais St Pk, St. Clair Co, June 16 - July 3, 1950 (SV-IAB108:6); young, Moredock Lake, early Sep 1963 (RA); 2, near Havana, July 6, 1974 (RS, HDB); 2 downy young and Ad, north of Cuba, Fulton Co, July 19, 1975 (HDB). *Other records:* 1, Long John Slough, Cook Co, Nov 2, 1968 (CC, PD); 1, near Havana, Oct 12, 1974 (HDB). *High count:* 28, Cook Co (SBC), May 8, 1976.

American Coot *(Fulica americana)*

Early March — Mid-May
Mid-September — Mid-November

Status: Abundant migrant. Common summer resident near Lake Michigan but less common in northwestern portion of state. Occasional winter resident in north. Uncommon summer resident and uncommon winter resident in central and south.
Documentation: Specimen(s) — ♀, 4 miles west of White Oak, Montgomery Co, Apr 19, 1972 (ISM 605246).
Remarks: Found on lakes and marshes. *Summer records:* 10, Rend Lake, July 10, 1971 (VK, Reuter-AB25:863); 50 nests, Jackson Co, summer 1973 (DH-AB27:779); nests and young, near Havana, summer 1974 (HDB).

49

High counts: 60,000, Chautauqua NWR, Oct 25, 1959 (Norman-AFN14:40); 45,000, Mark Twain NWR, Oct 11, 1965 (Bellrose); 1,500, Palos Park, Apr 15, 1967 (J.Probst); 16,000, McGinnis Slough, Cook Co, November 1, 1970 (CC); 5,000, Lake Decatur, Nov 5, 1974 (RS); 187,735, Mississippi River Valley, Nov 24, 1975 (IDOC).

CHARADRIIFORMES: Plovers, Sandpipers, Gulls, Terns and allies.

American Avocet *(Recurvirostra americana)*

Late April — Mid-May
Mid-July — Early November

Status: Rare migrant.
Documentation: Specimen(s) — ♀, Big Lake (now E. St. Louis, Madison Co) Oct 28, 1878 (WU Hurter collection 107).
Remarks: A large wader that seems to be increasing in numbers. Usually occurs on extensive mudflats and shallow water areas. *Records:* 1, Lake Decatur, Macon Co, Aug 30, 1955 (RS-AFN10:28); 1, Evanston, Apr 30, 1966 (CC-AFN20:514); 1, Mark Twain NWR, May 17, 1967 (SV); 1, McGinnis Slough, Cook Co, Sep 22 - Oct 4, 1969 (RR-AFN24:54); 1, Lake Nalbandov, Champaign Co, Aug 17, 1970 (R. Graber-AB25:65); 1, Sangchris St Pk, Nov 11, 1970 (HDB); 1, Meredosia Bay, Morgan Co, May 1, 1971 (PW, HDB); 1, Round Lake, Lake Co, June 2, 1973 (LB, CC-AB27:876); 1, Monroe Co, May 5, 1973 (RA); 1, Union County Refuge, Oct 17, 1976 (RQR, B. Adams, HDB). *High counts:* 11, Mark Twain NWR, Oct 8, 1969 (SV); 9, Carlyle Lake, Fayette Co, Sep 3, 1973 (VK, HDB, RS); 15, McHenry Co, Apr 23, 1974 (Fiske-AB28:808); 12, McDonough Co, May 2, 1975 (E. Franks); 14, Chautauqua NWR, Oct 26, 1975 (D. Friedman).

Black-necked Stilt *(Himantopus mexicanus)*

Late August — Early September
Status: Very rare fall migrant or vagrant.
Documentation: Specimen(s) — ♀, near Wood River, Madison Co, Aug 31, 1969 (INHS RE-b-1).
Remarks: *2 recent sight records:* 1, near Chicago, Aug 28 - Sep 2, 1959 (Fetter, Lane-AFN14:40); 1, Lake Calumet, Aug 23 - Sep 7, 1968 (CC, JG-AFN23:65).

American Golden Plover *(Pluvialis dominica)*

Late March — Mid-May
Late August — Late October

Status: Common migrant. More numerous in fall along Lake Michigan; more numerous in spring in remainder of state.
Documentation: Specimen(s) — Ad ♂, near Miller City, Alexander Co, Apr 26, 1969 (SIU A-1627).
Remarks: Found in wet fields and pastures and on grassy mudflats. *Records:* Ad collected, Lake Calumet, Nov 11, 1958 (PN); 2, Urbana, Nov 10, 1963 (PN);

1, Lake Calumet, July 15, 1972 (CC-AB26:865); Ad, Meredosia, Morgan Co, July 8, 1973 (HDB, RS); 1, Mason Co, May 31, 1974 (HDB); Ad, Lake Calumet, July 7, 1974 (CC-AB28:909). *High counts:* 365, Chicago, Sep 18, 1955 (Bi-AFN10:28); 1,200, Rock Falls, Whiteside Co, May 4, 1962 (RT-AFN16:419); 400, near Moweaqua, Apr 11, 1970 (HDB); 896, Union Co, Apr 10, 1971 (VK-AB25:752); 100, near Bloomington, Apr 17, 1971 (DBi-IAB159:16); 4,000, Livingston Co, May 6, 1972 (RR-AB26:767); 150, Chautauqua NWR, Sep 22, 1973 (HDB, VK, RS); 3,200, Marshall Co (SBC), May 4, 1974.

Black-bellied Plover *(Pluvialis squatarola)*

Early May — Early June
Early August — Early November

Status: Common migrant along Lake Michigan. Uncommon migrant in remainder of state.
Documentation: Specimen(s) — ♀, Illinois Beach St Pk, Lake Co, May 13, 1961 (NIU 113).
Remarks: Found on beaches and in wet fields. *Records:* 1, Crab Orchard NWR, Nov 30, 1960 (Bush-AFN15:45); 1, on levee below E. St. Louis, June 2, 1963 (Wally George, K. Stewart); 4 in breeding plumage, Evanston, July 31, 1964 (RR); 1, near Dickson Mounds, Fulton Co, June 3, 1973 (HDB); 2, Thomson, Whiteside Co, Nov 17, 1973 (Shaws-IAB168:28); 1, Jacksonville, Nov 29, 1973 (WO); 1, Lake Calumet, Dec 22, 1973 (KB-AB28:378); 1, Mason Co, Nov 11, 1974 (HDB). *High counts:* 100, Wolf Lake, Cook Co, Aug 16, 1959 (Grow-AFN14:40); 250, Wadsworth, Lake Co, May 26, 1962 (RR-AFN16:419); 750, Lake Co, May 21, 1966 (J. Probst); 200, Lake Calumet, Sep 9, 1968 (LC-IAB148:19).

Piping Plover *(Charadrius melodus)*

Early May — Mid-May
Late July — Late September

Status: Rare migrant. Very rare summer resident along Lake Michigan.
Documentation: Specimen(s) — Ad, Waukegan, Aug 6, 1933 (FMNH 97589).
Remarks: Found on beaches and sandbars. Population greatly reduced due to loss of habitat. *Recent nesting record:* Nest with 3 downy young, Waukegan, July 8, 1973 (CC-AB27:876), first known nest since 1955. *Other records:* 1, Waukegan, Aug 24, 1968 (CC-IAB148:18); 1, Lawrenceville, Lawrence Co, Oct 1, 1970 (R.E. Dolphin); 1, Chautauqua NWR, May 8, 1971 (HDB); 5, Mark Twain NWR, Sep 4, 1973 (SV-AB28:60); 1, Illinois Beach St Pk, Nov 10, 1973 (CC-AB28:60); 3, Lake Co (SBC), May 4, 1974; 1, Charleston, Coles Co, July 19, 1975 (LBH-AB29:980)

Semipalmated Plover *(Charadrius semipalmatus)*

Late April — Late May
Late July — Early October

Status: Fairly common migrant.

Documentation: Specimen(s) — ♀, Calumet Flats, Cook Co, Sep 13, 1961 (NIU 218).
Remarks: Found on drier parts of mudflats. *Records:* 1, Lake Calumet, June 18, 1966 (CC); 1, Waukegan, Oct 29, 1972 (CC, LB, GR-AB27:68); 1, Waukegan, Nov 10 - Dec 1, 1974 (CC-AB28:647). *High counts:* 25, Waukegan, Sep 5, 1971 (LB-IAB157:30); 20, St. Clair Co (SBC), May 6, 1972; 8, Pope Co (SBC), May 5, 1973; 90, Wadsworth, Lake Co, May 19, 1973 (LB); 32, Franklin Co (SBC), May 4, 1974; 40, Mason Co (SBC), May 10, 1975; 50, Chautauqua NWR, Sep 11, 1976 (HDB).

[Wilson's Plover *(Charadrius wilsonia)*]

Status: Hypothetical.
Remarks: Undocumented sight record of this southern coastal species at Glencoe, Cook Co, May 16-26, 1962. Said to have appeared after a hot spell and a heavy flow of warm Gulf air (RR & others-AFN16:418).

Killdeer *(Charadrius vociferus)*

Mid-March — Early November

Status: Common migrant and summer resident. Occasional winter resident in north and central. Uncommon winter resident in south.
Documentation: Specimen(s) — ♂, Franklin Twp, DeKalb Co, June 25, 1966 (NIU 2302).
Remarks: Found in wet areas in fields and pastures and on mudflats. The common nesting shorebird in the state. *Records:* 4, Barrington (CBC), Dec 17, 1973 (AB28:376); 1, Rockford, Dec 30, 1973 (AB28:386). *High counts:* 100, north of Sterling, Nov 6, 1960 (Max Hagans-IAB117:6); 43, Grundy Co (SBC), May 6, 1972; 103, Will Co (SBC), May 4, 1974; 500, Bedford Park, Cook Co, mid-Aug 1975 (LB).

American Woodcock *(Philohela minor)*

Early March — Early November

Status: Common migrant and uncommon summer resident. Occasional winter resident in south. Rare winter resident in central and north.
Documentation: Specimen(s) — ♂, Girard, Macoupin Co, July 22, 1972 (ISM 605245).
Remarks: Found in damp woods. Usually recorded in small numbers. *Summer records:* Nest and downy young, Urbana, summer, 1963 (PN-AFN17:464); nest with 4 eggs, Sangchris St Pk, May 11, 1974 (PW). *Winter records:* 1, Pere Marquette St Pk, Dec 26, 1965 (SV-AFN20:430); 4, Peoria, Dec 21, 1969 (AFN24:312); 1, Princeton (CBC), Dec 30, 1969 (AFN24:313); 1, Chicago North Shore (CBC), Dec 27, 1975 (AB30:428). *High count:* 15, Lake Co (SBC), May 10, 1975.

Common Snipe *(Capella gallinago)*

Late March — Early May
Late August — Late November

Status: Common migrant. Uncommon winter resident in south. Occasional winter resident in central and north. Rare summer resident.

Documentation: Specimen(s) — ♂, 6 miles southwest of Hull, Pike Co, Dec 12, 1953 (ISM 603783).

Remarks: Found in wet areas and along open creeks. *Summer records:* 1, Powderhorn Marsh, Cook Co, June 27 & July 18, 1965 (CC-AFN19:551); courtship flight, Goose Lake Prairie, June 6, 1971 (LB, CC-AB25:863); nest and young, Illinois Beach St Pk, May 21, 1972 (LB-AB26:767); 3 winnowing, Oakwood Bottoms, Jackson Co, June 6-9, 1973 (DH, VK-AB27:876); winnowing, Sangchris St Pk, May 21, 1974 (HDB). *High counts:* 24, western Mercer Co (CBC), Dec 30, 1962 (AFN17:206); 35, Chillicothe (CBC), Jan 2, 1967 (AFN21:253); 56, McHenry Co (SBC), May 4, 1974; 50, Union County Refuge, Oct 17, 1976 (RQR, B. Adams, HDB).

Long-billed Curlew *(Numenius americanus)*

Late April — Mid-June
July — Late September

Status: Very rare migrant. [Formerly very abundant(?) during migrations and a common summer resident (Ridgway, 1895).]

Documentation: Specimen(s) —♂, Lemont, Cook Co, July 1889 (ISM 604305).

Remarks: A species of the wet prairies. *Only 2 recent records:* 1 photographed, Villa Grove, Douglas Co, Apr 20-24, 1962 (H.W. Norton, W.D. Zehr, R. Graber—photo on file ISM); 1, Camargo, Douglas Co, Apr 21, 1963 (PN-AFN16:408).

Whimbrel *(Numenius phaeopus)*

Late April — Mid-June
Late July — Mid-October

Status: Rare migrant along Lake Michigan. Very rare migrant in remainder of state.

Documentation: Specimen — 1, Waukegan, Sep 16, 1923 (Ford, Sanborn, & Coursen, 1934).

Remarks: Found on beaches and near grassy pools of water. Especially prefers rear areas of beaches where grasses have begun to grow. Occurs in small numbers yearly along Lake Michigan. *Records:* 1, Moredock Lake, Monroe Co, May 24, 1964 (S. Hanselmann, J. Willet, RA); 1, across from St. Louis, Madison Co, Illinois, Apr 24, 1969 (RA, PB-AFN23:596); 1, Lake Calumet, Aug 25, 1969 (LC-IAB152:19); 1, Lake Calumet, May 13, 1972 (LB-AB26:767); 1, Waukegan, July 24-29, 1973 (LB-AB27:876); 1, Waukegan, Aug 25 - Sep 2, 1974 (LB, CC-AB29:66). *High count:* 15, 2 miles north of Bondville, Champaign Co, Apr 29, 1971 (J. & R. Graber).

Eskimo Curlew *(Numenius borealis)*

Mid-April — Mid-May
Late August — Late October

Status: Probably extinct. [Formerly common migrant (Ridgway, 1895).]

Documentation: Specimen(s) — 2, from McLean Co, both dated Sep 1879 (Hahn, 1963).

Remarks: This was a bird of the wet prairies. A recently discovered specimen, taken in Fayette Co, Mar 30, 1894, by E.F. Steinhauer (ISM 605948). Last sight record, group of 8, Lincoln Park, Chicago, May 22, 1923 (Ford, Sanborn, Coursen, 1934). No recent records; very unlikely that it will ever be seen again in the state.

Marbled Godwit *(Limosa fedoa)*

Late April — Mid-May
Mid-August — Late September

Status: Rare migrant.
Documentation: Specimen(s) — ♂, Lake Calumet, Sep 24, 1957 (UMMZ-Binford, 1958).
Remarks: A large shorebird that occurs on extensive mudflats and feeds in water, at times up to its belly. *Records:* 1, Calumet Lake, Aug 5-22, 1961 (RT, Fetter-AFN16:37); 1, Evanston, Apr 30, 1966 (CC, CW-IAB139:22); 1, Glencoe, Sep 15, 1966 (IAS-IAB140:6); 1, Thomson, Carroll Co, May 18, 1967 (Shaws); 1, Lake Calumet, May 16, 1970 (CC-AFN24:614); 1, Chautauqua NWR, Sep 14-25, 1971 (HDB); 4, Wilmette, May 1, 1972 (RR-AB26:767); 1, Lake Co, May 5, 1973 (LB-AB27:779); 1, Alexander Co, Aug 16, 1973 (DH-AB28:61); 1, Chautauqua NWR, Sep 13-29, 1973 (HDB); 1, Lake Calumet, Aug 23-24, 1974 (M. Myers, CC-AB29:66); 1, Charleston, July 19, 1975 (LBH-AB29:980). *High count:* 17 photographed, near Havana, Apr 20, 1975 (Bjorklund, Bellrose).

Hudsonian Godwit *(Limosa haemastica)*

Early May — Late May
Early September — Mid-October

Status: Rare migrant.
Documentation: Specimen(s) — ♂, Lake Calumet, June 23, 1956 (Levy-AFN10:387).
Remarks: Occurs on mudflats and at grassy pools of water. More records for spring than fall. *Records:* 1, Chicago, Apr 22, 1960 (Shepley-AFN14:392); 8, on levees below E. St. Louis, May 18, 1965 (S. Hanselmann, J. Willets); 1, Spring Lake, Whiteside Co, Oct 13, 1969 (Hagans, Shaws); 1, Lake Calumet, May 9-16, 1970 (CC-AFN24:614); 1, Carbondale Reservoir, Williamson Co, Oct 17, 1970 (VK-AB25:65); 5, near Bloomington, May 12, 1971 (DBi-IAB159:16); 1, Skokie Lagoon, Cook Co, May 22, 1971 (Nork-AB25:752); 1, Waukegan, May 28, 1971 (LB-AB25:752); 1, Morgan Co, May 13, 1973 (P. Gibson, WO-AB27:779); 5, Springfield, May 19, 1973 (HDB); 8, near Dalton City, Macon Co, May 17 & 18, 1974 (RS); 8, Mason Co, May 18, 1974 (HDB); 3, Meredosia, Morgan Co, May 19, 1974 (Funk); 2, Chautauqua NWR, Oct 1, 1975 (RS, HDB).

Short-billed Dowitcher *(Limnodromus griseus)*

Early May — Late May
Mid-July — Mid-September

Status: Uncommon spring migrant; fairly common fall migrant.

Documentation: Specimen(s) — 1, Hyde Lake, Cook Co, Aug 6, 1922 (FMNH 1364).
Remarks: Found on mudflats and in shallow water. Most or all records probably refer to the inland race, *L. g. hendersoni*. *Records:* 1, Champaign, July 16, 1961 (Brooks, 1965); 15, Lake Calumet, Aug 23, 1964 (CC); 8, Chautauqua NWR, July 10, 1971 (HDB); 1, Crab Orchard NWR, July 10, 1971 (VK, Reuter-AB25:864); 25, Waukegan, Sep 5, 1971 (LB-IAB157:30); 40, Lake Carlyle, Fayette Co, Aug 29, 1973 (VK-AB28:60); 23, Lake Co (SBC), May 10, 1975; 1, Jackson Co, July 12, 1975 (BP-AB29:980); *High counts:* 100, Waukegan, Aug 15, 1965 (RR); 125, Chautauqua NWR, Aug 25, 1973 (HDB, VK).

Long-billed Dowitcher *(Limnodromus scolopaceus)*

Mid-April — Early May
Early September — Mid-October

Status: Uncommon migrant.
Documentation: Specimen(s) — Ad, Barstow, Rock Island Co, Nov 1, 1959 (PM 1960-200).
Remarks: Found on mudflats and in shallow water. Very similar to Short-billed Dowitcher; should be identified with great care. Best way to separate is by flight call. Note that this species generally occurs earlier in spring and later in fall than Short-billed Dowitcher. No spring records in Chicago area. *Records:* 4, Lock 13, Whiteside Co, Nov 6, 1970 (Shaws-IAB157:28); 9, Chautauqua NWR, Oct 6, 1973 (HDB); 2, Champaign, Apr 24, 1976 (J. Frank-AB30:848). *High count:* 50, Chautauqua NWR, Oct 18, 1975 (RS, HDB).

Stilt Sandpiper *(Micropalama himantopus)*

Mid-May — Late May
Mid-July — Late October

Status: Common fall migrant and occasional spring migrant.
Documentation: Specimen(s) — 1, Chautauqua NWR, Mason Co, Sep 5, 1971 (ISM 604848).
Remarks: Feeds in shallow water off the mudflats. In fall resembles Lesser Yellowlegs and is at times overlooked; tends to probe when feeding, while the Yellowlegs feeds by picking. *Records:* 20, Champaign, Sep 13, 1961 (Brooks, 1965); 1-3, Carbondale, Sep 6-28, 1970 (VK-IAB158:23); 1, Chautauqua NWR, July 4, 1971 (HDB); 1, Skokie Lagoons, Cook Co, Nov 2, 1971 (GR-AB26:72); 11, Coles Co, July 31, 1973 (LBH-AB27:876); 1, Sangchris St Pk, Oct 21, 1973 (HDB); 41, Lake Calumet, Aug 3, 1974 (CC-AB29:66); 30, Whiteside Co, Aug 31, 1974 (Shaws-AB29:66); 1, Lake Shelbyville, Moultrie Co, Apr 23, 1976 (RS). *High counts:* 70, Lake Decatur, Sep 1955 (Kirby, RS, Chaniot-AFN10:28); 150, Chautauqua NWR, Aug 21, 1971 (HDB); 250, Chautauqua NWR, Aug 18 - Sep 13, 1973 (RS, VK, HDB).

Greater Yellowlegs *(Tringa melanoleucus)*

Early April — Mid-May
Mid-July — Early November

Status: Fairly common migrant.

Documentation: Specimen(s) — ♀, Shabbona, DeKalb Co, Apr 18, 1967 (NIU 2582).

Remarks: Found on mudflats, lakes, and small pools of water. *Records:* 1, near Findlay, Shelby Co, June 13, 1970 (HDB); 1, Evanston, Nov 13, 1970 (B. Tweit); 2, Rend Lake, Nov 8, 1975 (BP). *High counts:* 30, St. Clair Co (SBC) May 5, 1973; 48, Knox Co (SBC), May 4, 1974.

Lesser Yellowlegs *(Tringa flavipes)*

Early April — Late May
Mid-July — Late October

Status: Common migrant.

Documentation: Specimen(s) — 1, Chautauqua Lake, Mason Co, Aug 14, 1971 (ISM 604843).

Remarks: Found on mudflats and wet grassy fields. *Records:* 1, Urbana, June 16, 1961 (Brooks-AFN16:37); 1, Normal, Nov 4, 1971 (DBi-AB26:72); 2, Mason Co, June 15, 1974 (HDB). *High counts:* 125, Urbana, Sep 7, 1961 (Brooks-AFN16:37); 400, Chautauqua NWR, Aug 7, 1971 (HDB); 156, LaSalle Co (SBC), May 5, 1973; 60, McHenry Co (SBC), May 4, 1974; 490, Bedford Park, Cook Co, July 8, 1976 (LB, CC).

Solitary Sandpiper *(Tringa solitaria)*

Mid-April — Mid-May
Mid-July — Mid-September

Status: Common migrant.

Documentation: Specimen(s) — ♀, Horseshoe Lake, Alexander Co, May 6, 1961 (NIU 242).

Remarks: Found along creeks, sloughs, and ponds and on mudflats. Usually found away from other shorebirds. *Records:* 1, Northbrook, Cook Co, Oct 9, 1965 (R. Horwitz); 2, Springfield, July 3, 1974 (HDB); 1, Decatur, Oct 2, 1974 (RP); 1, Decatur, Mar 31, 1975 (RP). *High counts:* 65, Chautauqua NWR, Aug 7, 1971 (HDB); 24, LaSalle Co (SBC), May 6, 1972; 25, Will Co (SBC), May 5, 1973; 20, Pike Co (SBC), May 4, 1974.

Spotted Sandpiper *(Actitis macularia)*

Mid-April — Late September

Status: Common migrant. Common summer resident in north. Uncommon summer resident in central. A rare summer resident in south.

Documentation: Specimen(s) — ♂, 5 miles north Sycamore, DeKalb Co, Apr 17, 1966 (NIU 2216).

Remarks: Found along creeks, ponds, and beaches (especially rocky beaches). *Records:* 1, Chicago, Nov 20, 1965 (Brecklin-AFN20:54); 2, Springfield, Apr 13, 1974 (HDB). *High counts:* 31, Chautauqua NWR, July 31, 1971 (HDB); 71, Cook Co (SBC), May 6, 1972.

Willet *(Catoptrophorus semipalmatus)*

Mid-April — Mid-May
Mid-July — Mid-September

Status: Occasional migrant.

Documentation: Specimen(s) — ♂, southern Illinois, May 6, 1875 (NMNH 94719).

Remarks: Occurs on beaches and mudflats; seen yearly in state. *Records:* 2 photographed, near Sterling, Whiteside Co, Apr 30, 1958 (Shaws-IAB106:11); 4, on levees below St. Louis, Apr 27, 1963 (K. Arhos); 1, Chicago, June 18, 1966 (CC-AFN20:575); 1, Shelbyville Lake, May 2, 1971 (HDB); 1, Evanston, May 2, 1971 (Nork-IAB159:13); 1, Bloomington, May 19, 1971 (DBi-IAB159:16); 1, Saverton Dam, Pike Co, July 23, 1971 (JF-AB25:864); 10, Evanston, Aug 19, 1973 (LB, CC-AB28:60); 25, Pulaski Co, Apr 6, 1974 (Haw-AB28:808).

Upland Sandpiper *(Bartramia longicauda)*

Mid-April — Mid-September

Status: Uncommon migrant and summer resident.

Documentation: Specimen(s) — ♂, 3 miles northeast of Thebes, Alexander Co, May 6, 1961 (NIU 123).

Remarks: Found in pastures and hayfields. Population is declining (Graber and Graber, 1963). *Records:* 1, Chandlerville, Cass Co, Oct 2, 1971 (HDB); 30, LaSalle Co (SBC), May 5, 1973; 22, Boone Co (SBC), May 10, 1975; 10, Decatur, mid-Aug 1975 (RS). *High count:* 500, Olney, Apr 7, 1962 (PN-AFN16:491).

Buff-breasted Sandpiper *(Tryngites subruficollis)*

Late April — Early May
Mid-August — Late September

Status: Occasional fall migrant and very rare spring migrant.

Documentation: Specimen(s) — ♂, DeKalb Co, Sep 3, 1961 (NIU 266).

Remarks: Found on dryer flats that have grown up in short grass and other similar areas such as sod fields. No recent spring records but occurs yearly in the fall. *Records:* 2, Champaign, Sep 10, 1960 (Brooks, 1965); 1, Mark Twain NWR, Aug 21, 1973 (SV-AB28:61); 1, Chautauqua NWR, Oct 6, 1973 (HDB); 3, Alexander Co, Sep 6, 1975 (BP); 3, Chautauqua NWR, July 25, 1976 (HDB). *High counts:* 18, Chicago, Sep 18, 1955 (Bi-AFN10:28); 45, Chicago, Sep 8, 1960 (Fetter-AFN15:45); 25, Chautauqua NWR, Sep 4, 1971 (RQR, HDB); 19, Grand Tower, Jackson Co, Sep 3, 1973 (R. Zoanetti).

Ruff *(Philomachus pugnax)*

Late April — Early May
Mid-July — Mid-September

Status: Very rare migrant or vagrant.

Documentation: Photographic — Blackish ♂ in breeding plumage, Lodge Park, Piatt Co, May 3, 1969 (photo by R.R. Graber—on file ISM).

Remarks: Plumages of male birds vary considerably. Females (called reeves) closely resemble other species of shorebirds and should be identified with care. There are 11 records of this Old World species for Illinois. 8 are fall

57

(some very early fall), and 3 are spring. *Recent records:* ♂ in breeding plumage, Chicago, July 4 & 5, 1959 (Nork-AFN14:40); ♂, Lake Calumet, July 3, 1962 (Fetter-AFN17:37); ♂, Glencoe, July 21 & 22, 1964 (RR-AFN18:511); ♂, Rock Falls, Apr 26, 1969 (Shaws-IAB152:21); ♂ in breeding plumage, Powderhorn Marsh, July 18, 1971 (LB, CC-AB28:864); dark ♂, Bloomington, May 9, 1973 (RS-AB27:779); ♂, Lake Calumet, June 29, 1976 (CC, LC); ♂, Springfield, Sep 15-20, 1976 (RS, P. Gibson).

Curlew Sandpiper *(Calidris ferruginea)*

Status: Very rare vagrant.
Documentation: Sight record with acceptable details — Ad in breeding plumage, Rend Lake, Franklin Co, July 23, 1976 (BP & M. Morrison).
Remarks: 1 record. An Old World species. Several records in the U.S. but few inland records.

Dunlin *(Calidris alpina)*

Late April — Early June
Late September — Mid-November

Status: Fairly common fall migrant and uncommon spring migrant.
Documentation: Specimen(s) — ♂, near Springfield, Sangamon Co, May 25, 1972 (ISM 605184).
Remarks: Found on mudflats and beaches. *Winter records:* 1, Pere Marquette St Pk (CBC), Dec 26, 1965 (SV-AFN20:265); 1, Sangchris St Pk, Dec 12, 1970 (HDB); 1, Chicago, Dec 18, 1971 to early Jan 1972 (H. Blume-AB26:612). *Other records:* 1, Waukegan, July 4 & 22, 1972 (GR-AB26:866); 1, Springfield, June 1, 1974 (HDB). *High counts:* 200, Waukegan, May 27, 1961 (RR-AFN15:415); 75, Spring Lake, Whiteside Co, Nov 5, 1970 (Shaws); 3,100, Chicago, Oct 23, 1971 (LB-AB26:72); 1,200, Evanston, Oct 24, 1973 (GR-AB28:60); 120, Mason Co, May 8, 1974 (RS, HDB); 500, Chautauqua NWR, Oct 18, 1975 (RS, HDB).

Red Knot *(Calidris canutus)*

Late May — Early June
Late August — Late September

Status: Occasional fall migrant and rare spring migrant along Lake Michigan. Rare fall migrant and very rare spring migrant in remainder of state; no records south of E. St. Louis.
Documentation: Specimen(s) — ♀, Lake Calumet, Sep 1959 (PM 1959-138).
Remarks: Usually found on extensive flats, sandbars or beaches. *Records:* 9, south of Chicago, Sep 14, 1957 (Chandik-AFN12:35); 1, Lake Calumet, Aug 8, 1961 (RT-AFN16:37); 1, Urbana, Aug 11, 1963 (PN); 1, Skokie Lagoons, Cook Co, May 25, 1968 (CC); 1, E. St. Louis, Sep 22, 1968 (RA, JEC-AFN23:65); 8, Waukegan, Aug 31, 1969 (Coffin-IAB152:20); 1, Quiver Lake, Mason Co, Oct 11, 1971 (WO, HDB); 1, Waukegan, May 21, 1972 (LB-AB26:767); 1, Quiver Lake, Mason Co, Aug 17, 1974 (RS, HDB); 5, Chautauqua NWR, Sep 7, 1974 (HDB); 1, Waukegan, Oct 28, 1976 (LB, GR).

Sanderling *(Calidris alba)*

Mid-May — Early June
Mid-July — Early November

Status: Common migrant along Lake Michigan. Uncommon migrant in remainder of state.
Documentation: Specimen(s) — 1, Lake Decatur, Macon Co, Nov 13, 1973 (ISM 605810).
Remarks: Found on beaches and sandbars, at times on mudflats. *Records:* 6, Champaign, Aug 31, 1961 (Brooks, 1965); 1, Waukegan, Dec 1, 1968 (JG); 2, Crab Orchard NWR, Aug 3 & 5, 1972 (VK-AB27:866); 1, Chautauqua NWR, July 20, 1974 (HDB). *High counts:* 150, Waukegan, May 27, 1961 (RR-AFN15:415); 350, Waukegan, July 24, 1971 (LB); 200, Chicago, Oct 23, 1971 (LB); 15, Chautauqua NWR, Sep 22, 1973 (HDB).

Purple Sandpiper *(Calidris maritima)*

Mid-March — June
Late October — January

Status: Very rare migrant along Lake Michigan.
Documentation: Specimen(s) — 1, Cook Co, Nov 7, 1871; and 1, Cook Co, June 1895 (Cory, 1909).
Remarks: Occurs on rocky shores, especially where algae are prevalent. *Total records (except those above):* 1, Cook Co, Nov 1886 (Helmeyer & Conover, 1948); 1, Lincoln Park, Chicago, Nov 30, 1938 (Clark & Nice, 1950); 1, Camp Logan, Lake Co, June 2, 1951 (S & P, 1955, p. 28); 1, Wilmette, Cook Co, Dec 9, 1952 (S & P, 1955, p. 28); 1, Waukegan, Jan 1, 1961 (AFN15:215); 4, Wilmette, Mar 14, 1961 (RR-AFN15:415); 1 photographed (on file ISM), Montrose Harbor, Chicago, Nov 22, 1973 (Hogg-AB28:60); 1, Waukegan, Oct 27, 1976 (CC).

Sharp-tailed Sandpiper *(Calidris acuminata)*

Status: Very rare vagrant.
Documentation: Sight record with acceptable details — Im, Chautauqua NWR, Sep 28 & 29, 1974 (HDB & RS, 1975).
Remarks: 1 record. Asiatic species. Seen with increased frequency on the West Coast; recently found on the East Coast. Im are quite distinguishable in the field (Pough, 1957).

Pectoral Sandpiper *(Calidris melanotos)*

Late March — Mid-May
Mid-July — Early November

Status: Abundant migrant.
Documentation: Specimen(s) — ♂, 4 miles southwest of Hull, Pike Co, Apr 17, 1956 (ISM 603805).
Remarks: Inhabits mudflats and wet grassy areas. Sometimes lingers late in fall. *Records:* 1, Jackson Park, Chicago, Dec 31, 1954 (KB-IAB93:12); 1, Crab Orchard NWR, Dec 5, 1960 (LH-AFN15:333); flocks, Lawrence Co,

Mar 15 & 16, 1974 (P. Roush-AB28:647); 1, near Snicarte, Mason Co, June 15, 1974 (HDB). *High counts:* 2,500, McGinnis Slough, Cook Co, Apr 8, 1955 (Bi-AFN9:334); 600, Gilbert Lake, Aug 7, 1963 (SV); 2,500, Chautauqua NWR, Aug 14, 1971 (HDB, PW); 500, McLean Co (SBC), May 5, 1973; 600, Chandlerville, Cass Co, May 12, 1973 (VK, HDB).

White-rumped Sandpiper *(Calidris fuscicollis)*

Mid-May — Mid-June
Late July — Late September

Status: Uncommon migrant in spring and rare migrant in fall.
Documentation: Specimen(s) — ♂, Sangchris Lake, Christian Co, July 28, 1976 (ISM 606450).
Remarks: Found on mudflats and grassy pools. Late spring migrant occurring into June. More numerous in north along Lake Michigan in fall than downstate, suggesting that it migrates directly to East Coast in fall. *Records:* 1, Lake Nalbandov, Champaign Co, Oct 16, 1970 (J. Seets, R. Graber); 1, Chautauqua NWR, June 6, 1971 (HDB); 4, Chautauqua NWR, June 26, 1971 (HDB); 1, Waukegan, Sep 17-22, 1971 (LB-IAB157:30); 1, Waukegan, July 22, 1972 (CC-AB26:866); 2, Mason Co, June 15, 1974 (HDB). *High counts:* 8, Waukegan, Aug 13, 1967 (RR); 60, Chautauqua NWR, May 23, 1971 (HDB); 100, Mason Co, May 18, 1974 (RS, HDB).

Baird's Sandpiper *(Calidris bairdii)*

Late April — Mid-May
Mid-August — Late October

Status: Occasional spring migrant and uncommon fall migrant.
Documentation: Specimen(s) — ♀, Lake Co, Sep 14, 1930 (Stevenson & Brodkorb, 1933).
Remarks: Frequents mudflats, beaches, and grassflats. *Records:* 3, Champaign, Sep 3, 1961 (Brooks, 1965); 1, Waukegan, Nov 27, 1970 (Palmquist-AB25:65); 7, Sparta, Randolph Co, Aug 23 - Sep 6, 1971 (Morrison-AB26:72); 2, Mark Twain NWR, Aug 26, 1971 (SV-AB26:72); 7, Chautauqua NWR, Sep 22, 1973 (HDB); 1 photographed, Havana, Dec 2, 1972 (PW); 2, near Dalton City, Apr 25, 1974 (RS); 1 photographed, Jacksonville, Mar 19, 1977 (WO, B. Adams, RQR). *High counts:* 12, Calumet flats, Aug 26, 1962 (CC); 14, Illinois River Valley, Aug 18, 1975 (RS, HDB); 23, Chautauqua NWR, Sep 17, 1976 (RS).

Least Sandpiper *(Calidris minutilla)*

Late April — Late May
Mid-July — Late October

Status: Common migrant.
Documentation: Specimen(s) — ♂, north end of Carlyle Reservoir, Fayette Co, Aug 30, 1973 (ISM 605735).
Remarks: Found on mudflats. May linger late in fall. *Records:* 1, Crab Orchard NWR, Dec 4, 1960 (LH-AFN15:333); 1, Chautauqua NWR, July 4,

1971 (HDB); 1, Chautauqua NWR, Jan 1, 1975 (RS, HDB); 1, Rend Lake, Dec 6, 1975 (RP, RS, HDB); 2, Horseshoe Lake (CBC), Dec 29, 1976 (AB31:685). *High counts:* 700, Chautauqua NWR, Aug 14, 1971 (HDB); 47, Union Co (SBC), May 4, 1974; 98, Lawrence Co (SBC), May 10, 1975.

Semipalmated Sandpiper *(Calidris pusillus)*

Early May — Early June
Mid-July — Early October

Status: Common migrant. Rare (nonbreeding) summer resident.
Documentation: Specimen(s) — ♂, Chautauqua NWR, Sep 22, 1973 (ISM 605756).
Remarks: Frequents mudflats. *Records:* 1, Chautauqua NWR, July 10, 1971 (HDB); 1, Mason Co, June 15, 1974 (HDB); 25, St. Clair Co (SBC), May 6, 1972. *High counts:* 500, Chautauqua NWR, July 31, 1971 (HDB); 400, Mason Co and Fulton Co, May 22, 1976 (HDB).

Western Sandpiper *(Calidris mauri)*

Mid-May — Early June
Mid-July — Late September

Status: Occasional spring migrant and uncommon fall migrant.
Documentation: Specimen(s) — ♂, north end of Lake Carlyle, Fayette Co, Aug 30, 1973 (ISM 605743).
Remarks: May be more common than suspected since it is difficult to distinguish from other "peeps." Feeds on mudflats, usually in deeper water than the Semipalmated Sandpiper. *Records:* 3, Champaign, Sep 15, 1961 (Brooks, 1965); 5, Chicago, May 29, 1965 (CC-AFN19:481); 1, Chicago, May 16, 1971 (LB-AB25:752); 1, Springfield, May 21 & 26, 1971 (HDB); 1, Williamson Co (SBC), May 6, 1972; 1, Waukegan, July 22 & 30, 1972 (CC, LB, GR-AB26:866); 1, Chautauqua NWR, July 22, 1972 (HDB); 3, Springfield, Sep 2, 1972 (HDB); 3, Chicago, Sep 16, 1972 (CC-AB27:68); 1, Fulton Co, July 21, 1973 (HDB); 7, Chautauqua NWR, Aug 25, 1973 (VK, HDB); 1, Sangchris St Pk, Sep 30, 1973 (HDB); 15, Lake Carlyle, Aug 22, 1974 (VK); 1, Jackson Co, July 19, 1975 (BP-AB29:980); 1, Decatur, May 1, 1976 (RS).

Ruddy Turnstone *(Arenaria interpres)*

Mid-May — Early June
Early August — Early October

Status: Common migrant along lake shore in Lake Co and Cook Co. An occasional migrant in other section of state.
Documentation: Specimen(s) — ♀, Waukegan, Lake Co, July 28, 1973 (ISM 605715).
Remarks: Inhabits sandbars, beaches, and mudflats. *Records:* 1, Rockford, May 21, 1961 (LJ-AFN15:414); Ad ♀ collected, Lake Calumet, Oct 2, 1961 (PM); 1, Decatur, May 14, 1966 (D. Thompson, P. Stutsman); 1, Crab Orchard NWR, Aug 3, 1972 (VK-AB26:866); 9, Coles Co, July 30, 1973 (LBH-AB27:876); 2, Waukegan, Nov 11, 1973 (CC, HDB). *High counts:* 240, Waukegan, May 27, 1961 (RR-AFN15:414); 350, Illinois Beach St Pk, June 1, 1966 (J. Probst); 19, Chautauqua NWR, Sep 5, 1971 (PW, HDB); 200, Waukegan, May 21, 1972 (LB-AB26:767).

Red Phalarope *(Phalaropus fulicarius)*

Late April — Late May
Early September — Late November

Status: Rare fall migrant. Very rare spring migrant.
Documentation: Specimen(s) — ♂, Lake Calumet, Sep 24, 1957 (UMNZ-Binford, 1958).
Remarks: Usually occurs singly at small ponds, such as sewage lagoons, and on larger lakes. Prefers deeper water and swims more than other phalaropes but can occur on mudflats. Recently has been found yearly in very small numbers. *Records:* 1, E. St. Louis (CBC) Dec 27, 1952 (AFN7:135); 1 found dead, Salem, Marion Co, Apr 30, 1970 (W. Jones-IAB155:26); ♀, Lyndon, Whiteside Co, May 25, 1971 (Shaws-AB25:752); 1 photographed, Chautauqua NWR, Nov 18, 1972 (HDB, LB, GR); 1 photographed, Waukegan, Nov 19-24, 1972 (LB-AB27:68); 1, Jacksonville, Oct 28 - Nov 4, 1973 (HDB, WO); 1, Chautauqua NWR, Oct 12, 1974 (RP, RS, HDB); 1, Wilmette, Oct 27, 1974 (GR-AB29:66); 1, Chautauqua NWR, Nov 1, 1975 (RS, HDB).

Northern Phalarope *(Lobipes lobatus)*

Mid-May — Late May
Mid-August — Late September

Status: Occasional fall migrant and rare spring migrant.
Documentation: Specimen(s) — ♂, Lake Calumet, Cook Co, Sep 13, 1961 (NIU 264).
Remarks: Occurs in very shallow water, usually along mudflats; also can be found in sewage lagoons. *Records:* ♀, Lake Calumet, May 27, 1956 (Levy-AFN10:337); 1, Urbana, May 19, 1962 (PN-AFN16:419); ♂, Lyndon, Whiteside Co, May 27, 1968 (Shaws-IAB147:26); 1, Brussels, Calhoun Co, Sep 3, 1970 (SV, H. Wusetenfeld-IAB156:22); 1, Lock 13, Whiteside Co, Nov 13, 1970 (Shaws-IAB157:28); 7, Chautauqua NWR, Aug 21, 1971 (HDB); 1, Crab Orchard NWR, Aug 19, 1972 (VK-AB26:866); 1, Jacksonville, Aug 18, 1973 (RQR); 9, Evanston, Sep 3, 1973 (LB, GR-AB28:61); ♀, Jacksonville, May 11, 1974 (WO, PW); 13, Chautauqua NWR, Sep 7, 1974 (HDB); ♀, Mason Co, May 18, 1975 (RS, HDB).

Wilson's Phalarope *(Steganopus tricolor)*

Late April — Mid-May
Late July — Mid-September

Status: Uncommon migrant. [Formerly nested in north.]
Documentation: Specimen(s) — ♀, Clinton Twp, DeKalb Co, May 10, 1967 (NIU 2465).
Remarks: Prefers mudflats and very shallow pools of water with grassy edges. Last known breeding, cinder flats near Lake Calumet, 1968. *Summer records:* 12 nests with 29 young, Lake Calumet, summer, 1961 (Fetter, Lane-AFN15:472); possible nesting, Marshall Co, May 12 - June 29, 1973 (Princen, 1974); ♀, Lake Co, June 2 & 9, 1973 (LB & GR-AB27:876); ♂ (possible nesting), Mason Co, June 15 & June 23, 1974 (HDB); 1, Moline,

Rock Island Co, June 23, 1974 (EF-AB28:909). *Other records:* 1, Crab Orchard NWR, August 5, 1972 (VK-AB26:866); 1, Meredosia, Morgan Co, July 14, 1973 (HDB); 8, Chicago, July 28, 1973 (CC-AB27:876); 1, Chautauqua NWR, Oct 9, 1975 (RS). *High count:* 30, Chautauqua NWR, Aug 30, 1975 (RP, RS, HDB).

Pomarine Jaeger *(Stercorarius pomarinus)*

Status: Very rare fall migrant.
Documentation: Sight record with acceptable details — Ad, Illinois River below Kampsville, Calhoun Co, Aug 31, 1962 (W.C. Starrett—on file ISM).
Remarks: 2 records. Listing of specimen by Smith and Parmalee (p. 31) is erroneous. Old unverified records from Nelson (1876) and Sanborn (1922). *Other recent record:* Light phase, first-year bird, Evanston, Oct 14, 1974 (GR, RR).

Parasitic Jaeger *(Stercorarius parasiticus)*

Early September — Late November

Status: Rare fall migrant in north along Lake Michigan and very rare fall migrant in central along large rivers of state.
Documentation: Specimen(s) — Im ♀, Chicago, Oct 29, 1926 (FMNH 97330).
Remarks: Appear suddenly and fly in to harrass gulls and terns. Regular on Chicago lake front. No spring records, indicating that they make long high flights in spring or, more likely, use another route. *Recent records:* Dark phase Im, Chautauqua NWR, Sep 12, 1970 (HDB); 1, Wilmette, Oct 31, 1970 (RR, Ekert-AB25:65); light phase, Chautauqua NWR, Nov 28, 1970 (HDB); 1, Wilmette, Oct 17, 1971 (LB-AB26:72); 2 Ad, Chicago lake front, Oct 15, 1972 (LB, CC-AB27:68); 1, Chicago lake front, Sep 7, 1973 (GR-AB28:61); 5, Evanston, Oct 14, 1974 (LB); 8, Chicago lake front, fall, 1975 (AB30:79).

Long-tailed Jaeger *(Stercorarius longicaudus)*

Status: Very rare fall migrant in south.
Documentation: Specimen(s) — Im, Nashville, Washington Co, Oct 21, 1893 (SIU A-161).
Remarks: Should be found earlier in the fall than other jaegers. Only other record is a decayed bird, found near Cairo, Nov 1876, by W.H. Ballow; specimen was discarded (Ridgway, 1889, p. 218).

[Skua *(Catharacta skua)*]

Status: Hypothetical.
Remarks: Listed by Ridgway (1895) as "Accidental in Illinois." No records.

Glaucous Gull *(Larus hyperboreus)*

Late November — Mid-March

Status: Occasional winter resident along Lake Michigan and larger rivers. Very rare winter resident in remainder of state.

Documentation: Specimen(s) — Im, Lake Calumet, Cook Co, Mar 5, 1961 (PM 1961-38).

Remarks: A large white gull which appears on larger lakes and rivers with Herring Gulls. Usually associated with ice. Most in either 1st- or 2nd-year plumages, although adults can be found. *Records:* 3, Chicago, Jan 2, 1956 (Bi-AFN10:255); 1, Lake Decatur, Dec 22, 1956 (Chaniot-AFN11:269); 2nd-year, Lyndon, Whiteside Co, May 9, 1968 (Shaws-AFN22:532); 10, Lake Calumet, Jan 1971 (DE-AB25:586); 1st-year and 2nd-year, Chautauqua NWR, Nov 28, 1970, and Mar 13, 1971 (HDB); 1, Alton, May 10, 1971 (M. Shaeffer, RA-AB25:752); 5, Lake Calumet, Jan 13, 1973 (AB27:624); 1, Chicago, May 8, 1975 (GR-AB29:860); Ad, Crab Orchard NWR, Feb 4, 1976 (BP).

Iceland Gull *(Larus glaucoides)*

Early December — Mid-March

Status: Rare winter resident on Lake Michigan and along Illinois and Mississippi rivers. Not recorded in remainder of state.

Documentation: Sight record with acceptable details — 2nd-year, Chicago, Feb 5, 1972 (CC—on file ISM).

Remarks: Usually appears in Jan or Feb on large bodies of water in association with ice periods. Very similar to other "white-winged" gulls, all of which should be identified with care. *Records:* 1, Chicago, Jan 2, 1956 (Bi-AFN10:255); 1, Chicago, Dec 28 - Jan 27, 1960 (Fetter, Lane-AFN14:313); 1, Wilmette, Apr 4, 1961 (RR-AFN15:415); 1, Alton, Jan 30, 1969 (JEC-AFN23:487); 1st-year, Lake Calumet, Mar 8, 1969 (CC-AFN23:487); 3, Lake Calumet, Jan 3, 1971 (DE-AB25:586); 2nd-year, Quiver Lake, Mason Co, Feb 21, 1972 (HDB); 1st-year, Chautauqua NWR, Dec 13, 1975 (RS, HDB).

Subspecies: The Kumlien's Gull, *L. g. kumlieni*, subspecies of the Iceland Gull, was reported at Winnetka, Feb 27, 1949 (Ford, 1956).

Great Black-backed Gull *(Larus marinus)*

Early September — Mid-March

Status: Very rare migrant and winter resident on Lake Michigan and large rivers and lakes.

Documentation: Photographic — Ad, Crab Orchard NWR, Feb 5-8, 1976 (BP, D. Klem-on file ISM).

Remarks: Found on large bodies of water. *Records:* 1, Chicago, Feb 15 - Mar 17, 1959 (Fetter-AFN13:297); 2, Moline, Rock Island Co, Feb 10, 1963 (EF-AFN17:328); Ad, Mississippi River near Portage Des Sioux, Missouri, Feb 15, 1968 (JEC, SV-IAB146:29); 1st-year, Lincoln Park Feb 17, 1968 (Nork, Dean-AFN22:444); Subadult (3rd-year), Waukegan, Sep 9, 1972 (LB); Ad, Lake Calumet, Dec 8, 1974 (CC-AB29:698).

Western Gull *(Larus occidentalis)*

Status: Very rare vagrant.

Documentation: Specimen — 1 (of the race *L. o. wymani*), Lincoln Park, Chicago, Nov 17, 1927 (CAS 1663).

Remarks: 2 records of this West Coast species. *Other record:* 1, Randolph Street Harbor, Chicago, Feb 18, 1950 (S & P, 1955, p. 32).

Herring Gull *(Larus argentatus)*

Early October — Early April

Status: Abundant migrant and winter resident on large rivers and Lake Michigan. Common migrant and winter resident in remainder of state. Non-breeding birds common near Lake Michigan during summer but rare in remainder of state.

Documentation: Specimen(s) — Im ♀, Lake Calumet, Cook Co, Oct 1, 1961 (NIU 141).

Remarks: Found on large bodies of water. Nesting attempted, Lake Calumet, in 1976 but destroyed by heavy rains (LB). *High counts:* 10,594, southeast Cook Co (CBC), Dec 29, 1955 (AFN10:166); 3,310, Crab Orchard NWR, Dec 27, 1956 (AFN11:168); 1,280, Chautauqua NWR (CBC), Jan 3, 1960 (AFN14:202); 6,000, Peoria (CBC), Dec 26, 1966 (AFN21:256); 2,300, Chicago, Nov 21, 1971 (LB-IAB162:20); 350, Whiteside Co (SBC), May 5, 1973; 568, Lake Co (SBC), May 4, 1974; 3,000, Lake Michigan, Oct 11, 1975 (LB, RS, GR).

Thayer's Gull *(Larus thayeri)*

Status: Very rare migrant and winter resident.

Documentation: Specimen — 1, Chicago, Mar 27, 1876 (British Museum-Dwight, 1925).

Remarks: Considered a subspecies of the Herring Gull until recently. Very difficult to identify since field marks constitute extremely subtle differences from other species of gulls. May prove to be regular. *Records:* Ad, Lincoln Park, Chicago, Mar 20, 1939 (Clark & Nice, 1950); 1st-year, Chautauqua NWR, Dec 17, 1974 - Jan 1, 1975 (HDB, RS); 1st-year photographed (on file ISM), Mississippi River near Alton, Oct 11, 1975 (T. Barksdale); 1st-year, Chautauqua NWR, Dec 13, 1975 (RS, HDB).

California Gull *(Larus californicus)*

Status: Very rare vagrant.

Documentation: Sight record with acceptable details — 1st-year, Chicago, Oct 26, 1974 (LB, GR, LC—on file ISM).

Remarks: Breeds as close as east-central North Dakota, but only 2 records sufficiently documented in state. Im gulls difficult to identify; great care should be taken with sight records. *Other record:* 1 Ad, Chautauqua NWR, May 21, 1976 (RS, P. Gibson).

Ring-billed Gull *(Larus delawarensis)*

Late August — Late May

Status: Common migrant. Fairly common winter resident in central and south. Uncommon winter resident in north. Rare summer resident in north (along Lake Michigan). Occasional nonbreeding summer resident in remainder of state.

Documentation: Specimen(s) — Im ♀, Lake Decatur, Oct 29, 1972 (ISM 605340).

Remarks: Occurs wherever there is a large expanse of water; at times may be seen in fields following the plow. Much migration in winter, depending on ice conditions. *First Illinois breeding record:* 800, including 71 young of the year ranging in age from downy chicks to fledged juveniles, Lake Calumet, July 6, 1975 (CC). *Summer (nonbreeding) record:* 9, Springfield, summer, 1971 (HDB). *High counts:* 1,999, Murphysboro (CBC), Dec 27, 1955 (AFN10:164); 2,800, Pere Marquette St Pk (CBC), Dec 30, 1956 (AFN11:170); 5,000, Crab Orchard NWR (CBC), Dec 23, 1964 (AFN19:232); 2,000, Springfield (CBC), Dec 27, 1964 (AFN19:237); 12,000, Peoria (CBC), Dec 26, 1966 (AFN21:256); 1,428, Cook Co (SBC), May 10, 1975.

Black-headed Gull *(Larus ridibundus)*

Status: Very rare vagrant.
Documentation: Photographic — Ad, North Chicago, July 15, 1976 (LB—on file ISM).
Remarks: 2 records. Old World species which has become regular on Northeast Coast of North America. *Other record:* Im changing to Ad plumage, Quiver Lake, Mason Co, Feb 10, 1973 (HDB & VK, 1973-74).

Laughing Gull *(Larus atricilla)*

Mid-April — Early June
Mid-August — Mid-November

Status: Rare migrant or vagrant. Most records for the north and central. Evidently not recorded below E. St. Louis.
Documentation: Specimen — Ad ♂, Springfield, May 27, 1971 (ISM 604789).
Remarks: Appears about every year, its destinations and origins unknown. Gulf Coast is most likely place of origin. Frequents large lakes and rivers where it associates with other gulls. *Recent records:* Ad, New Boston, Mercer Co, May 19, 1971 (HDB); 1, Waukegan, May 28, and 2, May 31, 1971 (LB, RR, CC-AB25:752); 5, Nauvoo, Hancock Co, June 12, 1971 (JF-AB25:864); Im and Ad, Waukegan, Aug 28, 1971 (C. Olson, LB-AB26:72); 1, Chicago, Nov 18, 1972 (LB, GR-AB27:69); Im, Waukegan, Aug 4, 1973 (GR, JG-AB27:876); Ad, Chautauqua NWR, May 11, 1974 (RS, PW, RQR); Ad, Chicago, May 10, 1975 (LB-AB29:860).

Franklin's Gull *(Larus pipixcan)*

Late March — Late May
Late July — Early December

Status: Rare spring migrant. Uncommon fall migrant in central and south. Occasional fall migrant in north.
Documentation: Specimen(s) — ♀, Lake Calumet, Cook Co, July 21, 1956 (NMHS-S. Levy).
Remarks: Usually occurs on shallow lakes and mudflats but can occur on deep lakes. *Records:* 1, Chicago (CBC), Dec 26, 1959 (Huxford-AFN14:202); 1, Wilmette, Mar 24, 1963 (RR-AFN17:408); Ad, Waukegan, July 19, 1969 (CC); 1, Waukegan, May 31, 1971 (LB, RR, CC-AB25:752); 1, Springfield, Apr 30, 1972 (HDB); 2, Whiteside Co (SBC), May 6, 1972; 2, Fulton Co (SBC), May 5, 1973; 3, Decatur, May 28, 1973 (RS-AB27:779); 8, Nauvoo, Hancock Co, Apr 2, 1975 (G. Senn); 1, Chicago, May 10, 1975 (CC-AB29:860);

Ad, near Mississippi River, Alexander Co, June 7, 1975 (RS, HDB); Ad, Lake Springfield, Dec 21, 1975 (WO, D. Allyn). *High counts:* 100, Mark Twain NWR, Oct 1970 (SV-IAB158:23); 75, Quiver Lake, Oct 16, 1971 (HDB); 125, Chautauqua NWR, Oct 5, 1974 (RS, VK, HDB); 16, Chicago, Oct 31, 1970 (CC).

Bonaparte's Gull *(Larus philadelphia)*

Late March — Mid-May
Mid-August — Early December

Status: Abundant migrant along Lake Michigan. Fairly common migrant in remainder of state. Uncommon nonbreeding summer resident along Lake Michigan and rare nonbreeding summer resident downstate. Uncommon winter resident along Lake Michigan and occasional winter resident in remainder of state.
Documentation: Specimen(s) — Ad, Highland Park, Lake Co, Aug 16, 1933 (FMNH 74386).
Remarks: A small gull found on large lakes and rivers. Indications are that most of those found on Lake Michigan migrate to and from the East Coast. *Records:* Im, Lake Decatur, June 29, 1973 (RS); 30, Chicago area, summer, 1975 (LB-AB29:980). *High counts:* 2,500, Wilmette, Sep 13, 1955 (Bi-AFN10:28); 60, Crab Orchard NWR, Nov 13, 1959 (Bush-AFN14:40); 180, Chicago, Dec 27, 1969 (AFN24:307); 11,000, Chicago, Apr 22, 1971 (LB-AB25:752); 2,000, Cook Co (SBC), May 4, 1974; 1,300, Evanston, Nov 19, 1970 (LB).

Little Gull *(Larus minutus)*

Late April — Late May
Mid-August — Early December

Status: Rare migrant on Lake Michigan. Very rare migrant in remainder of state.
Documentation: Photographic — Ad in winter plumage, Calumet Harbor, Chicago, Dec 1971 (Jack Armstrong—on file ISM).
Remarks: Closely resembles and associates with Bonaparte's Gulls. Usually found in harbors along Lake Michigan. First appeared at Chicago in 1938 (Clark & Nice, 1950). More numerous in fall. *Recent records:* 2 Ad, Chicago, Sep 16, 1956 (Bi-AFN11:30); Im, Lincoln Park, Chicago, Oct 26 & Nov 1, 1958 (CC-AFN13:36); 1, Grand Marias St Pk, E. St. Louis, Nov 14 & 15, 1962 (RA-AFN17:37); 1, Chicago, Aug 15, 1964 (CC-AFN18:511); 5, Chicago, between Aug & Nov 14, 1970 (LB); 1, Chicago, Dec 20, 1970 (DE, Nork-AB25:586); 10, Chicago, Aug 15 - Dec 4, 1971 (LB-AB26:72); 1, Chicago, Nov 25, 1973 (CC-AB28:61); 2 Ad, Evanston, Nov 26, 1975 (RS); 1, Chicago, Apr 27, 1976 (GR, LB), 1, Crab Orchard NWR, Apr 9, 1976 (BP-AB30:849).

[Ivory Gull *(Pagophila eburnea)*]

Status: Hypothetical.
Remarks: 1 reported, Waukegan Harbor, Lake Co, Jan 1, 1949 (Mr. & Mrs. Al Campbell, KB, Baldwin, and others-AFN3:172). Record is probably correct, but unfortunately very little description was recorded and certainly not nearly enough for basis of a state record. It is interesting to note that 3 other Ivory Gulls were observed on the Great Lakes (from Wisconsin and Michigan) in 1947-49, one of which was collected (Ford, 1956).

Black-legged Kittiwake *(Rissa tridactyla)*

Early November — Early April

Status: Rare migrant and winter resident. None reported below E. St. Louis.
Documentation: Specimen(s) — Im ♀, Meredosia Lake, Morgan Co, Nov 25, 1898 (FMNH 94574).
Remarks: Occurs yearly in small numbers on large lakes and rivers. Most birds observed in distinct Im plumage. Usually found with Bonaparte's Gulls. *Records:* Ad, Chicago, Jan 24, 1965 (CC-AFN19:384); Im, Lake Decatur, Nov 21 - Dec 8, 1966 (HDB); Im, Chillicothe, Peoria Co, Jan 2 - Jan 13, 1967 (AFN21:253); Im, Alton Dam, Madison Co, Jan 29, 1967 (RA-AFN21:425); Im, Chicago, May 4, 1968 (Bi); Im photographed, Springfield, Apr 1-8, 1971 (J. Paul, HDB); Im, Evanston, Nov 13, 1971 (LB, GR, B. Tweit-AB26:72); Im, Chicago, Feb 27, 1972 (LB-AB26:612); Ad, Waukegan, Oct 27, 1974 (GR-AB29:68); Im, Hamilton, Nov 23, 1974 (RS, HDB).

Sabine's Gull *(Xema sabini)*

Early September — Early November

Status: Very rare fall migrant.
Documentation: Specimen(s) — Im ♀?, Lake Springfield, Sangamon Co, Sep 25, 1974 (ISM 605923).
Remarks: Found on large bodies of water. Recently has occurred yearly in small numbers in fall. Most or all recent records of Im birds. One old spring record for Apr 1873 (Nelson, 1876). Has been found on the extreme dates of July 24 & Jan 9. *Recent records:* 1, Wilmette, Sep 13, 1955 (Bi-AFN10:28); 1, Alton, Sep 12, 1965 (RA-AFN20:54); 1, Mark Twain NWR, Sep 28, 1967 (RA, SV-AFN22:49); Im, Wilmette, Oct 19, 1971 (LB, GR-AB26:72); Im, Navy Pier, Chicago, Nov 4, 1973 (HDB, GR, WO, RQR); Im, Lake Decatur, Sep 16-17, 1974 (RS); Im, Lake Decatur, Sep 11-12, 1975 (RS); Im, Rend Lake, Sep 26-28, 1975 (BP, P. Biggers); Im, Chautauqua NWR, Oct 6-13, 1976 (RS, P. Gibson, RP).

[Gull-billed Tern *(Gelochelidon nilotica)*]

Status: Hypothetical.
Remarks: Listed by Nelson (1876) and Ridgway (1881) but no records given. The A.O.U. Checklist (5th edition) lists it as casual or accidental in Illinois; but this is unwarranted since there are no specimens or acceptable records. *Of 2 recent sight records, the latter is probably correct:* 1, Chicago, Aug 15 & 26, 1959 (Fetter, Lane-AFN14:40); 1, Waukegan, Aug 13, 1967 (Eckert, RR-AFN21:578).

Forster's Tern *(Sterna forsteri)*

Late April — Mid-May
Late July — Mid-October

Status: Common migrant. Occasional summer resident in northeastern part of state.
Documentation: Specimen(s) — Ad ♂, Lake Calumet, Sep 11, 1926 (UMMZ 84808).

Remarks: Found on lakes and rivers during migration. Nests in marshes. There is much confusion in the literature between this species and the Common Tern. *Summer records:* 3 nests, Powderhorn Marsh, summer, 1965 (LB); Im, Waukegan, May 31, 1971 (CC-AB25:752); 3, Waukegan, July 9, 1972 (LB-AB26:866); Im, Fulton Co, June 20, 1973 (HDB); 1, McClure, Union Co, July 20, 1973 (DH-AB27:876). *Other records:* 1, Kane Co, Apr 10, 1974 (RM-AB28:808); 1, Lake Decatur, Oct 27, 1976 (RS); 1, E. St. Louis, Apr 8, 1976 (J. Eades-AB30:849). *High count:* 139, Cook Co (SBC), May 4, 1974.

Common Tern *(Sterna hirundo)*

Early May — Late May
Late July — Early October

Status: Common migrant and rare summer resident on Lake Michigan. Fairly common migrant in remainder of state.
Documentation: Specimen(s) — ♂, 2 miles north of Zion, Lake Co, May 13, 1961 (NIU 1120).
Remarks: Prefers lakes and large rivers. *Summer records:* 50 pairs, Lake Co, June 1, 1963 (RR); nest, Powderhorn Marsh, July 4, 1966 (LB, H. Blume); nest, Waukegan, July 23, 1967 (Bi, CC-AFN21:578). *Other records:* 1, Illinois Beach St Pk, Nov 3, 1970 (LB); 1, Chautauqua NWR, Oct 20, 1973 (HDB). *High counts:* 160, Illinois Beach St Pk, May 24, 1967 (J. Probst); 2,000, Chicago, May 8, 1971 (LB); 106, Lake Co (SBC), May 4, 1974.

[Roseate Tern *(Sterna dougallii)*]

Status: Hypothetical.
Remarks: 4 sight records, all with little or no documentation. All doubtful because of likeness of this species to other terns. It is interesting to note that there is a specimen from Indiana (Stoddard, 1917). A specimen is needed to confirm this species for the state. *Records:* 1, no date, Wilmette (RR, 1967); 1, Jackson Park, Chicago, May 7-18, 1934 (Ford, 1956); 1, Jacksonville, Apr 17, 1954 (S & P, p. 34); 1, Crab Orchard NWR, May 7, 1961 (LH-AFN15:415).

Least Tern *(Sterna albifrons)*

Mid-May — Early September

Status: Uncommon local migrant and summer resident in south. Rare summer resident in central. Rare migrant and postbreeding wanderer in remainder of state. [Formerly rare summer resident in north.]
Documentation: Specimen(s) — ♀, on Mississippi River, 6 miles southwest of Hull, Pike Co, Aug 31, 1957 (ISM 603812).
Remarks: Prefers rivers and lakes with sandbars on which it can nest. Due to flooding and overuse of sandbars by boaters, it is becoming less numerous. *2 nesting colonies:* 1, in Ohio River, Bell Island, near Shawneetown, Gallatin Co; 1, in Mississippi River, Mosenthein Island, near E. St. Louis, Madison Co. *Summer records:* 40 Ad and 11 young, Shawneetown, Aug 6, 1955 (AFN9:381); 2 eggs on sandbar, south of Hull, July 3, 1961 (Parmalee-IAB122:15); 8 pairs,

Mosenthein Island, Aug 8, 1971 (RA, PB-AB25:864). *Other records:* 3, Decatur, May 28, 1955 (Chaniot-AFN9:334); 1, Waukegan, May 10, 1959 (Lehman-AFN13:375); 8, Fulton, Whiteside Co, May 13, 1971 (Shaws-IAB159:13); 1, Charleston, June 4, 1972 (LBH-AB26:866); 3, Mark Twain NWR, Sep 1-4, 1973 (SV-AB28:61); 1, Decatur, Sep 13, 1974 (RS-AB29:67); 20, Cairo, Aug 11, 1974 (DH-AB29:66).

[Royal Tern *(Sterna maxima)*]

Status: Hypothetical.
Remarks: Nelson (1876) considered it "an exceedingly rare summer visitant to Lake Michigan." *1 recent undocumented sight record:* 1, Crab Orchard NWR, Sep 5, 1962 (Rice, Rose). Caspian Terns occur in summer and could have been mistaken for this species.

Caspian Tern *(Sterna caspia)*

Late April — Mid-May
Mid-July — Early October

Status: Uncommon migrant. Occasional nonbreeding summer resident.
Documentation: Specimen(s) — ♂, Mississippi River, 6 miles southwest of Hull, Pike Co, Sep 27, 1958 (ISM 603813).
Remarks: Found along lakes and rivers. *Summer records:* 2, Wilmette, July 5, 1961 (RR-AFN15:472); 1, Evanston, July 3, 1964 (RR-AFN18:511); 5, Lake Decatur, June 29, 1973 (RS-AB27:876). *High counts:* 50, Lake Calumet, Sep 9, 1968 (LC); 12, Madison Co (SBC), May 6, 1972; 15, Springfield, May 14, 1974 (HDB); 25, Chautauqua NWR, Sep 19, 1975 (RS); 42, Lake Calumet, Aug 8, 1976 (LB).

Large-billed Tern *(Phaetusa simplex)*

Status: Very rare vagrant.
Documentation: Sight record with acceptable details — 1, Lake Calumet, Cook Co, July 15 - Aug 28, 1949 (CC, also vague photographs — on file ISM).
Remarks: Only North American record of this South American species. Description plus sketches by R. Zusi (IAB71:4-5). Seen by many observers.

Black Tern *(Childonias niger)*

Early May — Late May
Late July — Late September

Status: Common migrant. Common summer resident in north and rare summer resident (locally) in central.
Documentation: Specimen(s) — 1, Mississippi River, 7 miles southwest of Hull, Pike Co, Aug 27, 1959 (ISM 603827).
Remarks: Occurs on lakes and marshes. *Summer records:* Several nests, Powderhorn Marsh, Cook Co, June 6, 1965 (LB); 1, Mason Co, June 15 & 23, 1974 (HDB). *High counts:* 150, Mason Co and Morgan Co, May 11, 1974 (WO, HDB); 100, Chautauqua NWR, Sep 1, 1973 (HDB).

Ancient Murrelet *(Synthliboramphus antiquus)*

Status: Very rare vagrant.
Documentation: Specimen — subadult ♀, 5 miles northeast of Macomb, McDonough Co, Nov 16, 1961 (ISM 603842).
Remarks: 1 record. Found alive on gravel road with broken wing (Balding, 1964). Regular range is Northwest Coast of North America.

COLUMBIFORMES: Doves and Pigeons.

Rock Dove *(Columba livia)*

Status: Initially introduced to North America; now abundant permanent resident.
Documentation: Specimen(s) — ♂, Springfield, Dec 27, 1974 (ISM 606107).
Remarks: The common pigeon of town and country, many of which can hardly be classified as wild birds.

Mourning Dove *(Zenaida macroura)*

Status: Abundant migrant and summer resident. Common winter resident.
Documentation: Specimen(s) — ♀, 7½ miles south of Springfield, July 1, 1971 (ISM 604815).
Remarks: A bird of open country; closely associated with agriculture. Tends to flock in colder weather and gather in river valleys for protection (Hanson & Kossack, 1963). *High counts:* 381, Olney (CBC), Dec 26, 1970 (AB25:350); 478, Bloomington (CBC), Jan 2, 1971 (AB26:369); 342, Barrington (CBC), Dec 29, 1971 (AB26:368); 318, Crawford Co (SBC), May 5, 1973; 435, Will Co (SBC), May 4, 1974; 149 (Route 46; BBS), Cumberland Co and Jasper Co, June 1, 1975 (M.C. Frazier — U.S. Fish & Wildlife Service, 1976, p. 639).

Passenger Pigeon *(Ectopistes migratorius)*

Status: Extinct. [Formerly abundant migrant. A common summer resident in north and uncommon summer resident in central.]
Documentation: Specimen(s) — young ♂, Calumet region, Sep 30, 1901 (Coale, 1925).
Remarks: Last bird of this species died in the Cincinnati Zoological Gardens, Cincinnati, Ohio, Sep 1, 1914. C.W.G. Eifrig wrote of seeing a single bird in River Forest, Cook Co, May 1, 1923, and then a pair, May 2, 11, 16 & July 18, 1923 (IAB50:6-7), but these probably refer to Mourning Doves. 2 specimens found recently in Steinhauer Collection: ♂ and Im, Fayette Co, Oct 2, 1892 (ISM 605930, 605931).

[Ringed Turtle Dove *(Streptopelia risoria)*]

Status: Hypothetical. Probable escapes.
Remarks: Commonly caged; has been found in the wild. *Nesting record:* Beardstown, Cass Co, 1963 (TEM-AFN19:45). *Other records:* 1, Springfield, Aug 23, 1957 (Thompson-AFN11:408); 1, Highland Park, Lake Co, June 17, 1967 (Bock-IAB144:17); 1, Decatur, July - Dec 1973 (RS).

Ground Dove *(Columbina passerina)*

Status: Very rare vagrant.
Documentation: Specimen — ♂, Lake Chautauqua, Jackson Co, Nov 10, 1974 (SIU uncatalogued).
Remarks: Normally found in southern U.S. *3 acceptable records:* 1, west of Meredosia in Brown Co, Aug 17, 1975 (RQR); 1, Springfield, Nov 23, 1975 (HDB). *2 undocumented records:* 1, Crab Orchard NWR, Oct 1964 (Rice, Rose); 2, near Harrisonville, Monroe Co, May 23, 1970 (Kraus-IAB155:28).

PSITTACIFORMES: Parrots and allies.

Carolina Parakeet *(Conuropsis carolinensis)*

Status: Extinct. [Formerly a common resident(?) especially in the south; less numerous in the north.]
Documentation: Specimen(s) — ♀, along Illinois River, May 8, 1879 (Rockbridge Alum Springs Biological Laboratory, Goshen, Virginia-Walley, 1966).
Remarks: Disappeared probably about 1890. Specimen (in CAS) collected in Union Co, May 18, 1857, by R. Kennicott; sight record of a flock near Kates Lake, Adams Co, about mid-Apr 1884 (S & P, 1955, p. 36).

[Monk Parakeet *(Myiopsitts monachus)*]

Status: Hypothetical. Probable escapes.
Remarks: Viewed as a possible agricultural pest and will probably be eliminated whenever it occurs. Illinois birds could have wandered from other states to the east instead of being released locally. Not firmly established at the present. *Records:* 4 Ad, and 3 fledged young, Hinsdale, DuPage Co, July 1973; 2 (with nest), Carlock, McLean Co, and 2, near Lockport, Will Co, 1973 (Larson, 1973); 1 specimen, Joliet, Will Co, Oct 30, 1974 (ISM 606072); 1 at feeder, Hinsdale, Dec 22, 1974 (AB29:414).

CUCULIFORMES: Cuckoos and allies.

Yellow-billed Cuckoo *(Coccyzus americanus)*

Early May — Early October

Status: Common migrant and summer resident.
Documentation: Specimen(s) — ♀, 3½ miles east of Petersburg, Menard Co, June 6, 1973 (ISM 605731).
Remarks: Found in woodland, woodland edge, and orchards. At times, linger late in fall. *Records:* 1, Bushnell, McDonough Co, Nov 6, 1954 (LH-AFN9:30); 1, Wilmette, Nov 1, 1970 (CC, RR, K. Eckert-AB25:66); 1, Mark Twain NWR, Nov 3, 1970 (SV-AB26:66); 1, Charleston, Coles Co, Nov 2, 1974 (LBH-AB29:67). *High counts:* 25 (Route 51, BBS), Madison Co and Clinton Co, June 16, 1973 (N.P. Lane — U.S. Fish & Wildlife Service, 1973, p. 591); 32 (Route 59, BBS), Pulaski Co and Alexander Co, June 20, 1973 (VK-U.S. Fish & Wildlife Service, 1973, p. 591).

Black-billed Cuckoo *(Coccyzus erythropthalmus)*

Early May — Early June
Late August — Early October

Status: A fairly common migrant. Uncommon summer resident in north. Rare summer resident in south and central.
Documentation: Specimen — ♂, Evanston, Cook Co, June 3, 1973 (ISM 605722).
Remarks: A woodland species. *Summer records:* Nest, Sangamon Co, June 18, 1959 (D. Allyn); 1, Crab Orchard NWR, July 29, 1975 (BP-AB29:980). *Other record:* 1, Urbana, Oct 16, 1963 (PN-AFN18:43). *High count:* 12, Cass Co (SBC), May 10, 1975.

STRIGIFORMES: Owls.

Barn Owl *(Tyto alba)*

Status: Occasional permanent resident in south. Rare permanent resident in north and central.
Documentation: Specimen(s) — ♂, near Elkhart Hill, Logan Co, Oct 8, 1977 (ISM 606687).
Remarks: Found in barns, steeples, and other high vacant structures as well as hollow trees. Definite population decrease in last 10 years. Probably migratory. *Records:* 1, DeKalb (CBC), Dec 27, 1970 (AB25:353); 1, Fenton, Aug 19, 1972 (Hagans-AB26:866); nests, Barnhill, Wayne Co, Dahlgren, Hamilton Co, 1973, and Mt. Vernon, Jefferson Co, Apr 27-28, 1974 (VK); 1, Blue Island, Cook Co, Apr 2-3, 1975 (KB-AB29:698).

Screech Owl *(Otus asio)*

Status: Common permanent resident.
Documentation: Specimen(s) — ♀ red phase, 2 miles east of Deer Plain, Calhoun Co, Feb 12, 1973 (ISM 605746).
Remarks: This woodland species can also be found in residential areas. *High counts:* 16, Joliet (CBC), Dec 15, 1973 (AB28:382); 26, Chicago North Shore (CBC), Dec 29, 1973 (AB28:379); 16, McHenry Co (SBC), May 4, 1974; 24, Morton Arboretum (CBC), Dec 21, 1975 (AB30:432).

Great Horned Owl *(Bubo virginianus)*

Status: Fairly common permanent resident.
Documentation: Specimen(s) — ♀, Wyanet, Bureau Co, Jan 12, 1971 (ISM 604807).
Remarks: Nocturnal woodland species. Can be found hunting in open places. Best seen at dawn and dusk sitting in the tops of trees. *High counts:* 9, Cook Co (SBC), May 6, 1972; 49, Beverly (CBC), Dec 22, 1973 (JF-AB28:377); 13, Crab Orchard NWR, Dec 29, 1973 (AB28:380); 24, Crane Lake (CBC), Dec 15, 1973 (AB28:380); 20, Pike Co (SBC), May 4, 1974.
Subspecies: The Arctic Horned Owl *(B. v. wapacuthu)*, which occurs rarely in the north, was taken in northeastern Illinois Dec 31, 1874 (Nelson, 1876). Observed in Chicago area from Jan 27 - Feb 4, 1973 (LB, CC-AB27:624).

Snowy Owl *(Nyctea scandica)*

Early November — Early March

Status: Occasional winter resident in north. Rare winter resident in central. Very rare winter resident in south.

Documentation: Specimen(s) — ♀, 2½ miles east of Chambersburg, Pike Co, Jan 4, 1975 (ISM 606062).

Remarks: A diurnal owl. Prefers open areas and sits on elevated perches such as haystacks and knolls. Occurrence is cyclic, depending on food supplies farther north. A fair influx occurred in the winter of 1974-75. *Records:* 1, Wolf Lake, Cook Co, Apr 17, 1966 (LB); 1, Bethany, Moultrie Co, Dec 29, 1967 (AFN22:266); 1, Lake Petersburg, Menard Co, Jan 11, 1971 - Feb 25, 1972 (HDB); 1, O'Hare Field, Chicago, Dec 18, 1973 (CC-AB28:647); 1, Montrose Harbor, Chicago, Oct 4-10, 1974 (T. Gatz-AB29:67); 1, Champaign, Nov 22, 1974 (R. Applegate-AB29:67); ♂ killed, near Yorkville, Kendall Co, Jan 1975 (ISM 606108); 1, near Elkhart, Logan Co, Mar 6, 1975 (RS); 1, Rend Lake, Dec 31, 1975 (BP). *High count:* 6, Chicago, Mar 16, 1975 (W. Krawiecz, D. Brenner).

Hawk-Owl *(Surnia ulula)*

Late November — Late April

Status: Very rare winter vagrant in north and central.

Documentation: Specimen(s) — ♀, Chicago, Dec 3, 1922 (FMNH-Sanborn, 1930).

Remarks: No recent records. *Only 5 records for this diurnal owl:* 1, Kane Co, Sep 1, 1869 (Nelson, 1876) (this seems extremely early in the fall?); 1, Chicago, Nov 27, 1928 (Sanborn, 1930); 1, near Clayton, Adams Co, Jan 1947 (TEM, 1948); 1, Rockford, Apr 24, 1950 (S & P, 1955, p. 37); 1 questionable record, from Morton Arboretum, DuPage Co, Apr 28, 1953 (Shawvan, Wasson).

Burrowing Owl *(Athene cunicularia)*

Late March — Early May

Status: Very rare spring vagrant in north and central.

Documentation: Specimen(s) — ♂, near Hamilton, Hancock Co, Apr 9, 1930 (Lambert, 1930).

Remarks: Appears in open, dry areas. Usually perches on or near the ground. *Records:* 1, Chicago, May 6, 1950 (CC, Nork-S & P, 1955, p. 37); 1, Lake Calumet, Mar 27, 1952, and 1, DuPage Co, Apr 8-23, 1953 (S & P, 1955, p. 37); 1 collected, Chicago, 97th & Torrence Ave (specimen supposedly in Bowen High School), Mar 27, 1953 (IAB86:2); 1 (with few details), near Fairbury, Livingston Co, Apr 18 & 19, 1966 (R. Phelps-IAB139:22); 1, near Springfield, Apr 18, 1975 (HDB).

Barred Owl *(Strix varia)*

Status: Common permanent resident in central and south. Uncommon permanent resident in north.

Documentation: Specimen(s) — ♀, 4 miles north of Greenfield, Greene Co, Nov 8, 1971 (ISM 605214).

Remarks: A bottomland forest species. *High counts:* 8, Rock Island (CBC), Dec 27, 1964 (IAB133:17); 10, Union Co (SBC), May 5, 1973; 16, Crane Lake (CBC), Dec 15, 1973 (AB28:380); 19, Pike Co (SBC), May 4, 1974.

[Great Gray Owl *(Strix nebulosa)*]

Status: Hypothetical.
Remarks: A large owl of northern coniferous forests. Kennicott (1855) and Nelson (1876) list this species but give no records. Musselman (S & P, 1955, p. 37) reported 1 collected, near Rockford, about 1930 by Dr. Lambert, but no specimen can be found. 2 reported on a Christmas count, Moline, Rock Island Co, Dec 27, 1946, but with no details (AFN1:90).

Long-eared Owl *(Asio otus)*

Late November — Early April

Status: Uncommon winter resident in north and central. Rare winter resident in south. Rare summer resident.
Documentation: Specimen(s) — ♂, 4 miles east of Beardstown, Cass Co, Mar 18, 1971 (ISM 604753).
Remarks: Usually observed roosting in dense evergreens. *Summer records:* Pair with fledged young, Winnebago Co, May 29, 1958 (LJ-IAB108:7); nested, Eggers Woods, Chicago, summer, 1963 (CC-AFN17:464); 1, Mason St Forest, June 1971 (Princen, 1972); nest with young photographed, Carlyle, Fayette Co, spring 1977 (M. Jantzen-AB31:1008). *Other records:* 20, Morton Arboretum, Jan 1955 (Campbell-AFN9:261); 38, Rockford, Nov 24, 1956 (LJ-AFN15:214); 10-15, near Carbondale, Jackson Co, Dec 29, 1956 - Apr 8, 1957 (DBi, 1958); 4, Crane Lake, Mason, Co, Mar 19, 1972 (HDB); 1, Rock Island Co (SBC), May 6, 1972; 6, Adams Co, Dec 1972 (JF-AB26:612); 1, Lee Co, and 1, McHenry Co (SBC), May 5, 1973; ♂ collected, 2 miles south of Makanda, in Union Co, Jan 12, 1974 (SIU).

Short-eared Owl *(Asio flammeus)*

Mid-October — Mid-April

Status: Uncommon migrant and winter resident. Rare summer resident in north and central.
Documentation: Specimen(s) — ♀, 2 miles southeast of New Minden, Washington Co, Nov 8, 1973 (ISM 605854).
Remarks: A crepuscular species found in open areas, usually marshy situations and overgrown fields. Often observed as diurnal migrant along shore of Lake Michigan. *Summer records:* 1, Lake Calumet, May 27, 1972 (CC-AB26:767); nest, Goose Lake Prairie, 1973 (DBi-AB27:877); 3, Lake Calumet, July & Aug 1976 (LB). *Other records:* 12-14, near Paris, Edgar Co, Feb & Mar 1972 (LBH-AB26:612); 7, Union Co, Jan 1973 (DH, MH, M. Swayne); 2, Grundy Co, and 2, Mercer Co (SBC), May 5, 1973; a flight of 13, Chicago Lakefront, Oct 14, 1973 (LB-AB28:61); 18, Waukegan (CBC), Jan 1, 1976 (AB30:438).

Boreal Owl *(Aegolius funereus)*

Mid-October — Early March

Status: Very rare winter vagrant in north.
Documentation: Specimen(s) — ♀, Chicago, Mar 5, 1914 (Coale, 1914).
Remarks: Inhabits coniferous woodland. *Only 5 records; none recent:* 1, Rockford, Oct 15, 1884 (Cory, 1909); 1, Sycamore, DeKalb Co, last week in Jan 1887 (Wyman, 1915); 1, Kenilworth, Cook Co, Dec 26, 1902 (Deane, 1903); 1, Cicero, Cook Co, Dec 1902 (Coale, 1914).

Saw-whet Owl *(Aegolius acadicus)*

Late October — Early April

Status: Uncommon winter resident in north. Rare winter resident in central and south. Very rare summer resident in north and central. [Formerly summer resident in south(?).]
Documentation: Specimen(s) — ♂, 7 miles north of Albion, Edwards Co, Mar 6, 1957 (INHS 0-W-2).
Remarks: Usually observed in winter roosting in conifers or tangled brush. Very rare south of St. Louis although some winter records for Kentucky. *Summer records:* Nest(?), Marion Co, 1890 (TEM, 1951); 1 young of the year shot, and 1 captured, near Evanston, June 1932 (Ford, 1932); 4 young, near Quincy, Adams Co, Apr 28, 1949 (TEM, 1951); Ad, June 4, and juvenile, June 18, 1966, Allerton Park, Piatt Co, (Roth, 1967). *Other records:* 4 banded, Urbana, fall, 1961 (Kendeigh-AFN16:41); 1, Decatur, Dec 31, 1967 (AFN22:269); 7 banded, Shirland, Winnebago Co, fall, 1972 (LJ-AB27:69); 1, Apple River Canyon St Pk, Jo Daviess Co, Jan 21, 1973 (LB-AB27:624); 1, Skokie Lagoon, Cook Co, Feb 25, 1973 (GR-AB27:624); 1, Sterling, Whiteside Co, Oct 21, 1974 (Shaws-AB29:67); 1, Winnebago Co, Oct 6, 1975 (LJ-AB30:80); 1 banded, Springfield, Oct 31, 1975 (VK); 1, Pere Marquette St Pk (CBC), Dec 20, 1975 (AB30:434).

CAPRIMULGIFORMES: Goatsuckers.

Chuck-will's-widow *(Caprimulgus carolinensis)*

Late March — Mid-September

Status: Common migrant and summer resident from Jackson Co south. Occasional migrant and summer resident in remainder of south. Rare migrant and summer resident in central. Rare vagrant in north.
Documentation: Specimen(s) — ♂, Willow Springs, Cook Co, Apr 26, 1967 (CAS).
Remarks: Nocturnal woodland species. Best identified by its call. Most north and central records probably constitute over-migrants. *Summer records:* Nest with eggs, Peoria Co, Apr 20, 1963 (Schweitzer); nest with 2 eggs and later 2 fledged young, north of Liberty, Pike Co, June 10, 1966 (TEM, 1968). *Other records:* 1, Chicago, Apr 29, 1962 (CC-AFN16:419); 1, Urbana, May 3 & 14, 1962 (PN-AFN16:419); 1, Lake Forest, Lake Co, May 19, 1962 (Clow-AFN16:419); 1, Glenview, Cook Co, Aug 1964 (Palmquist-AFN19:45);

1, Olney, Richland Co, May 19, 1967 (V. Shaw-AFN21:513); 4, Decatur, May 15, 1974 (RP); 1 calling, Mason St Forest, May 10, 1975 (R. Bjorklund). *High count:* 7, Union Co (SBC), May 6, 1972.

Whip-poor-will *(Caprimulgus vociferus)*

Mid-April — Late September

Status: Common migrant and summer resident in south. Common migrant and fairly common summer resident in central and north.
Documentation: Specimen(s) — ♀, 2 miles north of Cobden, Union Co, Oct 6, 1967 (SIU A-1572).
Remarks: A nocturnal woodland species. Difficult to detect in fall. *Records:* 1, Illinois Beach St Pk, Oct 1, 1965 (J. Probst); 1, Evanston, Oct 10, 1970 (GR); 1 banded, Carbondale, Oct 7, 1971 (VK-AB26:72); 1 heard, Pope Co, Mar 23, 1975 (R. Graber-AB29:698). *High counts:* 50, Pope Co (SBC), May 6, 1972; 57, Pike Co (SBC), May 4, 1974; 55, Pope Co (SBC), May 10, 1975.

Common Nighthawk *(Chordeiles minor)*

Early May — Late September

Status: Common migrant and summer resident.
Documentation: Specimen(s) — ♂, 2½ miles west of Moweaqua, Christian Co, May 13, 1973 (ISM 605648).
Remarks: Found in residential areas. Can be observed migrating in flocks, especially in fall. *Records:* 1, Wilmette, Oct 12, 1961 (RR-AFN16:41); 1 specimen of *C. m. sennetti* collected, Blairsville, Williamson Co, Oct 15, 1961 (W. Ettling — SIU collection); 1, Chicago, Nov 2 & 3, 1968 (RR); 1, Springfield, Oct 17, 1971 (HDB); 1, Vermilion Co, Oct 10, 1974 (M. Campbell-AB29:67). *High counts:* 100, Rockford, May 30, 1958 (LJ-AFN12:358); 1,000, Lake Forest, Lake Co, Aug 31, 1958 (Clow-AFN13:36); 734, Charleston, Sep 6, 1971 (LBH-AB26:72); 600, Rockford, Sep 11, 1972 (JD-AB27:69).

APODIFORMES: Swifts and Hummingbirds.

Black Swift *(Cypseloides niger)*

Status: Very rare vagrant.
Documentation: Sight record with acceptable details — 1, Saganashkee Slough, Cook Co, Sep 5, 1951 (CC-on file ISM).
Remarks: *1 record:* This bird of western North America observed at close range in comparison with Chimney Swifts (also seen by T. Nork). *2 other records lack sufficient documentation:* 4, Evanston, early Sep 1953 (S & P, 1955, p. 38); 1, Chicago, May 15, 1956 (Wasson, 1956).

Chimney Swift *(Chaetura pelagica)*

Mid-April — Early October

Status: Common migrant and summer resident.
Documentation: Specimen(s) — ♀, Lake Springfield, May 31, 1973 (ISM 605670).

Remarks: Found in residential areas. In south, can be found in swamps where it nests in hollow trees. Gathers in large flocks in fall. *Records:* 1, Chicago, Apr 1, 1972 (B. Tweit-AB26:767); 1, Petersburg, Menard Co, Apr 1, 1973 (Dunn); 1, Rockford, Oct 13, 1973 (LJ-AB28:61); 1, Carbondale, Jackson Co, Nov 23, 1974 (D. Klem-AB29:67). *High counts:* 242, Logan Co (SBC), May 6, 1972; 214, Jersey Co (SBC), May 5, 1973; 220, Monroe Co (SBC), May 4, 1974; 200, Springfield, Sep 24, 1975 (HDB); 271, Cook Co (SBC), May 8, 1976.

Ruby-throated Hummingbird *(Archilochus colubris)*

Late April — Early October

Status: Common migrant and fairly common summer resident.
Documentation: Specimen(s) — ♂, Springfield, May 19, 1965 (ISM 604046).
Remarks: Frequents woods edge, weedy areas, and gardens. *Records:* 1, Sterling (snowed same night) Oct 25, 1967 (Shaws-IAB145:15); 1, Charleston, Coles Co, Oct 20, 1970 (LBH). *High counts:* 50, in 1-mile drive near Quincy, Sep 7, 1960 (TEM-AFN15:45); 23, Springfield, Sep 4, 1974 (VK-AB29:67); 22, Marshall Co (SBC), May 4, 1974.

[Black-chinned Hummingbird *(Archilochus alexandri)*]

Status: Hypothetical.
Remarks: 1 report with few details — ♂, Beall Woods, Wabash Co, first week in Aug 1967 (Norman McClain). Also, a report from Mt. Carmel at the same time. More details needed to add this western species to the state list.

CORACIIFORMES: Kingfishers.

Belted Kingfisher *(Megaceryle alcyon)*

Early April — Late October

Status: Common migrant and uncommon summer resident. Uncommon winter resident in north and central. Common winter resident in south.
Documentation: Specimen(s) — ♀, 6 miles southwest of Hull, Pike Co, Sep 29, 1959 (ISM 603830).
Remarks: Found near ponds, lakes, and rivers. Usually recorded in small numbers. *High counts:* 12, Decatur (CBC), Dec 28, 1958 (AFN13:187); 12, Will Co (SBC), May 4, 1974; 13, Crab Orchard NWR (CBC), Dec 28, 1974 (AB29:411); 13, Lake Co (SBC), May 10, 1975.

PICIFORMES: Woodpeckers.

Common Flicker *(Colaptes auratus)*

Late March — Mid-October

Status: Common migrant and common summer resident. Common winter resident in south. Uncommon winter resident in central and north.
Documentation: Specimen(s) — ♀, near Lincoln, Logan Co, Oct 9, 1972 (ISM 605757).

Remarks: Found in both open areas and woodland. Definite loose flocks of migrants obvious in early spring. Fall migration usually less detectable. *High counts:* 91, Pere Marquette St Pk (CBC), Dec 26, 1965 (AFN20:265); 204, Will Co (SBC), May 4, 1974; 124, Union Co, Dec 29, 1974 (AB29:418); 241, Cook Co (SBC), May 10, 1975.

Subspecies: An intergrade (Red-shafted x Yellow-shafted) flicker taken in Highland Park, Apr 27, 1940 (Ford, 1956, p. 54). *2 banding records of intergrades:* 1, Waukegan, Lake Co, Aug 30, 1934 (Barnes, 1935); 1, Blue Island, Cook Co, Sep 22, 1940 (S & P, 1955, p. 38). *Recent sight records of supposedly pure Red-shafted Flickers (C. a. cafer):* 1, Chautauqua NWR, winter, 1966-67 (Bellrose-IAB143:18); 1, Beverly, Adams Co, Jan 1, 1967 (JF-AFN21:425); 1, Chicago, Apr 16, 1971 (W. Krawiec, CC-AB25:752).

Pileated Woodpecker *(Dryocopus pileatus)*

Status: Uncommon permanent resident in south and along Illinois and Mississippi river bottoms in central and north. Rare in remainder of state.

Documentation: Specimen(s) — ♀, Carbondale, Jackson Co, Aug 1, 1971 (ISM 605449).

Remarks: Found in heavily wooded bottomland. Usually not found in northeastern portion of state. *Record:* 1, Chicago area, Jan 6 & 7, 1977 (CC-AB31:338). *High counts:* 15, Pere Marquette St Pk (CBC), Dec 26, 1965 (AFN20:265); 12, Georgetown (CBC), Dec 29, 1971 (AB26:374); 18, Randolph Co (SBC), May 6, 1972; 51, Union County Refuge (CBC), Dec 29, 1974 (AB29:418).

Red-bellied Woodpecker *(Melanerpes carolinus)*

Status: Common permanent resident in south and central. Uncommon permanent resident in north.

Documentation: Specimen(s) — ♂, East Peoria, Tazewell Co, Apr 30, 1971 (ISM 605055).

Remarks: A woodland species. Some migration or dispersion seems to occur. *Records:* 111, Decatur (CBC), Dec 26, 1955 (AFN10:164); 89, Pere Marquette St Pk (CBC), Dec 26, 1966 (AFN21:257); 94, Livingston Co (SBC), May 6, 1972; 3, Waukegan (CBC), Jan 1, 1973 (AB27:377); 14, McHenry Co (CBC), Dec 29, 1973 (AB28:384).

Red-headed Woodpecker *(Melanerpes erythrocephalus)*

Late April — Mid-October

Status: Common migrant and summer resident. Common winter resident in central and south and uncommon winter resident in north.

Documentation: Specimen(s) — ♂, New Salem St Pk, Menard Co, Feb 21, 1972 (ISM 605098).

Remarks: Found in woodland with standing dead trees. Acorn crop may influence wintering population in a given area. *Records:* 41 migrating, Mason St Forest, Sep 22, 1973 (VK, HDB). *High counts:* 217, Beverly, Adams Co (CBC), Dec 22, 1972 (AB27:366); 206, La Salle Co (SBC), May 5, 1973; 384, Pere Marquette St Pk (CBC), Dec 29, 1973 (AB28:385); 267, Bureau Co (SBC), May 4, 1974.

[Lewis' Woodpecker *(Melanerpes lewis)*]

Status: Hypothetical.
Remarks: 2 undocumented sight records of this western species. *Records:* 1, north side of Chicago, May 26, 1923 (Hine, 1924); 1, Argo, Cook Co, May 14, 1932 (Ford, Sanborn & Coursen, 1934). Although these records are probably correct, there are no specimens, photographs or descriptions.

Yellow-bellied Sapsucker *(Sphyrapicus varius)*

Early April — Early May
Mid-September — Early November

Status: Common migrant. Fairly common winter resident in south. Occasional winter resident in central and north. A rare summer resident in north.
Documentation: Specimen(s) — ♂, Quincy, Adams Co, Oct 4, 1974 (ISM 606270).
Remarks: A woodland species. Frequently found in parks and cemeteries in winter. *Summer records:* 3 old nesting records, Tazewell Co (Loucks, 1892), Putnam Co (Gault, 1922), and Cook Co (Ford, 1956); 3 nests, Henderson State Forest, June 19, 1955 (PCP, Sheets-AFN9:381). *High counts:* 14 killed at TV tower, Piatt Co, Sep 27, 1972 (Seets); 39, Cook Co (SBC), May 5, 1973; 12, Crane Lake, Mason Co (CBC), Dec 15, 1973 (AB28:380); 12, Springfield (CBC), Dec 16, 1973 (AB28:386); 77, Union Co (CBC), Jan 2, 1976 (AB30:437).
Subspecies: A Red-naped Sapsucker *(S. v. nuchalis)* observed by Dreuth at Lincoln Park, Chicago, Apr 27, 1930 (Clark & Nice, 1950).

Hairy Woodpecker *(Picoides villosus)*

Status: Fairly common permanent resident.
Documentation: Specimen(s) — ♀, Mark Twain NWR, Jan 6, 1972 (ISM 605054).
Remarks: A woodland species. Some migration may occur. Species seems more numerous in winter. *High counts:* 24, Peoria (CBC), Dec 26, 1965 (AFN20:265); 40, Chicago (CBC), Dec 30, 1967 (AFN22:268); 69, Chicago (CBC), Dec 26, 1971 (AB26:370).

Downy Woodpecker *(Picoides pubescens)*

Status: Common permanent resident.
Documentation: Specimen(s) — ♂, 5 miles south Timewell, Brown Co, Nov 10, 1971 (ISM 604953).
Remarks: A forest species. Visits open areas more than the Hairy Woodpecker. Some migration may occur. *High counts:* 123, Chicago (CBC), Dec 26, 1965 (AFN20:261); 144, Pere Marquette St Pk, Dec 30, 1967 (AFN22:272); 100, Bureau Co (SBC), May 4, 1974; 79, Cook Co (SBC), May 10, 1975; 183, Union Co (CBC), Jan 2, 1976 (AB30:437).

[White-headed Woodpecker *(Picoides albolarvatus)*]

Status: Hypothetical.
Remarks: This western species supposedly seen near Quincy, but no date or details available for this unlikely species for Illinois (TEM, 1916-17).

Black-backed Three-toed Woodpecker *(Picoides arcticus)*

Late October — Early April

Status: Rare winter resident in north and very rare winter resident in central.
Documentation: Specimen(s) — ♀, on campus of ISU at Normal, McLean Co, Oct 22, 1965 (ISU 381).
Remarks: Usually occurs in conifers, although can be found in deciduous trees. Prefers dead trees where it can strip off the bark. Seems to be certain influx years. Recently these have been 1956-57: 1 photographed, Rockford, Dec 9, 1956 (R. Olson, LJ-AFN11:269); ♀, Chicago, Apr 28 - May 19, 1957 (A. Montaque-AFN11:350); 1965-66: Above specimen; 2, Rockford, Jan 1, 1965 (AFN19:236); 1, Morton Arboretum, May 2, 1965 (R. Hoger, IAB135:12); 1, Peoria, Nov 19, 1965 (Tjaden-IAB137:4); ♀, Glenview, Cook Co, Feb 27, 1966 (J. Ware-IAB138:5); 1969-70: ♂, Techny, Dec 27, 1969 (CC-AFN24:510); 1, Rockford, Jan 1, 1970 (Seal, McFall-AFN24:314). *Other records:* 1, Wilmette, Jan 6, 1960 (RR-AFN14:313).

Ivory-billed Woodpecker *(Campephilus principalis)*

Status: Extirpated and probably extinct. [Formerly was probably a rare permanent resident in south.]
Documentation: Specimen — Only definite evidence, a tarsometatarsal bone discovered in midden deposits in Madison Co, Illinois (Parmalee, 1958).
Remarks: Other evidence very slight. Audubon (1831:341) states, "Descending the Ohio, we meet with this splendid bird for the first time near the confluence of that beautiful river and the Mississippi." Holder (1861) lists it in his "Birds of Illinois" but gives no date or place. Ridgway (1889) says, "The writer has a distinct recollection of what he believes to have been this species in White Co, some forty miles south of Mt. Carmel." Since this species is virtually extinct, the occurrence in Illinois ever again is extremely unlikely.

PASSERIFORMES: Perching or passerine birds.

TYRANNIDAE: Flycatchers.

Eastern Kingbird *(Tyrannus tyrannus)*

Late April — Late September

Status: Common migrant and summer resident.
Documentation: Specimen(s) — ♀, 5 miles south of Timewell, Brown Co, July 14, 1971 (ISM 604823).
Remarks: A flycatcher of open and semiopen areas. Diurnal migrations may be observed. *Records:* 1, near Sanganois Refuge, Cass Co, Oct 16, 1971 (RQR-AB26:72); 1, Crab Orchard NWR, Apr 8, 1972 (VK, GC-AB26:767). *High counts:* 50, Fayette Co (SBC), May 6, 1972; 53, Adams Co (SBC), May 5, 1973; 69, Fulton Co (SBC), May 10, 1975.

Western Kingbird *(Tyrannus verticalis)*

Early May — Early October

Status: Rare migrant throughout state. Occurs more often in western portion. Very rare summer resident in central and north.

Documentation: Specimen — 1, Highland Park, Lake Co, June 6, 1924 (specimen at Lincoln Avenue Grammar School, Highland Park-Coale, 1924).

Remarks: Found in open areas. Usually on fences and telephone wires. *Summer records:* Nest, near Kilbourne, Mason Co, June 9, 1965 (Graber, Graber & Kirk, 1974); nest, northwest of Kilbourne, Mason Co, Aug 14, 1967 (Graber, Graber & Kirk, 1974); nest, Winnetka, Aug 13, 1970 (CC-AFN24:690); 1, east of Springfield, June 20, 1973 (HDB). *Other records:* 1, near Quincy, Oct 8, 1957 (TEM-AFN12:36); 1, Herrin, Williamson Co, May 25, 1965 (Mitchell-IAB135:22); 1, Mark Twain NWR, Sep 18, 1966 (RA-AFN21:45); 1, west of Moweaqua, Christian Co, May 16, 1971 (HDB); 1, Skokie Lagoons, Cook Co, May 13-14, 1972 (LB-AB26:767); 1, Illinois Beach St Pk, May 29, 1974 (CC, GR-AB28:809).

Scissor-tailed Flycatcher *(Muscivora forficata)*

Mid-April — Early August

Status: Rare vagrant.

Documentation: Photographic — 1, 8 miles east of Havana, July 3-5, 1965 (J. & R. Graber, 1965).

Remarks: Prefers open areas. Probably occurs as an over-migrant. A species of the southwestern plains. Seems to be expanding its breeding range north and east. *Records:* 1, Danville, June 15, 1958 (Bursewicz, 1958). 1, Neponset, Bureau Co, Apr 15, 1967 (Gould-AFN21:513); 1, Lacon, Marshall Co, Apr 26, 1967 (Collins, Princen-IAB143:20); 1, Fults, Monroe Co, May 20, 1967 (RA, 1968); 1, between Cobden and Anna, July 25, 1970 (SV, William George-IAB156:21); 1 photographed, 6 miles southwest of Chandlerville, Cass Co, May 9, 1970 (PW, RQR, Crabtree, Leonhard).

Great Crested Flycatcher *(Myiarchus crinitus)*

Late April — Mid-September

Status: Common migrant and summer resident.

Documentation: Specimen(s) — ♂, 2½ miles east of Union County Refuge, July 19, 1972 (ISM 605221).

Remarks: A forest species feeding from mid-height to high. *Records:* 1, Springfield, Apr 20, 1976 (HDB). *High counts:* 19, along Cache River, Johnson Co, Apr 24, 1973 (VK, HDB); 21, Pope Co (SBC), May 5, 1973; 52, Cook Co (SBC), May 10, 1975.

Ash-throated Flycatcher *(Myiarchus cinerascens)*

Status: Very rare vagrant.

Documentation: Specimen — ♀, Springfield, Sangamon Co, Nov 9, 1973 (ISM 605794).

Remarks: *1 record:* This western species first observed Nov 2, 1973, in deciduous trees in a city park (HDB, 1975).

Eastern Phoebe *(Sayornis phoebe)*

Mid-March — Late October

Status: Common migrant and uncommon summer resident. Rare winter resident in north and central. Occasional winter resident in south.
Documentation: Specimen(s) — ♂, 6 miles southwest of Hull, Pike Co, Apr 18, 1956 (ISM 603800).
Remarks: Found along streams and forest edge. *Winter records:* 1, Rockford, Dec 26, 1955 (AFN10:166); 1, Decatur, Dec 27, 1956 (RS-AFN11:168); 1, Lake Co, Dec 23, 1961 (AFN16:211); 2, Pere Marquette St Pk (CBC), Dec 26, 1965 (AFN20:265); 1, Grundy Co, Dec 26, 1971 (PD, Lehman-AB26:375). *High count:* 24, Madison Co (SBC), May 6, 1972.

Say's Phoebe *(Sayornis saya)*

Status: Very rare vagrant.
Documentation: Sight record with acceptable details — 1, along the Ohio River, near Joppa, Massac Co, Dec 30, 1966 (RM & LH-on file ISM).
Remarks: 2 records. The other record of this western species was from Park Forest, Will Co, May 5, 1973 (Duke, Patterson). Supposedly there were specimens of which Nelson (1876) states, "Two specimens of this species are registered in the catalogue of birds in the museum of the Northwestern University at Evanston from West Northfield, Illinois, collected by R. Kennicott." He also says, "These specimens are not in the collection at present."

Yellow-bellied Flycatcher *(Empidonax flaviventris)*

Mid-May — Early June
Mid-August — Early October

Status: Fairly common migrant.
Documentation: Specimen(s) — ♀, east of Springfield, Sep 27, 1972 (ISM 605583).
Remarks: Found during migrations in a variety of habitats but seems to prefer forest edge. *Records:* 1, Waukegan, Aug 4, 1963 (CC); 1, Springfield, Oct 9, 1973 (HDB). *High count:* 12, Illinois Beach St Pk, May 25, 1964 (J. Probst).

Acadian Flycatcher *(Empidonax virescens)*

Early May — Mid-September

Status: Common migrant and summer resident in south. Uncommon migrant and summer resident in north and central.
Documentation: Specimen(s) — ♂, Lusk Creek, Pope Co, July 28, 1971 (ISM 604835).
Remarks: Inhabits river bottom forests and feeds at mid-height. Can be best recognized by its song. *Records:* Nest, 3 miles east of Woodstock, McHenry Co, June 16, 1964 (Carroll); 1, McGraw Wildlife Area, July 6, 1971 (Dillon, 1973); 1 singing, Chicago area, Aug 10, 1974 (CC). *High count:* 13, Johnson Co (SBC), May 4, 1974; 47, Jackson Co (SBC), May 10, 1975; 13, (Route 63, BBS), Massac Co and Pope Co, June 19, 1975 (VK-U.S. Fish & Wildlife Service, 1976, p. 647).

Alder Flycatcher *(Empidonax alnorum)*

Mid-May — Mid-June
Late August — Early October

Status: Common migrant.
Documentation: Specimen(s) — ♂, east of Springfield, Sep 2, 1972 (ISM 605260).
Remarks: Prefers woodland edge and hedge rows. Difficult and often impossible to separate from Willow Flycatcher unless singing. *Records:* 6 heard, north of Chicago, June 6, 1971 (RR-AB25:752); 1 recorded song, LaRue Swamp, Union Co, May 20, 1972 (JF); 1 heard, Beverly, Adams Co, May 28, 1973 (JF, HDB).

Willow Flycatcher *(Empidonax traillii)*

Mid-May — Late September

Status: Common migrant. Common summer resident in north and central. Rare summer resident in south.
Documentation: Specimen(s) — ♂, 2½ miles southeast of New City, Sangamon Co, Aug 15, 1974 (ISM 606067).
Remarks: Found in willow thickets and scrub areas. Almost impossible to separate from Alder Flycatcher (even in the hand) except by song. *Records:* Small breeding colony, Jackson Co, summer, 1972 (DH, VK-AB26:866); 7 singing males, Sangchris St Pk, May 30, 1975 (HDB).

Least Flycatcher *(Empidonax minimus)*

Late April — Late May
Mid-August — Early October

Status: Common migrant. Uncommon summer resident in north and very rare summer resident in central.
Documentation: Specimen(s) — ♂, east of Springfield, Sep 27, 1972 (ISM 605584).
Remarks: A deciduous edge species. *Summer record:* Nests, McHenry Co, June 3 & June 29, 1963 (Carroll). *Other records:* 1 banded, Carbondale, Jackson Co, July 22, 1971, and 1 collected, Aug 4, 1971 (VK-AB25:864); ♂ collected, near Crane Lake, Mason Co, Dec 15, 1973 (HDB, JF-ISM 605838); 1 collected, 2 miles north of Springfield, Oct 17, 1974 (VK). *High counts:* 30, McLean Co (SBC), May 6, 1972; 60, Cook Co (SBC), May 10, 1975.

Eastern Wood Pewee *(Contopus virens)*

Early May — Early October

Status: Common migrant and summer resident.
Documentation: Specimen(s) — ♂, 1½ miles east of Union County Refuge, July 18, 1972 (ISM 605220).
Remarks: A woodland species. *Records:* 1, Carbondale, Jackson Co, Oct 17, 1971 (DH-AB26:72); 1, Springfield, Nov 8, 1972 (HDB). *High counts:* 20, Coles Co (SBC), May 6, 1972; 37, Lawrence Co (SBC), May 10, 1975; 24 (Route 63, BBS), Massac Co and Pope Co, June 19, 1975 (VK-U.S. Fish & Wildlife Service, 1976, p. 448).

Olive-sided Flycatcher *(Nuttallornis borealis)*

Mid-May — Early June
Mid-August — Late September

Status: Uncommon migrant.
Documentation: Specimen(s) — ♂, Kingston Twp, DeKalb Co, May 22, 1966 (NIU 2191).
Remarks: Usually found in dry upland woods, along the edge, sitting high in dead trees. *Records:* 1, Shelby County State Forest, Aug 1, 1970 (HDB); 1, Skokie Lagoons, Cook Co, Sep 23, 1971 (LB, GR); 1, Jonesboro, Union Co, May 6, 1973 (VK-AB27:780); 1, Springfield, May 1, 1975 (VK). *High counts:* 8, Chicago, May 28, 1973 (LB, M. Smith-AB27:780); 5, Mason Co, Sep 8, 1973 (HDB).

Vermilion Flycatcher *(Pyrocephalus rubinus)*

Status: Very rare vagrant.
Documentation: Sight record with acceptable details — Ad ♂, Botanic Gardens, Glencoe, Cook Co, May 4, 1973 (Pat Ware-on file ISM).
Remarks: 2 records of this southwestern species. May appear in fall since St. Louis area has several fall records. *Other record:* Ad ♂, University of Illinois campus, Urbana, spring, 1962 (Graber, Graber, & Kirk, 1974).

ALAUDIDAE: Larks.

Horned Lark *(Eremophila alpestris)*

Status: Common permanent resident.
Documentation: Specimen(s) — ♂, near Jacksonville, Morgan Co, June 5, 1971 (ISM 605693).
Remarks: Has benefited from man because it is associated with agricultural land. During snowstorms many come up to roads to feed. Some migration, especially of northern birds in winter. *High counts:* 5,000, Urbana (CBC), Dec 29, 1956 (AFN11:171); 525, Decatur (CBC), Dec 28, 1957 (AFN12:176); 365, western Mercer Co (CBC), Jan 1, 1967 (AFN21:260); 1,000, near Watseka, Iroquois Co, Jan 15, 1968 (KB); 300, Livingston Co (SBC), May 6, 1972; 144, Douglas Co (SBC), May 4, 1974; 183 (Route 34, BBS), Iroquois Co and Vermilion Co, June 19, 1975 (R. Gruenewald-U.S. Fish & Wildlife Service, 1976, p. 649).
Subspecies: The breeding subspecies is *E. a. praticola.* During winter there is an influx of Northern Horned Larks, *E. a. alpestris,* but to what extent is unknown.

HIRUNDINIDAE: Swallows.

Violet-green Swallow *(Tachycineta thalassina)*

Status: Very rare vagrant.
Documentation: Specimen — ♂, Calumet region of Chicago, May 4, 1897 (Coale, 1925).
Remarks: Only 1 record. Specimen presented to Bryn Mawr High School by collector, George F. Clingman, but cannot be located. (Important Note: specimens should be placed in known collections at museums or universities).

Tree Swallow *(Iridoprocne bicolor)*

Late March — Late October

Status: Abundant migrant. Common summer resident in north. Uncommon and local summer resident in central and south.
Documentation: Specimen(s) — ♂, Horseshoe Lake, Alexander Co, May 6, 1961 (NIU 371).
Remarks: Found near water both in nesting season and during migration. At times lingers late. *Records:* 1, Chicago, Nov 1, 1969 (RR); 1, Chautauqua NWR, Mar 19, 1972 (HDB); 4, Chautauqua NWR, Nov 24, 1972 (HDB); 2, McHenry Co, Jan 1, 1974 (AB28:384); *High counts:* 5,000, Mark Twain NWR, Sep 12, 1965 (SV); 40,000, Chautauqua NWR, Oct 5, 1974 (RS, HDB); 518, Cook Co (SBC), May 8, 1976.

Bank Swallow *(Riparia riparia)*

Late April — Mid-September

Status: Common migrant and local common summer resident.
Documentation: Specimen(s) — ♂, near Roots, Randolph Co, July 26, 1971 (ISM 604828).
Remarks: Found near sand pits and road cuts where it nests in colonies. During migration congregates near water; also sits in roads. *Records:* 1, Rockford, Apr 11, 1959 (LJ-AFN13:375); 1, Skokie Lagoons, Cook Co, Apr 14, 1973 (LB-AB27:780); 1, Illinois Beach St Pk, Oct 25, 1975 (GR, LC). *High counts:* About 300 banded, Milan, Rock Island Co, June 7, 1966 (PCP); 800, Chautauqua NWR, July 31, 1971 (HDB); 2,000, Wolf Lake, Union Co, July 31, 1971 (VK, F. Reuter-AB25:864); 510, Rock Island Co (SBC), May 6, 1972; 470, Jersey Co (SBC), May 4, 1974.

Rough-winged Swallow *(Stelgidopteryx ruficollis)*

Mid-April — Mid-September

Status: Common migrant and uncommon summer resident.
Documentation: Specimen(s) — ♂, Kingston Twp, DeKalb Co, July 8, 1966 (NIU 2334).
Remarks: Found near rivers and lakes with high banks and near water during migrations. Seems to be more numerous in spring, but this may be due to the fact that they migrate down major river valleys and may go undetected unless observer is present at right time. *Records:* 1, Spring Lake St Pk, Tazewell Co, Oct 27, 1967 (PW, RQR). *High counts:* 500, Lock No. 13, Whiteside Co, Sep 1, 1958 (PCP-IAB108:17); 90, McHenry Co (SBC), May 6, 1972; 85, Peoria Co (SBC), May 5, 1973; 79, Lake Co (SBC), May 4, 1974.

Barn Swallow *(Hirundo rustica)*

Early April — Mid-October

Status: Abundant migrant and summer resident.
Documentation: Specimen(s) — ♂, 4 miles south of Easton, Mason Co, July 8, 1972 (ISM 605612).

Remarks: Found near farms, meadows, and water. *Records:* 2, Carbondale, Jackson Co, Dec 19, 1956 (Brewer, Ellis, Bell-AFN9:172); 1, Normal, McLean Co, Oct 30, 1971 (DBi-AB26:72); 1, Lincoln Park, Chicago, Nov 6, 1971 (CC, HDB); 1, Crab Orchard NWR, Mar 21, 1972 (VK-AB26:767); 1, Chautauqua NWR, Nov 9, 1975 (HDB). *High count:* 227, Jersey Co (SBC), May 5, 1973; 367, Cook Co (SBC), May 8, 1976.

Cliff Swallow *(Petrochelidon pyrrhonota)*

Late April — Late May
Mid-July — Late September

Status: Fairly common migrant and rare summer resident.
Documentation: Specimen(s) — ♀, Brookville Twp, Ogle Co, July 18, 1966 (NIU 2337).
Remarks: Has declined as a breeding species; only large colonies remaining are in northwestern part of state along Fox and Apple rivers. Usually observed on telephone lines or flying over water during migration. *Nesting records:* Nest, Libertyville, Lake Co, July 4, 1964 (RR); 40 pairs nesting under bridges, Crab Orchard NWR, 1975 (VK). *Other records:* 1, Christian Co, Apr 16, 1972 (HDB). *High counts:* 100, Decatur, May 14, 1966 (P. Stutesman); 400, Mason Co, May 18, 1974 (HDB).

Purple Martin *(Progne subis)*

Late March — Mid-September

Status: Common migrant and summer resident.
Documentation: Specimen(s) — ♀, Wheaton, DuPage Co, June 26, 1961 (NIU 385).
Remarks: Particularly numerous in residential areas where nesting boxes form nesting colonies. Sometimes gathers in large flocks in late summer. *Records:* 1, Wilmette, Oct 12, 1961 (RR-AFN16:41); 1, Mark Twain NWR, Mar 13, 1964 (SV); 12, Virginia, Cass Co, Sep 22, 1973 (Calhoun-AB28:62); 1, Chicago, Mar 20, 1975 (AB29:698). *High counts:* 4,000, Montrose Harbor, Chicago, Aug 12 - Sep 1, 1962 (CC); 8,000-10,000, Rock Island, Aug 10-24, 1969 (Frink, Wickstrom-IAB152:20); 246, St. Clair Co (SBC), May 6, 1972; 175, Kane Co (SBC), May 5, 1973; 770, Cook Co (SBC), May 8, 1976.

CORVIDAE: Crows, Magpies and Jays.

[Gray Jay *(perisoreus canadensis)*]

Status: Hypothetical.
Remarks: *2 records, neither with documentation:* 1, Peoria, winter (no date), by a Mr. Cobleigh (Loucks, 1892); 1 at feeder, Highland Park, Lake Co, Jan 1, 1959 (AFN13:190). Nelson (1876) lists this species but gives no definite records.

Blue Jay *(Cyanocitta cristata)*

Status: Common permanent resident.

Documentation: Specimen(s) — ♂, 1 mile east of Chautauqua Lake, Mason Co, Jan 27, 1973 (ISM 605515).
Remarks: A woodland species that also occurs in residential areas. Migrations take place especially along the major rivers of state. More numerous from south to north in winter. *Migration:* 2,000 in 1 hour, Mason Co, Sep 22, 1973 (VK, HDB). *High counts:* 429, Olney (CBC), Dec 26, 1967 (IAB145:28); 494, Will Co (SBC), May 4, 1974; 764, Cook Co (SBC), May 10, 1975.

Steller's Jay *(Cyanocitta stelleri)*

Status: Very rare vagrant.
Documentation: Specimen — 1, Lincoln Park, Chicago, June 12, 1911 (CAS 414).
Remarks: 2 records of this western mountain jay. Possibly escaped pets. Above specimen is *C. s. macrolopha* (Ford, 1956). *Other records:* 1 banded, Highland Park, Lake Co, July 13, 1952. This bird stayed several months and was determined to be *C. s. annectens* (S & P, 1955, p. 41); 1 reported with no documentation, Palos Hills Forest Preserve, Cook Co, May 25, 1965 (PD).

Black-billed Magpie *(Pica pica)*

Early October — Late April

Status: Very rare vagrant.
Documentation: Specimen — Ad ♂ (1 of 2 birds), Lake Forest, Lake Co, Nov 10, 1918 (Coale, 1919).
Remarks: Several old records of this western species. Some possibly escaped pets. *Records:* 1, Elmhurst, DuPage Co, and 1, Highland Park, Lake Co (maybe same bird?), Dec 13 & 16, 1957 (RM, Lappen-AFN12:283); 1, Palos Hills, Cook Co, Oct 28, 1959 (Shaughnessy, PD-IAB113:9); 1, Waukegan, Oct 5, 1963 (Campbell-IAB128:23); 1, Chicago, Apr 17, 1967 (CC-IAB143:20); 1 photographed at feeder, Barrington, mid-Sep 1973 - Jan 5, 1974 (RQR-ISM).

Common Raven *(Corvus corax)*

Status: Extirpated. [Probably formerly an uncommon permanent resident.]
Documentation: Specimen(s) — ♀, Meredosia, Morgan Co, Oct 23, 1892 (FMNH-Woodruff, 1896).
Remarks: Could occur again in north as winter resident. Kennicott (1855) listed it as "known to nest in Cook County" and Nelson (1876) said it "frequents the sandhills along the lake [Michigan] shore." 1 specimen, Fayette Co, taken Jan 10, 1901 (Steinhauer Collection-ISM 605940). Last sight record, near Chicago, Oct 13, 1953 (S & P, 1955, p. 42), but may have been escaped caged bird. No recent records.

Common Crow *(Corvus brachyrhynchos)*

Status: Common permanent resident.
Documentation: Specimen(s) — 1, near Chatham, Sangamon Co, April 9, 1970 (ISM 604485).
Remarks: Found in open and semiopen areas. Migration does occur, often as a large influx from north during the winter that form roosts. *High counts:*

10,000, Waukegan (CBC), Jan 1, 1961 (AFN15:215); 5,000, Pere Marquette St Pk (CBC), Dec 26, 1965 (AFN20:265); 1,740, western Mercer Co (CBC), Dec 26, 1971 (AB26:379); 1,200, near Elgin, Kane Co, Dec 27, 1973 (VK, PW); 1,000, Gifford, Champaign Co, Nov 28, 1975 (M. Campbell).

Fish Crow *(Corvus ossifragus)*

Status: Uncommon summer resident along Mississippi River in south, north as far as St. Louis, and along the Ohio River to Mound City, Pulaski Co.
Documentation: Specimen — Ad ♀, near Mound City, Pulaski Co, Apr 20, 1968 (SIU A-1643).
Remarks: Stays along rivers and flat areas adjacent to the rivers. Migratory and winter status are unknown. *Records:* 17, below E. St. Louis, May 12, 1968 (RA-IAB147:28); 5, Grand Tower, Jackson Co, Aug 5, 1970 (HDB); 17, Fults, Monroe Co, Aug 20, 1971 (RA-AB25:864); flocks of over 20, Union Co and Jackson Co, May 6 & 15, 1972 (VK-AB26:768); 13, Alexander Co and Union Co, Mar 5, 1974 (VK, HDB); 5, Monroe Co (SBC), May 4, 1974.

[Clark's Nutcracker *(Nucifraga columbiana)*]

Status: Hypothetical.
Remarks: A bird, supposedly of this species, shot at Gross Point, Cook Co, Oct 9, 1894 (Coale, 1911). Evidently specimen not kept and Coale obtained information secondhand. However, record probably correct since there were other extralimital records that year. A dispersal flight in fall of 1972, but none confirmed from Illinois even though there were many records from Iowa.

PARIDAE: Titmice.

Black-capped Chickadee *(Parus atricapillus)*

Status: Common permanent resident in north and central and upper part of south (see Carolina Chickadee).
Documentation: Specimen(s) — ♀, Forest Park Nature Center, Peoria, Dec 4, 1971 (ISM 605567).
Remarks: Mainly a woodland species. Little definite evidence that this species migrates into southern zone in winter. 1 observed, Rend Lake, Nov 15, 1975 (BP). *High counts:* 374, Pere Marquette St Pk (CBC), Dec 30, 1967 (AFN22:272); 500, Chicago (CBC), Dec 29, 1973 (AB28:379); 106, Cook Co (SBC), May 6, 1972; 231, Beverly, Adams Co (CBC), Dec 21, 1974 (AB29:407); 450, Chautauqua NWR (CBC), Dec 23, 1975 (AB30:427).

Carolina Chickadee *(Parus carolinensis)*

Status: Common permanent resident in south and eastern part of central. Very rare vagrant in north.
Documentation: Specimen(s) — ♂, Thebes, Alexander Co, Dec 21, 1961 (NIU 1344).
Remarks: A woodland species not easily separated in the field from Black-capped Chickadee, except by song. Borderline counties between Carolina and Black-capped Chickadees are: Madison, Bond, Fayette, Shelby, Moultrie,

Champaign, Ford, and Kankakee (Brewer, 1963). *Records:* 2, Urbana, Dec 30, 1961 (AFN16:213); 5, Pere Marquette St Pk, Dec 21, 1974 (T & K Barksdale-AB29:416). *High counts:* 103, Murphysboro (CBC), Dec 27, 1955 (AFN10:164); 61, Marion Co (SBC), May 6, 1972; 50, Clark Co (SBC), May 5, 1973.

Boreal Chickadee *(Parus hudsonicus)*

November — February

Status: Very rare winter resident in north.
Documentation: Specimen(s) — ♀, Beach, Lake Co, Nov 5, 1906 (FMNH 21755).
Remarks: Usually inhabits coniferous forests. Several old records. *Only recent records are:* 1 banded and photographed in a pine grove, Fulton, Whiteside Co, Nov 19, 1961 (PCP-AFN16:41); 1 observed daily at feeder, Dixon, Lee Co, during Feb 1963 (J. Keegan-AFN17:329).

Tufted Titmouse *(Parus bicolor)*

Status: Common permanent resident in south and central. Uncommon permanent resident in north.
Documentation: Specimen(s) — ♀, 5 miles south Timewell, Brown Co, Apr 18, 1972 (ISM 605151).
Remarks: A woodland species. *High counts:* 92, Rockford (CBC), Jan 1, 1962 (AFN16:212); 336, Pere Marquette St Pk (CBC), Dec 30, 1967 (AFN22:272); 102, Vermilion Co (SBC), May 4, 1974; 146, Union County Refuge (CBC), Jan 2, 1976 (AB29:418).

SITTIDAE: Nuthatches.

White-breasted Nuthatch *(Sitta carolinensis)*

Status: Common permanent resident.
Documentation: Specimen(s) — ♀, 1 mile southeast of Rockford, Winnebago Co, Sep 25, 1975 (ISM 606341).
Remarks: A woodland species. Probably some migration but little evidence available. *High count:* 74, Rockford (CBC), Jan 1, 1962 (AFN16:212); 99, Peoria (CBC), Jan 3, 1965 (AFN19:325); 65, Crane Lake (CBC), Jan 2, 1971 (AB25:353); 86, Chillicothe (CBC), Jan 2, 1972 (AB26:371); 66, Bureau Co (SBC), May 5, 1973; 78, Pere Marquette St Pk (CBC), Dec 29, 1973 (AB28:385); 114, Princeton (CBC), Dec 27, 1975 (AB30:434).

Red-breasted Nuthatch *(Sitta canadensis)*

Early September — Early May

Status: Uncommon migrant and winter resident. Very rare summer resident in north.
Documentation: Specimen(s) — ♂, Evanston, Cook Co, June 9, 1973 (ISM 605726).

Remarks: An invasion species with definite year-to-year fluctuation. Found mostly in coniferous trees especially in winter; during migration can be found in deciduous trees. *Summer records:* Pair nested, Sterling, Whiteside Co and the pair and 4 young present on June 20, 1970 (Shaws); pair summered, Max McGraw Wildlife Foundation, 1972 (RM-AB26:866). *Other records:* 1, Illinois Beach St Pk, May 25, 1964 (J. Probst); 1 in hemlocks, 1½ miles north of Cobden, Union Co, Aug 31, 1965 (William George); 6, Cook Co, 6, Lake Co and 6, McLean Co (SBC), May 5, 1973; 1, Normal, Sep 5, 1975 (DBi). *High counts:* 200, Lisle, Nov 17, 1957 (Shaws-AFN12:35); 300, White Pines St Pk, Ogle Co, winter, 1959-60 (J. Keegan-AFN14:313); 200, Crab Orchard NWR (CBC), Jan 4, 1976 (AB30:429).

[Brown-headed Nuthatch *(Sitta pusilla)*]

Status: Hypothetical.
Remarks: DuMont (1935) relates a letter from Mr. E. S. Currier of Portland, Oregon, in which Mr. Currier reported having seen 6 of these birds in and near Keokuk, Iowa, on May 9, 1893, 2 of which were shot, but no specimens were kept. 3 others were seen in Keokuk, May 10 and "on May 12 two were seen in Hancock County, Illinois across from Keokuk." Since no specimens and no description of the birds were kept there is not enough evidence to add this Southeastern species to the list of Illinois birds.

CERTHIIDAE: Creepers.

Brown Creeper *(Certhia familiaris)*

Late September — Late April

Status: Common migrant and winter resident. Occasional summer resident.
Documentation: Specimen(s) — ♀, Cobden, Union Co, Aug 20, 1968 (SIU-George, 1972).
Remarks: Found in woodland. Summer habitat is floodplain forest and cypress swamps. *Summer records:* 1 collected, Glen Ellyn, DuPage Co, Aug 17, 1961 (NIU); nest photographed, Keithsburg, Mercer Co, June 14, 1966 (Greer-AFN20:575); 1, Macomb, McDonough Co, June 27, 1967 (Franks-AFN21:578); 4, Horseshoe Lake, Alexander Co, June 9, 1969 (Haw-AFN23:666); pair netted, ♀ with brood patch, Williamson Co, June 4, 1970 (VK-AFN24:690); 1, Shirland, Winnebago Co, Aug 20, 1972 (LJ-AB27:69); 1, Heron Pond, Johnson Co, July 18, 1973 (MH-AB27:877); 1, Charleston, Coles Co, Aug 28, 1973 (LBH-AB28:62). *High counts:* 31, DeKalb (CBC), Jan 2, 1972 (AB26:373); 36, Chicago (CBC), Dec 29, 1973 (AB28:379); 14, Cook Co (SBC), May 6, 1972.

TROGLODYTIDAE: Wrens.

House Wren *(Troglodytes aedon)*

Mid-April — Mid-October

Status: Common migrant and summer resident. Rare winter resident in south.

Documentation: Specimen(s) — ♂, near Bluffs, Scott Co, Oct 7, 1972 (ISM 605633).
Remarks: Found in woodland and residential areas. *Winter records:* 1, Crab Orchard NWR, Dec 30, 1972 (DH-AB27:369); 1, Union Co (CBC), Jan 2, 1976 (AB30:437). *High count:* 151, Will Co (SBC), May 4, 1974.

Winter Wren *(Troglodytes troglodytes)*

Late September — Late April

Status: Fairly common migrant. Uncommon winter resident in south and central. Occasional winter resident in north.
Documentation: Specimen(s) — ♂, Kishwaukee Park near Rockford, Sep 26, 1975 (ISM 606337).
Remarks: Found in river-bottom forest, usually in log jams and brush piles where it occurs in small numbers. Sometimes sings even in mid-winter. *Records:* 2, Morton Arboretum (CBC), Dec 17, 1972 (AB27:372); 1, Barrington (CBC), Dec 27, 1973 (AB27:365); 1, Monroe Co (SBC), May 4, 1974; 1, Normal, McLean Co, May 10, 1975 (DBi-AB29:861); 1 singing, Allerton Park, Piatt Co, May 20, 1976 (D. Friedman-AB30:849). *High counts:* 22, Urbana (CBC), Dec 21, 1974 (AB29:419); 5, Rockford (CBC), Dec 22, 1974 (AB29:417); 14, Crab Orchard NWR (CBC), Dec 28, 1974 (AB29:411).

Bewick's Wren *(Thryomanes bewickii)*

Mid-April — Late October

Status: Uncommon migrant and summer resident (locally) in central and south. Rare migrant and summer resident in north. Occasional winter resident in south, and rare winter resident in central.
Documentation: Specimen(s) — 1, Pittsfield, Pike Co, Apr 9, 1959 (ISM 603826).
Remarks: Found in dry, scrubby areas. Once common in the south but has been mostly replaced by the House Wren. *Summer records:* Nest, Rock Island Co, June 28, 1959 (PCP-IAB115:10); 5 young, Bureau Co, Aug 6, 1966 (Cater-IAB142:19); nest and young, Geneva, Kane Co, May - July 1976 (LB). *Winter records:* 2, Murphysboro, Jackson Co, Dec 27, 1955 (AFN10:164); 1, Decatur, from mid-Dec - Dec 31, 1966 (AFN15:213); 1, near Pere Marquette St Pk, Dec 20, 1969 (Stricklings-AB24:313); 1, Mason State Forest, Nov 23, 1973 (HDB); 1, Beverly, Adams Co, Dec 22, 1973 (JF). *Other records:* 2, Bureau Co (SBC), May 6, 1972; 1, Sterling, May 15, 1973 (Shaws-IAB166:24); 7 banded, Pope Co, June 21, 1973 (VK, DH).

Carolina Wren *(Thryothorus ludovicianus)*

Status: Common permanent resident in south and central. Irregular migrant and uncommon summer resident in north. Occasional winter resident in north.
Documentation: Specimen(s) — ♂, 4 miles south of Hardin, Calhoun Co, Jan 10, 1971 (ISM 604672).
Remarks: Primarily a woodland species. Prefers log jams and brush piles. At times found in residential areas. Extremely cold and snowy winters diminish the population as was very evident in 1977. In central the population suffered

90% to 95% losses. *Records:* 1, Barrington, Dec 29, 1964 (AFN19:231); 2 at feeder, Chicago, Dec 26, 1965 (AFN20:261). *High counts:* 90, Pere Marquette St Pk (CBC), Dec 26, 1971 (AB26:376); 50, Pike Co (SBC), May 5, 1973; 58, Jackson Co (SBC), May 10, 1975; 209, Union Co (CBC), Jan 2, 1976 (AB30:437).

Long-billed Marsh Wren *(Cistothorus palustris)*

Late April — Late May
Early September — Mid-October

Status: Fairly common migrant. Common summer resident in north. Rare summer resident in central and south. Rare winter resident.
Documentation: Specimen(s) — ♀?, Dickson Mounds, Fulton Co, Sep 17, 1971 (ISM 604850).
Remarks: Found in marshes, primarily cattails, also during migration in weed patches. *Winter records:* 1, McGinnis Slough, Cook Co, Nov 8, 1970 (CC-AB25:66); 1, Beverly, Adams Co, Dec 23, 1971 (PW, HDB); 1, Sangchris St Pk, Dec 3, 1972 (HDB); 1, Goose Lake Prairie, Feb 18, 1973 (LB, CC-AB27:624); 1, Quiver Creek, Mason Co, Mar 3, 1973 (VK, HDB); 1, Morton Arboretum (CBC), Dec 21, 1975 (AB30:433). *Summer records:* Pair with young, near Havana, Mason Co, Sep 9, 1974 (HDB). *High counts:* 15, Lake Co (SBC), May 10, 1975; 21, Cook Co (SBC), May 8, 1976.

Short-billed Marsh Wren *(Cistothorus platensis)*

Late April — Mid-October

Status: Uncommon migrant and uncommon local summer resident. Very rare winter resident in south.
Documentation: Specimen(s) — ♂, near Bluffs, Scott Co, Oct 7, 1972 (ISM 605632).
Remarks: Found in wet grassy meadows and marsh areas. *Records:* 1, Pere Marquette St Pk, Dec 21, 1968 (Wiese-AFN23:300); 1, Normal, McLean Co, Nov 4, 1971 (DBi-AB26:72); 2, Pere Marquette St Pk (CBC), Dec 26, 1971 (AB26:376). *High count:* 14, McLean Co (SBC), May 4, 1974.

Rock Wren *(Salpinctes obsoletus)*

Status: Very rare vagrant.
Documentation: Specimen — 1, found near a greenhouse, ISU campus, Normal, McLean Co, Nov 2, 1970 (ISM 604982).
Remarks: 3 records. A western species. Most often found near dams and rocky places. *Records:* 1, Urbana, Champaign Co, May 30, 1926 (Hyde, 1927); 1 (later photographed) in burned tree stumps near Olive Branch, Alexander Co, Dec 30, 1974 - Jan 28, 1975 (VK, RS).

MIMIDAE: Thrashers and Mockingbirds.

Mockingbird *(Mimus polyglottos)*

Status: A common permanent resident in central and south. An occasional permanent resident in north.

93

Documentation: Specimen(s) — ♂, 8 miles east of Springfield, Sep 30, 1973 (ISM 605773).

Remarks: Some migration does occur. Range seems to be extending northward. Usually occurs in multiflora rose hedges and around farmyards. *Records:* 1, western Mercer Co (CBC), Dec 28, 1956 (AFN11:172); 1, Plainfield, Will Co, Dec 9 & 24, 1961 (LB-AB26:612); 1, Blue Island, Cook Co, May 5, 1966 (A. Baldwin); 1, Rockford (CBC), Dec 26, 1966 (AFN21:257). *High counts:* 65, Crab Orchard NWR (CBC), Dec 30, 1957 (AFN12:176); 66, near Olney (CBC), Dec 26, 1966 (AFN21:251); 199, Crab Orchard NWR (CBC), Dec 18, 1971 (AB26:371); 68, Crawford Co (SBC), May 5, 1973; 69, Jefferson Co (SBC), May 4, 1974.

Gray Catbird *(Dumetella carolinensis)*

Late April — Late October

Status: Common migrant and summer resident. Rare winter resident.

Documentation: Specimen(s) — ♀?, 5 miles north of Hamilton, Hancock Co, Oct 19, 1974 (ISM 606119).

Remarks: Found on forest edge low in the brush. *Winter records:* 1, Kenilworth, Cook Co, Nov 19, 1969 (B. Tweit); 1, near Urbana, Jan 2, 1970 (AB25:361); 1, Barrington, Dec 29, 1971 (CW-AB26:368); 1, Mark Twain NWR, Jan 7, 1972 (SV-AB26:612); 1, Waukegan, Jan 1, 1973 (KB-AB27:377). *High count:* 323, Will Co (SBC), May 10, 1975.

Brown Thrasher *(Toxostoma rufum)*

Early April — Late October

Status: Common migrant and summer resident. Rare winter resident in north. Occasional winter resident in central and uncommon winter resident in south.

Documentation: Specimen(s) — ♂, Beverly Twp, Adams Co, Apr 17, 1973 (ISM 606363).

Remarks: Inhabits brush areas. Stays low to the ground except when singing. *Winter records:* 1 at feeder, Barrington, Dec 27, 1972 (AB27:365); 4, Chicago, Dec 23, 1972 (AB27:368); 6 in 1½-miles of hedge, Horseshoe Lake, Alexander Co, Jan 25, 1973 (VK-AB27:624); 1, north of Mt. Carroll, Jo Daviess Co, Jan 24, 1974 (Shaws-IAB168:29). *High count:* 239, Will Co (SBC), May 4, 1974.

Sage Thrasher *(Oreoscoptes montanus)*

Status: Very rare vagrant in north.

Documentation: Photographic — 1, Winnetka, Jan 17, 1970 (Jack Armstrong-photo on file ISM).

Remarks: 3 records. A western species. Has occurred several times in the east. The record at Winnetka was first found Dec 26, 1969 and observed by many (Bi). *Other records:* 1, Lincoln Park, Chicago, May 11, 1940 (Clark & Nice, 1950); 1 photographed, Northwestern University, Chicago, Oct 24, 1974 (GR, LB).

TURDIDAE: Thrushes.

American Robin *(Turdus migratorius)*

Late February — Late November

Status: Abundant migrant and summer resident. Uncommon winter resident in north and central and common winter resident in south.

Documentation: Specimen(s) — Im ♂, 2 miles west of Ashland, Cass Co, Oct 12, 1971 (ISM 605047).

Remarks: Inhabits residential areas and woodland. *Winter records:* 296, Chicago (CBC), Dec 26, 1964 (AFN19:232); 598, Pere Marquette St Pk (CBC), Dec 21, 1968 (AFN23:300); 108, Decatur, Dec 26, 1971 (AB26:372). *High counts:* 3,000, Blue Island, Cook Co, Oct 24, 1964 (KB); 1,500 in spruce windbreak, Fall Creek, Adams Co, Jan 26, 1965 (TEM); 1,200, Will Co (SBC), May 4, 1974.

Varied Thrush *(Ixoreus naevius)*

Mid-December — Late March

Status: Rare winter resident in north. Very rare winter resident in central and south.

Documentation: Photograph(s) — ♂, Decatur, Dec 27, 1956 - Mar 30, 1957 (RS, TN-ISM).

Remarks: A western species. Usually appears singly at feeding stations. Also feeds on various fruit and berry trees and shrubs. There are 20 or more records, only 1 of which was before 1950. *Records:* 1, Chicago, Dec 26, 1955 (Montaque, Pearson-AFN10:165); 1, Rock Island, mid-Dec 1956 - mid-Jan 1957 (RT-AFN11:270); 1, Libertyville, Lake Co, Dec 18, 1962 (Greaves-AFN17:329); 1, Crystal Lake, Dec 1963 (Brecklin-AFN18:360); 1, Lisle, DuPage Co, Apr 11, 1964 (Swink, n.d.); ♂, Green River Preserve, Lee Co, Jan 11, 1967 (Shaws-AFN21:425); ♀, Dixon, Lee Co, Dec 28, 1969 - Mar 18, 1970 (Shaws-AFN24:510); 1, Freeport, Stephenson Co, late Dec 1969 - early Jan 1970 (Armstrong-AFN24:510); ♂ photographed, Rockford, Jan 2, 1970 - Mar 18, 1970 (Graber, Graber & Kirk, 1971); 1, Illinois Beach St Pk, Nov 10, 1973 (CC-AB28:62); 1 photographed, Barrington, Feb 1, 1974 (Zimmer, RM-AB28:648); ♂, Springfield, Jan 7 - Feb 12, 1975 (VK, HDB); 1, Brussels, Calhoun Co, Dec 19, 1976 (RA-AB31:338).

Wood Thrush *(Hylocichla mustelina)*

Late April — Late September

Status: Common migrant and summer resident.

Documentation: Specimen(s) — ♂, Evanston, May 17, 1973 (ISM 605692).

Remarks: Prefers bottomland woods. *Records:* 1, Chicago, Nov 6, 1965 (Horowitz-AFN20:54); 1, Dixon, Lee Co, Nov 15, 1969 (Shaws, Greaves); 1, Springfield, Oct 27, 1970 (HDB); 1 photographed, Westville, Vermilion Co, Mar 29, 1975 (D. Watson-AB29:699). *High counts:* 45, Vermilion Co (SBC), May 4, 1974; 47, Will Co, and 47, Cook Co (SBC), May 10, 1975.

Hermit Thrush *(Catharus guttatus)*

Late March — Early May
Late September — Early November

Status: Common migrant. Uncommon winter resident in south. Occasional winter resident in north and central.

Documentation: Specimen(s) — ♂, Chicago Loop, Cook Co, Oct 14, 1974 (ISM 606332).

Remarks: Found in woodland and thickets. *Records:* 1, Chicago, Dec 26, 1955 (AFN10:163); 1, Morton Arboretum (CBC), Dec 30, 1956 (AFN11:169); 1, Urbana, Jan 2, 1971 (AB25:361); 4, Mark Twain NWR, Calhoun Co, Jan 15, 1972 (PW, HDB); 1, Chicago, Jan 30, 1972 (B. Tweit-AB26:612); 1, Decatur, Jan 7, 1974 (RS); 5, Chicago North Shore (CBC), Dec 27, 1976 (AB30:428). *High counts:* 14, Iroquois Co (SBC), May 6, 1972; 40, Sterling, Apr 17, 1975 (Shaws); 28, Cook Co (SBC), May 10, 1975; 21, Union County Refuge (CBC), Jan 2, 1976 (AB29:418).

Swainson's Thrush *(Catharus ustulatus)*

Late April — Early June
Late August — Mid-October

Status: Common migrant.

Documentation: Specimen(s) — ♂, Peoria, May 16, 1972 (ISM 605721).

Remarks: Inhabits woodland. *2 reported winter records:* 1, Winnetka, Cook Co, Jan 2, 1950 (Ford, 1956); 1, western Mercer Co (CBC), Jan 3, 1966 (RT-AFN19:238). *Other records:* 2, Waukegan, Aug 4, 1963 (CC); singing ♂, Wilmette, June 8, 1967 (RR); 1, Shirland, Winnebago Co, July 29, 1972 (LJ-AB27:69); 1, Springfield, Apr 14, 1974 (HDB); 1, Normal, McLean Co, June 12, 1973 (DBi-AB27:877). *High counts:* 107 killed at TV tower, Sangamon Co, Sep 16-17, 1958 (Parmalee & Parmalee, 1959); 91, Vermilion Co (SBC), May 10, 1975; 80, McLean Co (SBC), May 6, 1972.

Gray-cheeked Thrush *(Catharus minimus)*

Late April — Late May
Early September — Early October

Status: Common spring migrant, uncommon fall migrant.

Documentation: Specimen(s) — ♂, east of Springfield, Sep 27, 1972 (ISM 605823).

Remarks: A woodland species. Stays close to ground. *Records:* 1, Decatur, Apr 18, 1976 (RS, HDB); 1, Springfield, Oct 12, 1976 (VK). *High counts:* 145 killled at TV tower, Sangamon Co, Sep 16-17, 1958 (Parmalee & Parmalee, 1959). 33, Cook Co (SBC), May 6, 1972; 19, Marion Co (SBC), May 5, 1973; 40, Vermilion Co (SBC), May 10, 1975.

Veery *(Catharus fuscescens)*

Early May — Late May
Early September — Late September

Status: Common migrant in spring. Uncommon migrant in fall. Occasional summer resident in north and very rare summer resident in upper part of central.

Documentation: Specimen(s) — ♂, Evanston, May 17, 1973 (ISM 605707).
Remarks: Inhabits both upland and bottomland woods. (For detailed habitat of nesting areas, see Graber & Graber, 1973.) *Summer records:* Nest, Lake Co, July 4, 1964 (RR-IAB134:14); nest, Kankakee Co, June 23, 1972, and 2 ♂ singing, Lee Co, June 30 & July 6, 1972 (Graber and Graber, 1973); 1, Normal, McLean Co, June 19, 1973 (DBi-AB27:877). *High counts:* 59 killed at TV tower, Sangamon Co, Sep 2, 1972 (HDB); 58, Cook Co (SBC), May 10, 1975.

Eastern Bluebird *(Sialia sialis)*

Early March — Late October

Status: Common migrant and summer resident (locally uncommon in some areas). Fairly common winter resident in south and uncommon winter resident in central. Rare winter resident in north.
Documentation: Specimen(s) — ♂, Irving, Montgomery Co, Mar 16, 1974 (ISM 606086).
Remarks: Inhabits orchards and open woodlots. Has been replaced near residential areas by House Sparrows and Starlings. Also suffers population losses from late winter storms. *Records:* 83, near Olney (CBC), Dec 26, 1966 (AFN21:251); 92, Pere Marquette St Pk (CBC), Dec 26, 1971 (AB26:376); 1, Starved Rock St Pk (CBC), Dec 19, 1971 (AB26:378); 4, western Mercer Co (CBC), Dec 26, 1971 (AB26:379); 3, Waukegan (CBC), Jan 1, 1971 (AB25:361); 24, near Georgetown (CBC), Dec 29, 1973 (AB28:382); *High count:* 134, Adams Co (SBC), May 4, 1974.

[Mountain Bluebird *(Sialia currucoides)*]

Status: Hypothetical.
Remarks: 1 report with no details from Peoria Co, May 10, 1969 (Princen, 1970).

Townsend's Solitaire *(Myadestes townsendi)*

Late November — Early April

Status: Very rare winter vagrant.
Documentation: Specimen — 1, Waukegan, Dec 16, 1875 (in collection of S.S. Gregory Jr.-Ford, 1956).
Remarks: 9 records. Western species found in protected areas, especially those with red cedar, crabapple, and hawthorn trees. *Records:* 1, Morton Arboretum, Dec 27, 1953 - Mar 28, 1954 (KB-IAB89:6); 1, Morton Arboretum, Nov 23, 1958 - Feb 1959 (Campbell, Grow-AFN13:36); 1, Morton Arboretum, Feb 1960 (AFN14:313); 1, 7 miles south of Rock Falls, Whiteside Co, Apr 6, 1969 (Hagans-IAB152:21); 1, Beall Woods, Wabash Co, Dec 17, 1969 - Feb 22, 1970 (Norman McClain); 1, southwest of Chicago, Feb 17, 1972 (KB-AB26:612); 1, west of Prentice, Morgan Co, Dec 27-28, 1972 (P. Gibson, WO); 1, Sterling, Whiteside Co, Apr 8, 1977 (Shaws-AB31:1008).

SYLVIIDAE: Gnatcatchers and Kinglets.

Blue-gray Gnatcatcher *(Polioptila caerulea)*

Mid-April — Early September

Status: Common migrant and summer resident in south. Common spring migrant and uncommon summer resident in central. Uncommon spring migrant and summer resident in north. Occasional fall migrant in central and north.

Documentation: Specimen(s) — ♀, Lusk Creek, Pope Co, July 28, 1971 (ISM 604834).

Remarks: A woodland species. *Records:* Nest, 3 miles east of Woodstock, McHenry Co, June 16, 1964 (Carroll); 1, Unity, Alexander Co, Mar 28, 1975 (RP); 1, Springfield, Sep 23, 1977 (HDB). *High counts:* 43, Coles Co (SBC), May 6, 1972; 69, along Cache River, Apr 24, 1973 (VK, HDB); 42, Randolph Co (SBC), May 5, 1973; 60, Jackson Co (SBC), May 10, 1975.

Golden-crowned Kinglet *(Regulus satrapa)*

Early October — Late April

Status: Common migrant. Common winter resident in south. Fairly common winter resident in north and central.

Documentation: Specimen(s) — ♂, east of Springfield, Oct 18, 1972 (ISM 605326).

Remarks: Usually found in conifer trees but occurs also in deciduous growth especially during migration. *Records:* 1, Springfield, May 16-18, 1972 (HDB); 13, Boone Co (SBC), May 5, 1973; 1, Cook Co, May 27, 1975 (M. Smith-AB29:861). *High counts:* 62, Chicago, Dec 23, 1972 (AB27:368); 189, Crab Orchard NWR, Dec 28, 1974 (AB29:411).

Ruby-crowned Kinglet *(Regulus calendula)*

Mid-April — Mid-May
Mid-September — Early November

Status: Abundant migrant. Occasional winter resident in north and central. Fairly common winter resident in south.

Documentation: Specimen(s) — ♀, east of Springfield, Oct 28, 1972 (ISM 605453).

Remarks: Found in woodland and at woodland edge. In winter occurs most often in coniferous trees. Was becoming more numerous in winter until 1977. *Winter records:* 1, Chicago (CBC), Dec 26, 1965 (AFN20:261); 1, DeKalb (CBC), Dec 30, 1967 (AFN22:269); 5, Morton Arboretum (CBC), Dec 17, 1972 (AB27:372); 1, Morris-Wilmington (CBC), Dec 23, 1972 (AB27:373); 40, Horsehsoe Lake (CBC), Jan 3, 1976 (AB30:431); 53, Crab Orchard NWR (CBC), Jan 4, 1976. *High count:* 391, Cook Co (SBC), May 10, 1975.

MOTACILLIDAE: Wagtails and Pipits.

Water Pipit *(Anthus spinoletta)*

Late March — Early May
Mid-September — Mid-November

Status: Irregular and uncommon migrant.
Documentation: Specimen(s) — ♂, 2 miles east of Edinburg, Christian Co, Apr 7, 1973 (ISM 605587).
Remarks: Found in wet, open areas and occasionally in upland fields. In spring migration there seems to be an early and late population. *Records:* 3, Murphysboro (CBC), Dec 26, 1953 (AFN8:159); 1, Princeton, Bureau Co, Dec 28, 1961 (Kramer-IAB121:8-9); 26, East Cape levees, Alexander Co, May 9-11, 1969 (R. Rowlett); 1, Evanston, Nov 28, 1970 (CC-AB25:66); 4, Macon Co, May 4, 1974 (RS); 18, Lake Co (SBC), May 10, 1975. *High counts:* 80, Union County Refuge, Apr 20, 1971 (VK); 75, Rockford, Oct 28, 1972 (Dunn-AB27:69); 60, Mason Co, Nov 16, 1974 (RS); 120, Saverton Dam, Pike Co, Nov 17, 1974 (JF).

Sprague's Pipit *(Anthus spragueii)*

Mid-April — Early May
Late September — Late October

Status: Rare migrant. Rare winter resident in south.
Documentation: Specimen(s) — Im ♂, Cora, Jackson Co, Jan 10, 1957 (INHS-Graber, 1957).
Remarks: Probably occurs more often than suspected; but because it is usually found alone and available habitat is extensive, few are detected. Also, observers do not check open-field habitat (short grass and fallow fields) in which species is found. *Recent records:* 4, in alfalfa fields, Omaha, Gallatin Co, Jan 13, 1957 (Graber, 1957); 1, near Chicago, Apr 17, 1966 (Brecklin-AFN20:514); 1, near Jacksonville, Morgan Co, Apr 23, 1972 (HDB, WO); 1, west of Decatur, Oct 20, 1975 (RS); 5, on a golf course, Springfield, Oct 22, 1975 (VK, HDB).

BOMBYCILLIDAE: Waxwings.

Bohemian Waxwing *(Bombycilla garrulus)*

Late November — Late March

Status: Irregular and rare winter resident in north and central. Very rare winter resident in south.
Documentation: Specimen(s) — ♂, Springfield, Dec 22, 1972 (ISM 605448).
Remarks: Usually appears in small numbers, occurring alone, in small groups, or with Cedar Waxwings. Can be found feeding on variety of fruit and berry trees and bushes. *Only record for south:* 1 collected, Villa Ridge, Pulaski Co, Dec 18, 1879 (Ridgway, 1889). *Records:* 7, Kenilworth, Cook Co, Mar 25, 1963 (RR-AFN17:408); 1, Waukegan, Nov 22, 1969 (CC-AFN24:55); 1, Wadsworth, Lake Co, Dec 13, 1970 (LB, GR-AB25:587); 1, Decatur, Dec 23, 1972 (HDB); 3, Sterling, Dec 25, 1972 (Shaws-AB27:625). *High count:* 75, Morton Arboretum, Mar 1962 (Swink, n.d.).

Cedar Waxwing *(Bombycilla cedrorum)*

Late February — Mid-October

Status: Common but erratic migrant. Uncommon summer resident. Irregular and uncommon winter resident throughout state.

Documentation: Specimen(s) — ♀, Peoria, Oct 6, 1971 (ISM 605066).

Remarks: Erratic. Inhabits many woodland situations; frequently found in residential areas. Its numbers fluctuate with the availability of berries and fruits. Usually found in flocks. *Summer records:* Nest, Decatur, June 21, 1965 (TN); nest, Brown Co, June 10, 1965 (Schaeffer). *High counts:* 655, western Mercer Co (CBC), Jan 1, 1956 (AFN10:167); 421, Crab Orchard NWR (CBC), Dec 19, 1962 (AFN17:202); 300, Illinois Beach St Pk, Mar 30, 1966 (J. Probst); 102, Olney (CBC), Dec 26, 1966 (AFN21:251); 500, Lock 16, Rock Island Co, Nov 2, 1969 (Wickstroms-IAB153:18); 245, Springfield (CBC), Dec 27, 1970 (AB25:360); 110, Springfield, May 19, 1975 (HDB).

LANIIDAE: Shrikes.

Northern Shrike *(Lanius excubitor)*

Late October — Early March

Status: Uncommon winter resident in north. Very rare winter resident in central. [Formerly occurred in south.]

Documentation: Specimen(s) — 1, Lake Co, Nov 7, 1929 (CAS-Ford, 1956, p. 69).

Remarks: Prefers open areas with some woodland, especially marshy areas with many bushes. Numbers in Illinois may be due to cyclic eruptions. An old specimen from Fayette Co, Mar 27, 1896 in Steinhauer collection (ISM 605947) indicates this species occurred farther south than it does at the present; in fact, Mengel (1965) lists it as a casual winter visitant for Kentucky. *Records:* 1, Chicago, Dec 26, 1955 (AFN10:163); 1, Quincy, Oct 17, 1961 (TEM-AFN16:42); 1, Rockford, Nov 19, 1961 (LJ-AFN16:42); 1, Urbana, Mar 3, 1963 (PN); 1, DeKalb, Jan 3, 1965 (AFN19:233); 1, Chillicothe, Peoria Co, Jan 2, 1971 (AB25:352); 1, Lake Calumet, Jan 16, 1971 (LB, CC, GR-AB25:587); 1, Thomson, Carroll Co, Jan 18, 1973 (Shaws, VK-AB27:625); 1, Whiteside Co, Dec 29, 1973 (Shaws-AB28:648); 1, Illinois Beach St Pk, Oct 16, 1976 (LB).

Loggerhead Shrike *(Lanius ludovicianus)*

Late March — Early October

Status: Common permanent resident in south. Uncommon migrant and occasional summer resident in central and north. Occasional winter resident in central and rare winter resident in north.

Documentation: Specimen(s) — ♂, west side of Crab Orchard Lake, Williamson Co, Jan 28, 1961 (SIU A-1217).

Remarks: Prefers open areas. Tends to perch on power lines, fences, and in hedgerows. A dramatic decline of this species recently in central and northern Illinois (Graber, Graber & Kirk, 1973). North and central populations are probably much more migratory than south populations, with the winter population in south being increased by northern migrants during winter. *Records:* 1, Will Co, Jan 25-26, 1956 (Levy-AFN10:255); 1, Chicago, Dec 31, 1960 (Bi, Steffen-AFN15:212); 1, western Mercer Co (CBC), Jan 2, 1961

100

(AFN15:215); 1, Barrington, Dec 31, 1969 (T. Dillon-AFN24:306); 1, Morton Arboretum (CBC), Dec 21, 1969 (AFN24:311); 1, Chicago lakefront, Apr 3, 1974 (LB-AB28:809). *High counts:* 18, Union Co (CBC), Dec 30, 1973 (AB28:387); 15, Crab Orchard NWR (CBC), Dec 29, 1973 (AB28:380).

STURNIDAE: Starlings.

Starling *(Sturnus vulgaris)*

Status: Introduced and now an abundant permanent resident.
Documentation: Specimen(s) — ♂, Springfield, Feb 2, 1971 (ISM 604689).
Remarks: This "pest" was successfully introduced in New York about 1890. First report from Illinois was flock of 7 or 8 seen several times at Urbana during Jan & Feb 1922 (Ford, 1956). Stays near man; has adapted to both urban and rural habitats. Present all year but migrates in large flocks throughout state.

VIREONIDAE: Vireos.

White-eyed Vireo *(Vireo griseus)*

Mid-April — Mid-September

Status: Common migrant and summer resident in south. Uncommon migrant and summer resident in central. Occasional migrant and summer resident in north.
Documentation: Specimen(s) — ♂, 1 mile east of Olive Branch, Alexander Co, Apr 26, 1973 (ISM 605605).
Remarks: Prefers woods edge and thickets. Range seems to be expanding northward. *Records:* 1, Rockford, May 5, 1962 (LJ-AFN16:420); 1, New Boston, Mercer Co, May 30, 1963 (RT-AFN17:408); 1, Skokie Lagoons, Cook Co, May 3, 1969 (CC-AFN23:596); 1, Waukegan, Sep 22, 1970 (LB-AB25:70); 2, Chicago, May 16, 1971 (CC-AB25:752); 6, McGraw Wildlife Area, May 16, 1971 (RM-AB25:752); 1, Sanganois Refuge, Cass Co, Oct 16, 1971 (RQR-AB26:72); 2 banded, Rockford, Apr 20 & 27, 1974 (LJ-AB28:809); 1, Clark Co, Sep 29, 1974 (VK-AB29:67); 1, Jackson Co, Apr 5, 1975 (P. Biggers). *High counts:* 29, Alexander Co (SBC), May 6, 1972; 35, along Cache River, Apr 24, 1973 (VK, HDB); 69, Jackson Co (SBC), May 10, 1975.

Bell's Vireo *(Vireo bellii)*

Early May — Early September

Status: Uncommon migrant and summer resident. Very local in north.
Documentation: Specimen(s) — Im ♀, Carbondale, Jackson Co, Sep 1, 1966 (SIU A-1683).
Remarks: Inhabits thickets and hedgerows, staying low and inconspicuous except for its song. *Records:* 2 on territory, Rockford, Sep 7, 1958 (LJ-AFN13:36); 1, near Barrington, Nov 14, 1964 (CW-IAB133:4). *High count:* 6, Pike Co (SBC), May 10, 1975.

Yellow-throated Vireo *(Vireo flavifrons)*

Late April — Late September

Status: Uncommon migrant and summer resident.
Documentation: Specimen(s) — ♂, east of Springfield, Sep 27, 1972 (ISM 605333).
Remarks: Inhabits woodland. Tends to stay high in trees. Observed singly or in small groups. *Records:* 1, Charleston, Coles Co, Nov 16, 1974 (LBH-AB29:67); 1, Springfield, Mar 28, 1975 (HDB). *High counts:* 26, along Cache River, Johnson Co, Apr 24, 1973 (VK, HDB); 13, Jefferson Co, and 13, Union Co (SBC), May 4, 1974.

Solitary Vireo *(Vireo solitarius)*

Late April — Late May
Early September — Late October

Status: Uncommon migrant.
Documentation: Specimen(s) — ♂, 1 mile northeast of Bluffs, Scott Co, Oct 7, 1972 (ISM 605646).
Remarks: Prefers upland woods where it feeds at moderate heights. Sometimes lingers late in fall. *Records:* 1, Dixon, Nov 24, 1960 (Shaws-IAB117:6); 1, Volo Bog, Lake Co, Nov 28, 1967 (RR); 1, Springfield, Apr 22, 1974 (HDB); 1, Decatur, Nov 5, 1974 (RS). *High counts:* 21, McHenry Co (SBC), May 6, 1972; 19, Cook Co (SBC), May 10, 1975.

Red-eyed Vireo *(Vireo olivaceus)*

Late April — Early October

Status: Abundant migrant and common summer resident.
Documentation: Specimen(s) — ♂, Decatur, Sep 13, 1974 (ISM 606152).
Remarks: Found in woodland or wherever fairly large trees are available. *Records:* 1, Springfield, Nov 30, 1973 (HDB); 1, Chicago, Oct 19, 1974 (GR, RR-AB29:67). *High counts:* 153 killed at TV tower, Sangamon Co, Sep 22, 1972 (HDB); 57, Jackson Co (SBC), May 10, 1975.

Philadelphia Vireo *(Vireo philadelphicus)*

Early May — Late May
Early September — Early October

Status: Fairly common migrant.
Documentation: Specimen(s) — ♀, 1 mile southeast of Rockford, Winnebago Co, Sep 25, 1975 (ISM 606322).
Remarks: Found in woodland and along woodland edge. Nelson (1876) refers to possible nesting 60 miles south of Chicago. More common than realized; TV tower kills show it to be fairly numerous in fall. *Records:* 1, Illinois Beach St Pk, Oct 22, 1965 (J. Probst); 1, 2 miles northwest of Carbondale, Jackson Co, Oct 8, 1968 (Paul Gurn). *High counts:* 11 killed at TV tower, Champaign Co, Sep 19-20, 1960 (Graber, 1968); 12, Cook Co (SBC), May 6, 1972; 14 killed at TV tower, Macon Co, Sep 27, 1972 (Seets).

Warbling Vireo *(Vireo gilvus)*

Late April — Mid-Spetember

Status: Common migrant and summer resident.
Documentation: Specimen(s) — ♂, east of Springfield, May 8, 1972 (ISM 605173).
Remarks: Occurs in open woods, usually along streams and beside ponds and lakes. Stays in tops of tall trees. *Records:* 1, Gilbert Lake, Jersey Co, Apr 15, 1972 (HDB); 1, Springfield, Oct 15, 1977 (HDB). *High counts:* 31, Fulton Co and 31, Jersey Co (SBC), May 6, 1972; 40, Pike Co (SBC), May 10, 1975.

PARULIDAE: Wood Warblers.

Black-and-White Warbler *(Mniotilta varia)*

Late April — Late May
Late August — Early October

Status: Common migrant and rare summer resident.
Documentation: Specimen(s) — ♀, Evanston, Cook Co, May 17, 1973 (ISM 605689).
Remarks: Found in woodlands where it feeds by creeping along branches like a nuthatch. *Summer records:* Ad feeding young, Rock Island Co, July 12, 1959 (PCP, EF-IAB115:11); Pair, DesPlaines River, near Chicago, July 4, 1965 (CC-AFN19:552); 1, Pope Co, July 9 & Aug 9, 1973 (DH-AB27:877 & AB28:62); Im, Springfield, July 3, 1974 (HDB); ♂ singing, Charleston, Coles Co, June 21, 1975 (LBH-AB29:981). *Other records:* 1, Chicago, Nov 6, 1966 (CC-IAB137:4); 1, Springfield, Apr 3, 1973 (HDB); Ad ♀, Horseshoe Lake, Alexander Co, Dec 30, 1974 (RS, HDB). *High counts:* 70, McHenry Co (SBC), May 6, 1972; 31 killed at TV tower, Piatt Co, Sep 27, 1972 (Seets); 139, Cook Co (SBC), May 10, 1975.

Prothonotary Warbler *(Protonotaria citrea)*

Late April — Early September

Status: Common migrant and summer resident in south. Fairly common migrant and summer resident in central. Uncommon migrant and summer resident in north.
Documentation: Specimen(s) — ♂, Dickson Mounds, Fulton Co, May 11, 1971 (ISM 604744).
Remarks: Found in swamps and riverbottom forest. *Records:* 1 collected, Glen Ellyn, DuPage Co, May 17, 1967 (NIU); 1 banded, Carbondale, Sep 20, 1970 (VK-IAB158:23); nested, Skokie Lagoons, Cook Co, summer, 1975 (GR). *High counts:* 35, along Cache River, Pulaski Co, Apr 23, 1973 (VK, HDB); 37, Union Co (SBC), May 4, 1974; 32, Monroe Co (SBC), May 10, 1975.

Swainson's Warbler *(Limnothlypis swainsonii)*

Late April — Early September

Status: Occasional migrant and local summer resident in south. Very rare vagrant in north and central.

Documentation: Specimen(s) — ♀, 2 miles north of Pomona, Jackson Co, Aug 8, 1966 (SIU A-1394).
Remarks: Occurs in swampy areas. Usually associated with cane *(Arundinaria).* North and central records are probably over-migrants. *Records:* 1, Urbana, May 3, 1963 (Wallace-AFN17:409); 1, McGraw Wildlife Area, May 16, 1970 (Dillon, 1971); 4, Cave Creek, Jackson Co, Apr 27 - May 30, 1972 (VK-AB26:768); pair, near Roots, Randolph Co, July 8, 1972 (RA-AB26:866); 4, Union Co, May 5, 1973 (VK); pair feeding young, Heron Pond Nature Preserve, Johnson Co, Aug 31, 1973 (MH-AB28:62); 1, Monroe Co, May 4, 1974 (RA); 1, Pope Co, May 4, 1974 (P. & M. Biggers). *High count:* 12, Cedar Creek, Jackson Co, June 1975 (M. Swayne, MH).

Worm-eating Warbler *(Helmitheros vermivorus)*

Late April — Early September

Status: Fairly common migrant and summer resident in south. Uncommon migrant and summer resident in central. Occasional migrant in north.
Documentation: Specimen(s) — Ad ♀, 2 miles north of Pomona, Jackson Co, July 7, 1966 (SIU A-1396).
Remarks: Inhabits steep, wooded hillsides and ravines. Probably occurs in north as over-migrant since usually found only in early spring. *Summer record:* Pair feeding young Cowbird, Coles Co, summer, 1972 (LBH-AB26:866). *Other records:* 1, Skokie Lagoons, Cook Co, May 12, 1968 (RR-AFN22:533); 1, McGraw Wildlife Area, June 1, 1970 (Dillon, 1971); 1, Sterling, Apr 30, 1972 (Shaws-IAB163:18); 1, Oregon, Ogle Co, May 16, 1972 (J. Ware-AB26:768); 1, Winnetka, Cook Co, May 20, 1972 (Tweit-AB26:768); 4, Pike Co (SBC), May 5, 1973; 1, Normal, McLean Co, Apr 22 & May 8, 1974 (DBi-AB28:809). *High count:* 5, Jackson Co (SBC), May 10, 1975.

Golden-winged Warbler *(Vermivora chrysoptera)*

Late April — Mid-May
Late August — Late September

Status: Fairly common migrant. Very rare summer resident in north.
Documentation: Specimen(s) — ♂, Evanston, May 17, 1973 (ISM 605686).
Remarks: Found in woodland feeding at mid-heights. Ridgway (1889) claims he found this species breeding in Richland Co, June 1885, and Butler (1897) states that A.C. Poling found it nesting in the Mississippi Bottoms in Illinois. Both records, if true, are south of present breeding range. Only recent summer records are of nestings with Blue-winged Warblers in northern Illinois which should be considered a zone of hybridization between the Blue-winged and Golden-winged warblers. *Records:* 3, Decatur, Apr 18, 1976 (RS). *High counts:* 13, Cook Co (SBC), May 6, 1972; 12, St. Clair Co (SBC), May 5, 1973; 27, Will Co (SBC), May 10, 1975.
Hybrids: 2 hybrid types exist between the Golden-winged and Blue-winged warblers, the rare Brewster's Warbler and the very rare Lawrence's Warbler. *Records for Brewster's hybrid:* 1, north of Loxa, Coles Co, Apr 27, 1965 (HDB); 1, Deerfield, Lake Co, Aug 16, 1967 (M. Stolte, W. Vogl-IAB142:31); 2 banded, Winnebago Co, May 13 & 26, 1975 (LJ). *Records for Lawrence's hybrid:* Family group, Custer Park, Will Co, June 26, 1949 (Ford, 1956); ♀, Chicago, May 8, 1969 (CC-IAB151:16).

Blue-winged Warbler *(Vermivora pinus)*

Mid-April — Mid-September

Status: Uncommon migrant. Uncommon summer resident in north and south. Very rare summer resident in central.
Documentation: Specimen(s) — Ad ♂, Bald Knob, Union Co, Apr 30, 1966 (SIU A-1356).
Remarks: Found on dry bushy hillsides. *Summer records:* Nest with young, Carroll Co, June 9, 1962 (PCP-IAB126:13); pair, near Charleston Lake, Coles Co, June 8, 1966 (HDB); nest, Vermilion Co, summer, 1975 (M. Campbell-AB29:982). *Other records:* 1, Pere Marquette St Pk, Apr 27, 1970 (SV). *High counts:* 7, Pike Co (SBC), May 5, 1973; 6, Coles Co (SBC), May 4, 1974.

[Bachman's Warbler *(Vermivora bachmanii)*]

Status: Hypothetical.
Remarks: Several sight records, listed by Ridgway (Gault, 1922), Fawks, Bush (S & P, 1955, p. 48), and Lilly (Smith, 1941); all lack satisfactory documentation. According to E.T. Smith (1941), there was a specimen from Decatur in 1899. This specimen, if it existed, cannot be found. Probably occurrred as over-migrant when its population was greater; or might have occurred in southern Illinois as summer resident since habitat is similar to that in Missouri where first nest was found. This rare warbler appears to be on the verge of extinction.

Tennessee Warbler *(Vermivora peregrina)*

Late April — Late May
Late August — Mid-October

Status: Abundant migrant.
Documentation: Specimen(s) — ♂, Quincy, Adams Co, May 12, 1974 (ISM 606263).
Remarks: In spring frequents woodland; ranges from low to high in vegetation. In fall likes weed patches and woods edge; stays mainly low. *Records:* 2, Deerfield, Lake Co, July 21, 1963 (CC, Bi-AFN18:43); 1, Springfield, Nov 5, 1974 (HDB); 1, Decatur, Nov 11, 1974 (RS); 1, Charleston, Coles Co. Jan 27 - Mar 6, 1975 (LBH-AB29:699). *High counts:* 107 killed at TV tower, Sangamon Co, Sep 16-17, 1958 (Parmalee & Parmalee, 1959); 134, McLean Co (SBC), May 6, 1972; 177 killed at TV tower, Sangamon Co, Sep 2, 1972 (HDB); 98 killed at TV tower, Piatt Co, Sep 27, 1972 (Seets); 184, Monroe Co (SBC), May 10, 1975.

Orange-crowned Warbler *(Vermivora celata)*

Mid-April — Mid-May
Mid-September — Late October

Status: Uncommon migrant. Rare winter resident.
Documentation: Specimen(s) — ♀, east of Springfield, Oct 18, 1972 (ISM 605334).
Remarks: Occurs on the forest edge and also inhabits conifers. Occurs later in fall and its numbers usually peak after most of the other warblers have departed. *Winter records:* 1, Decatur, Dec 27, 1959 (Kirby-AFN14:203); 1 photographed, Barrington, Dec 31, 1969 (AFN24:306). 1, Springfield, Jan 9, 1972 (HDB); 1, Barry, Pike Co, Dec 28, 1975 (JF); 1, Crab Orchard (NWR) (CBC), Jan 4, 1976 (BP). *High count:* 46, Cook Co (SBC), May 6, 1972.

Nashville Warbler *(Vermivora ruficapilla)*

Late April — Mid-May
Late August — Late October

Status: Common migrant. Very rare summer resident in north.

Documentation: Specimen(s) — ♂, east of Springfield, Sep 29, 1972 (ISM 605552).

Remarks: Found in woodland and woodland edge; in fall also in weedy areas. Old nesting records from Lake Co (Pitelka, 1940) and Fulton Co (Smith, 1888) although latter record seems unlikely. *Summer records:* ♂ singing, Lake Co, summer, 1962 (RR-AFN16:480). *Other records:* 1, Rockford, Nov 5, 1972 (Dunn-IAB164:42); 1, Charleston, Coles Co, Nov 24-26, 1972 (LBH-AB27:69); 1, Rockford, Nov 2, 1973 (LJ-AB28:62); 1, Charleston, Coles Co, Nov 20, 1973 (LBH-AB28:62); 1, Champaign, Nov 15, 1974 (D. Friedman-AB29:67); 1, Charleston, Coles Co, Jan 6, 1975 (LBH-AB29:699). *High counts:* 189, McHenry Co (SBC), May 6, 1972; 48 killed at TV tower, Piatt Co, Sep 27, 1972 (Seets); 251, Will Co (SBC), May 10, 1975.

Northern Parula *(Parula americana)*

Mid-April — Early October

Status: Common migrant and summer resident in south. Fairly common migrant and uncommon summer resident in central. Uncommon migrant in north.

Documentation: Specimen(s) — ♂, east of Springfield, Sep 17, 1971 (ISM 604873).

Remarks: Occurs in swamps and river-bottom forest, where it stays in the treetops. *Records:* 1, southern Illinois (no specific locality) Mar 31, 1954 (Mengel, 1965); 1, Rockford, Apr 11, 1959 (LJ-AFN13:374); ♂ singing, Daniel Wright Woods, Cook Co, Oct 1, 1967 (CC); 1, Springfield, Oct 13, 1974 (HDB); ♂ singing, Ryerson Preserve, Lake Co, last week of June 1975 (GR). *High counts:* 8 killed at TV tower, Piatt Co, Sep 27, 1972 (Seets); 61, along Cache River, Johnson Co, Apr 24, 1973 (VK, HDB); 18, Pike Co (SBC), May 5, 1973.

Yellow Warbler *(Dendroica petechia)*

Late April — Early September

Status: Common spring migrant and uncommon fall migrant. Fairly common summer resident.

Documentation: Specimen(s) — ♂, east of Springfield, Sep 2, 1972 (ISM 605635).

Remarks: Found associated with willows along streams and lakes. May be decline in this species as summer resident in some sections of state. *Records:* 1, west of Charleston, Coles Co, Nov 17, 1965 (HDB); 1, Waukegan, Sep 27, 1970 (LB); 1, Springfield, Sep 30, 1974 (VK-IAB172:32). *High counts:* 65, Will Co (SBC), May 4, 1974; 145, Cook Co (SBC), May 10, 1975.

Magnolia Warbler *(Dendroica magnolia)*

Early May —Late May
Late August — Early October

Status: Common migrant.
Documentation: Specimen(s) — ♂, Evanston, May 17, 1973 (ISM 605678).
Remarks: Found from low to mid-height in wooded areas. In fall may occur in more open situations. In certain years could be classified as abundant migrant. *Records:* ♂ singing, Lake Forest, Cook Co, June 30, 1959 (Clow-AFN13:434); 1, Chicago area, Apr 10, 1966 (PD-IAB138:8). 1, Springfield, Oct 23, 1974 (HDB). *High count:* 133 killed at TV tower, Piatt Co, Sep 27, 1972 (Seets).

Cape May Warbler *(Dendroica tigrina)*

Early May — Late May
Early September — Mid-October

Status: Uncommon spring migrant. Occasional fall migrant.
Documentation: Specimen(s) — ♂, Momence, Kankakee Co, May 11, 1968 (NIU 2796).
Remarks: Prefers conifers especially spruce. Can be found also in oak and other deciduous trees. More numerous on eastern side of state. *Records:* 1, Chicago, Oct 25, 1969 (Krawiec-AFN24:55); 1, Springfield, Oct 19, 1971 (HDB); 6, Decatur, Oct 22, 1973 (TN-AB28:62); 1, Carterville, Williamson Co, Nov 11-21, 1973 (MH-AB28:62); 1, Decatur, Nov 16, 1974 (RS); 1, Bath, Mason Co, Nov 22, 1975 (RP, RS, HDB); 1, Springfield, Apr 23, 1976 (WO). *High count:* 10, Cook Co (SBC), May 10, 1975.

Black-throated Blue Warbler *(Dendroica caerulescens)*

Early May — Late May
Early September — Early October

Status: Fairly common migrant in north. Occasional migrant in central and south.
Documentation: Specimen(s) — ♂, Kishwaukee Park, Winnebago Co, Sep 25, 1975 (ISM 606249).
Remarks: Found in woodland with dense undergrowth. More common on northeastern edge of Illinois, suggesting that it migrates northwest in spring and southeast in fall across northern part of state. More numerous in fall. *Records:* ♂, Sinnissippi Park, Winnebago Co, May 1, 1969 (Shaws); 1, Charleston, Coles Co, Oct 21, 1970 (LBH); 1, Sparta, Randolph Co, Sep 11, 1971 (Morrison-AB26:73); 1, Springfield, Oct 19, 1971 (HDB); ♂, Decatur, Apr 28, 1975 (RS-AB29:861); 1, Winnebago Co, Aug 27, 1975 (LJ). *High counts:* 6 Ad ♂, Waukegan, Sep 22, 1970 (LB); 18, Cook Co (SBC), May 10, 1975; 5 killed at TV tower, Macon Co, Sep 27, 1972 (Seets).

Yellow-rumped Warbler *(Dendroica coronata)*

Early April — Mid-May
Mid-September — Late November

Status: Abundant migrant. Uncommon winter resident in south and occasional winter resident in central and north.

Documentation: Specimen(s) — ♂, Edinburg, Christian Co, May 18, 1972 (ISM 605193).

Remarks: Found in woodland, parkland, and forest edge. In winter usually stays in protected areas where it feeds mainly on poison ivy berries. *Records:* 355, Crab Orchard NWR, Dec 19, 1962 (AFN17:202); 10, Morris-Wilmington (CBC), Dec 28, 1963 (AFN18:224); 2, Rockford, February 2 1969 (WS-AFN23:488); 177, Union County Refuge (CBC), Dec 19, 1971 (AB26:378); 31, Chicago (CBC), Dec 26, 1971 (AB26:370); 42, Crane Lake, Mason Co, Dec 18, 1972 (HDB, JF); 1, Waukegan, Aug 12, 1975 (CC). *High counts:* 426, McHenry Co (SBC), May 6, 1972; 111 killed at TV tower, Piatt Co, Oct 31, 1972 (Seets); 719, Will Co (SBC), May 10 1975.

Subspecies: 3 records of Audubon's Warbler *(D. c. auduboni).* 1 listed from Buffalo Prairie, Rock Island Co, no date (AOU, 1957); 1 photographed, Sanganois WR, Cass Co, Dec 19, 1970 (HDB, 1971); ♀, Chicago, May 7 & 8, 1971 (CC, LB, Pulliam-AB25:753).

Black-throated Gray Warbler *(Dendroica nigrescens)*

Status: Very rare vagrant.

Documentation: Sight record with acceptable details — ♂ observed at close range in deciduous woods, Springfield, May 3, 1975 (RS, HDB).

Remarks: 3 other records of this western warbler. *Records:* ♂, Lincoln Park, Chicago, Apr 24, 1946 (H. Bennett); ♂, Winnetka, Cook Co, Oct 9, 1968 (T.K. Boyd); ♀, University of Illinois campus, Urbana, Sep 6, 1975 (J.C. Franks).

Black-throated Green Warbler *(Dendroica virens)*

Late April — Late May
Late August — Late October

Status: Common migrant.

Documentation: Specimen(s) — ♂, east of Springfield, Sep 29, 1972 (ISM 605642).

Remarks: Found in conifers as well as deciduous trees. *Records:* 1, Chicago, Oct 26, 1958 (CC-AFN13:36); ♂ singing, Wilmette, June 16, 1968 (RR); ♂ singing, Castle Rock, Ogle Co, June 28, 1969 (WS, LaBonty-AFN23:666); 1, Johnson Co, Apr 9, 1972 (VK-AB27:768); ♂, Deerfield, Lake Co, June 9, 1973 (CC, LB-AB27:877); 1, Springfield, Nov 8, 1973 (HDB); 1, Fulton Co, Nov 1, 1974 (VK-AB29:67); 1, Chautauqua NWR, Nov 18, 1975 (WO). *High counts:* 58, McHenry Co (SBC), May 6, 1972; 81 killed at TV tower, Macon Co, Sep 27, 1972 (Seets); 104, Will Co (SBC), May 10, 1975.

Cerulean Warbler *(Dendroica cerulea)*

Late April — Early September

Status: Common migrant and summer resident in south. Uncommon migrant and local summer resident in central and north.

Documentation: Specimen(s) — ♂, Glenwood, Cook Co, Apr 18, 1955 (NMNH-S. Levy).

Remarks: Found in river bottoms in tops of tall trees. *Records:* ♂, Cook Co and Will Co, July 1956 (Levy-AFN10:387); many near Rockford, summer, 1958 (LJ-AFN12:471); nest, Saganashkee Slough and St. Mary Woods, Cook Co, summer, 1963 (F. Brechlin); 1 banded, Carbondale, Sep 16, 1970 (VK-AB25:66); 1, Sterling, Apr 24, 1973 (Shaws-IAB166:23); 1, Decatur, Apr 12, 1974 (RS). *High count:* 58, along Cache River, Johnson Co, Apr 24, 1973 (VK, HDB).

Blackburnian Warbler *(Dendroica fusca)*

Early May — Late May
Late August — Late September

Status: Common migrant.
Documentation: Specimen(s) — ♀, Evanston, June 3, 1973 (ISM 605760).
Remarks: Usually found in tops of trees in woodland and parkland. In fall can be seen at moderate heights along forest edge. *Records:* 1, Quincy, Oct 25, 1964 (TEM-AFN19:45); 1, Springfield, Aug 7, 1972 (HDB). *High counts:* 21 killed at TV tower, Sangamon Co, Sep 2, 1972 (HDB); 25, McLean Co (SBC), May 10, 1975.

Yellow-throated Warbler *(Dendroica dominica)*

Mid-April — Early September

Status: Common migrant and summer resident in south. Uncommon migrant and local summer resident in central. Rare vagrant in north.
Documentation: Specimen(s) — Ad ♂, Pine Hills, Union Co, Apr 2, 1966 (SIU A-1365).
Remarks: In south, found in cypress swamps and conifers. In central and north, closely associated with sycamore trees in river bottoms. Usually found in tops of these tall trees. Northern records, probably over-migrants. *Records:* 1, Chicago, Apr 10-15, 1959 (AFN13:374); 1, Illinois Beach St Pk, Apr 13, 1964 (J. Probst); 1, Waukegan, Apr 30, 1972 (LC-AB26:768); 1. Carbondale, Jackson Co, Oct 7, 1972 (VK-AB27:69); 1, Charleston, Coles Co, Sep 13, 1973 (LBH-AB28:62); 1, Springfield, Nov 11, 1975 (HDB). *High counts:* 18, along Cache River, Johnson Co, Apr 24, 1973 (VK, HDB); 10, Madison Co (SBC), May 5, 1973; 11, Jackson Co (SBC), May 4, 1974.

Chestnut-sided Warbler *(Dendroica pensylvanica)*

Early May — Late May
Late August — Early October

Status: Common migrant. Rare summer resident in north.
Documentation: Specimen(s) — ♂, east of Springfield, Sep 27, 1972 (ISM 605783).
Remarks: Found in woodland and on forest edge. *Summer records:* Ad carrying food, Will Co, July 1956 (Levy-AFN10:387); 6 pairs, near Rockford, summer, 1958 (LJ-AFN12:417); 2 ♂ and 1 ♀, DesPlaines River, summer, 1962 (CC-AFN16:480); nest, 3 miles east of Woodstock, McHenry Co, May 26, 1965 (Carroll). *High counts:* 67 killed at TV tower, Sangamon Co, Sep 16-17, 1958 (Parmalee & Parmalee, 1959); 34, Sangamon Co (SBC), May 10, 1975.

Bay-breasted Warbler *(Dendroica castanea)*

Early May — Late May
Early September — Mid-October

Status: Fairly common spring migrant. Common fall migrant.
Documentation: Specimen(s) — ♂, Springfield, May 21, 1976 (ISM 606430).
Remarks: Usually found in upper levels of tall trees. More common in eastern part of state in spring. *Records:* Ad, Illinois Beach St Pk, Aug 1, 1972 (Smith-AB26:866); 1, Springfield, Oct 28, 1974 (HDB); 1, Winnebago Co, Nov 2, 1975 (LJ). *High counts:* 24 killed at TV tower, Sangamon Co, Sep 16-17, 1958 (Parmalee & Parmalee, 1959); 79 killed at TV tower, Vermilion Co, Sep 27, 1972 (Seets).

Blackpoll Warbler *(Dendroica striata)*

Late April — Late May
Late August — Mid-October

Status: Common migrant in north. Common spring migrant and uncommon fall migrant in central and south.
Documentation: Specimen(s) — ♂, Evanston, Sep 6, 1973 (ISM 605848).
Remarks: Found in deciduous and coniferous trees. Migrates primarily up the Mississippi River Valley in spring and east along the New England coast in fall (Nisbet, 1970). *Records:* 1, Lisle, DuPage Co, Nov 22, 1956 (KB-AFN11:30); 1, Chicago, Oct 23, 1971 (CC-AB26:73). *High counts:* 26 killed at TV tower, Vermilion Co, Sep 27, 1972 (Seets); 55, Skokie Lagoons, Cook Co, Sep 22, 1974 (LB); 87, Monroe Co (SBC), May 10, 1975.

Pine Warbler *(Dendroica pinus)*

Late March — Mid-October

Status: Uncommon migrant. Uncommon summer resident in south. Rare winter resident.
Documentation: Specimen(s) — ♂, east of Springfield, Sep 29, 1972 (ISM 605287).
Remarks: Prefers conifer stands; can also be found in deciduous trees. Seems to be more common on eastern side of state. *Records:* 1, Olney, Richland Co, Dec 26, 1967 (Bridges, Silva-AFN22:267); 1, York Park, DuPage Co, Dec 19 & 24, 1971 (LB-AB26:612); 2 ♂, Crab Orchard NWR, Mar 11, 1972 (VK-AB26:612); 1, Crab Orchard NWR, Jan 18 - Feb 2, 1975 (BP-AB29:699). *High counts:* 8, Boone Co (SBC), May 6, 1972; 7, Lake Co (SBC), May 10, 1975.

Kirtland's Warbler *(Dendroica kirtlandii)*

Status: Extirpated. [Formerly very rare migrant.]
Documentation: Specimen(s) — ♂, Chicago, May 22, 1899 (Blackwelder, 1899).
Remarks: Stays low in dense vegetation on migration. Not likely to be found again in Illinois because of decline in population. Reason to believe that specimens collected in Illinois were on their way to an expanded breeding

range (in Wisconsin?) that does not now exist (Mayfield, 1960). *2 other specimens:* ♂, Glen Ellyn, DuPage Co, May 7, 1894 (Gault, 1894); 1, Winnebago Co, May 25, 1894 (Dickinson, 1897). A few undocumented sight records, none recent.

Prairie Warbler *(Dendroica discolor)*

Mid-April — Late September

Status: Common migrant and summer resident in south. Rare migrant and summer resident (very locally) in central and north.

Documentation: Specimen(s) — ♂, 2½ miles west of Herod, Pope Co, July 27, 1971 (ISM 604832).

Remarks: Found in shrubby, open, upland areas. Occurs most abundantly in Shawnee Hills. Distribution is strange in that many suitable-appearing areas contain none of this species. *Records:* 1, Crab Orchard NWR, Nov 23, 1959 (Bush-AFN14:41); Ad and Im, Wilmette, Aug 4, 1964 (RR, K. Eckert-AFN18:512); ♂, Saganashkee Slough, Cook Co, June 13 & 19, 1965 (CC-AFN19:552); Im banded, Morrisonville, Christian Co, July 23, 1966 (Varner-IAB140:7); ♂, Mason State Forest, May 20, 1973 (HDB); 1, Decatur, Apr 28, 1975 (RS-AB29:861). *High count:* 24, Pope Co (SBC), May 4, 1974.

Palm Warbler *(Dendroica palmarum)*

Mid-April — Mid-May
Mid-September — Mid-October

Status: Abundant spring migrant. Common fall migrant in north. Uncommon fall migrant central and south. Very rare winter resident.

Documentation: Specimen(s) — ♀, Evanson, May 17, 1973 (ISM 605679).

Remarks: Likes woodland edge in spring. In fall occurs in more open areas such as weed patches, fence rows, and even fields. *Records:* 1 found dead, Decatur, Jan 27, 1956 (Chaniot-AFN10:254); 1, Sangchris St Pk, Sangamon Co, Nov 18, 1973 (HDB); 4, Decatur, Nov 11, 1974 (RS); 1, Charleston, Coles Co, Dec 27, 1974 (B. James-AB29:699); 1, Springfield, Apr 13, 1977 (VK). *High counts:* 20 killed at TV tower, Vermilion Co, Sep 27, 1972 (Seets); 264, Will Co (SBC), May 4, 1974; 100, Wilmette, Sep 20, 1974 (RR-AB29:67); 322, Cook Co (SBC), May 10, 1975.

Ovenbird *(Seiurus aurocapillus)*

Late April —Late May
Late August — Mid-October

Status: Abundant migrant. Locally uncommon summer resident.

Documentation: Specimen(s) — ♂, Evanston, June 3, 1973 (ISM 605779).

Remarks: Found in woodland. Nests more often in north than central or south. *Records:* Ad birds with 1 young, Belle Smith Springs, Pope Co, July 10, 1951 (Bennet, 1952); pair, near Cobden, July 16, 1966 (George, 1969); 1, Illinois Beach St Pk, Nov 9, 1968 (CC); 1, Brown Co, Apr 21, 1971 (HDB). *High counts:* 71 killed at TV tower, Sangamon Co, Sep 2, 1972 (HDB); 143 killed at TV tower, Piatt Co, Sep 27, 1972 (Seets); 92, Cook Co (SBC), May 10, 1975.

Northern Waterthrush *(Seiurus noveboracensis)*

Mid-April — Mid-May
Mid-August — Early October

Status: Common migrant.
Documentation: Specimen(s) — ♀, 1 mile northeast of Bluffs, Scott Co, Sep 2, 1972 (ISM 606164).
Remarks: Found in moist, wooded areas; stays near the ground. More than one subspecies found in Illinois but probably not safely separable in the field. Kennicott (1855) listed this species as known to breed in Cook Co (?). *Winter records:* 1 (undocumented), Springfield, Dec 23, 1956 (AFN11:171); 1, Caldwell Forest Preserve, Chicago, Dec 28, 1975 (D. Brenner, W. Krawiec). *Other records:* 1, Chautauqua NWR, Aug 5, 1972 (HDB); 1, west of Moweaqua, Christian Co, Apr 11, 1971 (HDB). *High counts:* 52 killed at TV tower, Sangamon Co, Sep 2, 1972 (HDB); 85, Cook Co (SBC), May 10, 1975.

Louisiana Waterthrush *(Seiurus motacilla)*

Early April — Late August

Status: Common migrant and summer resident in south. Uncommon spring migrant and rare fall migrant and summer resident in central and north.
Documentation: Specimen(s) — Ad ♀, 3 miles north of Alto Pass, Union Co, Apr 16, 1966 (SIU A-1374).
Remarks: Found in woodland along streams; seems to prefer streams with rock bottom. Some spring migrants in north and central are probable over-migrants. Fall migration almost undectable. *Records:* 1 pair, Deerfield, Lake Co, June 23, 1963 (CC); 1, McGraw Wildlife Area, May 6, 1968 (Dillon, 1971); 1, Springfield, Mar 31, 1973 (HDB); 1, Pope Co, Mar 23, 1975 (R. Graber-AB29:699). *High count:* 8, Monroe Co (SBC), May 4, 1974.

Kentucky Warbler *(Oporornis formosus)*

Late April — Mid-September

Status: Common migrant and summer resident in south and central. Rare spring migrant and summer resident in north.
Documentation: Specimen(s) — Im, Lusk Creek, Pope Co, July 28, 1971 (ISM 604836).
Remarks: Likes damp woods; more often heard than seen. *Records:* Nested, near New Boston, Mercer Co, summer, 1959 (RT-AFN13:434); ♂, near Half Day, Lake Co, July 4, 1965 (CC); 1, 1½ miles north of Cobden, Union Co, Oct 1-6, 1967 (William George); 1, McGraw Wildlife Area, May 28, 1970 (Dillon, 1971); nested, Oregon, Ogle Co, summer, 1973 (Shaws-AB27:780); 1, near Decatur, Oct 4, 1974 (RP). *High counts:* 18, along the Cache River, Johnson Co, Apr 24, 1973 (VK, HDB).

Connecticut Warbler *(Oporornis agilis)*

Mid-May — Early June
Early September — Late September

Status: Uncommon migrant.

Documentation: Specimen(s) — ♂, east of Springfield, Sep 2, 1972 (ISM 605255).

Remarks: Likes open thicket areas and weed patches. Much more difficult to find and identify in fall. *Records:* 1, Chicago, Nov 1, 1967 (RR-IAB145:15); 3, Springfield, Sep 18-26, 1971 (HDB); 4, Chicago, Sep 23, 1971 (LB, GR-AB26:73); 6, Chicago, May 28, 1972 (LB); 5, Springfield, May 19, 1974 (WO, HDB); 1 banded, Springfield, Oct 1, 1974 (VK); 1, Clark Co (SBC), May 10, 1975.

Mourning Warbler *(Oporornis philadelphia)*

Mid-May — Early June
Late August — Mid-September

Status: Uncommon migrant. Occasional summer resident in north.

Documentation: Specimen(s) — ♂, 2 miles north of Springfield, Sep 16, 1974 (ISM 605922).

Remarks: In spring likes open thickets and forest edge; in fall also found in weed patches. *Summer records:* 2, Lake Co, July 4, 1959 (CC-AFN13:434); 3 Ad and ♀ carrying food, Des Plaines River, June 30, 1962 (CC-AFN16:480); 3 ♂ singing, Daniel Wright Woods, Lake Co, June 26, 1966 (CC); 1, Lake Co, July 30 & Aug 1, 1972 (LB, GR-AB26:866). *Other records:* 1 banded, Carbondale, Jackson Co, Oct 10, 1970 (VK); 1, Mark Twain NWR, Oct 4, 1972 (SV-IAB164:41). *High count:* 15, Chicago, May 28, 1972 (LB).

Common Yellowthroat *(Geothlypis trichas)*

Mid-April — Mid-October

Status: Common migrant and summer resident. Rare winter resident.

Documentation: Specimen(s) — ♂, Jacksonville, Morgan Co, Apr 21, 1973 (ISM 605868).

Remarks: Likes low, wet areas with shrubby growth. *Winter records:* 1, east of Stonington, Christian Co, Jan 15, 1966 (HDB); 1, Champaign, Nov 20, 1962 (PN-AFN17:37); 1, Evanston, Nov 22, 1969 (CC-AFN24:55); ♀, Harrison, Winnebago Co, Nov 30, 1969 (LJ); 1, Mark Twain NWR, Dec 26, 1970 (Gast-AFN25:358); 1, Decatur, Jan 11, 1974 (RP); 1, Charleston, Coles Co, Nov 21, 1974 (LBH-AB29:67); 1, Jackson Co, Mar 8, 1975 (BP-AB29:699). *High count:* 166, Will Co (SBC), May 10, 1975.

Yellow-breasted Chat *(Icteria virens)*

Late April — Early September

Status: Common migrant and summer resident in south. Fairly common migrant and summer resident in central. Uncommon migrant and summer resident in north. Very rare winter resident.

Documentation: Specimen(s) — ♂, Murphysboro, Jackson Co, May 5, 1971 (ISM 605432).

Remarks: This large warbler inhabits shrubby upland areas. *Winter records:* 1, near Findlay, Shelby Co, Dec 27, 1967 (AFN22:274); 1, Urbana, winter,

1967-68 (Kendeigh-AFN22:275). *Other records:* 1 collected, DeKalb, DeKalb Co, May 11, 1963 (NIU); 1, northeast of Charleston, Coles Co, Apr 21, 1976 (LBH). *High counts:* 25, Fayette Co (SBC), May 6, 1972; 35, Jackson Co (SBC), May 10, 1975.

Hooded Warbler *(Wilsonia citrina)*

Mid-April — Mid-August

Status: Uncommon migrant and summer resident in south. Occasional spring migrant in central and north; very rare fall vagrant in central and north.
Documentation: Specimen(s) — ♂, 2 miles north of Pomona, Jackson Co, Apr 29, 1967 (SIU WGG-2204).
Remarks: Found on shaded hillsides in bottomland forest. Those appearing in the north and central are probably over-migrants; however, some evidence suggests that this species breeds in northern Illinois. *Records:* ♂, Pere Marquette St Pk, July 11, 1968 (SV-AFN22:613); 1, Skokie Lagoons, Cook Co, June 2, 1973 (CC, LB-IAB166:24); 1, Lincoln Park, Chicago, Oct 4, 1973 (Hogg-AB28:62); 1, Normal, McLean Co, Apr 15, 1974 (DBi-AB28:809); ♂, Decatur, Apr 13, 1975 (RS); 4, Douglas Co (SBC), May 10, 1975; ♂, near Chautauqua NWR, June 26, 1976 (HDB).

Wilson's Warbler *(Wilsonia pusilla)*

Early May — Late May
Late August — Early October

Status: Fairly common migrant.
Documentation: Specimen(s) — ♀, east of Springfield, May 30, 1973 (ISM 605672).
Remarks: Forest-edge species. Also found in weedy areas in fall. *Records:* 1, Morton Arboretum, Dec 1, 1963 (M. Lehmann-IAB129:6); 1, Carbondale, Jackson Co, Oct 24, 1970 (IAB158:23); 1, Kankakee River St Pk, Kankakee Co, Nov 23, 1973 (C. Shaw-AB28:62); *High counts:* 10, Chicago, May 26, 1974 (LB); 11, Champaign Co (SBC), May 10, 1975.

Canada Warbler *(Wilsonia canadensis)*

Mid-May — Early June
Late August — Mid-September

Status: Fairly common spring migrant and common fall migrant. Rare summer resident in north.
Documentation: Specimen(s) — ♂, Evanston, June 3, 1973 (ISM 605734).
Remarks: Inhabits bottomland forest and forest edge. *Summer records:* ♀, near Deerfield, Lake Co, June 27, and 1 ♂ singing, July 4, 1959 (CC-AFN13:434); 2 ♂ singing, Des Plaines River, June 24, 1962 (CC-AFN16:480); 1, Elmhurst, DuPage Co, July 29, 1972 (LB-AB26:866). *Other records:* 1 banded, Springfield, Oct 4, 1973 (HDB); 1, Chautauqua NWR, Aug 17, 1974 (HDB); 1, Cook Co, Apr 26, 1976 (Cal Snyder). *High counts:* 18, Chicago, May 28, 1972 (LB); 11, Springfield, Sep 1, 1974 (HDB).

American Redstart *(Setophaga ruticilla)*

Early May — Early October

Status: Common migrant and locally common summer resident.
Documentation: Specimen(s) — ♂, east of Springfield, Sep 27, 1972 (ISM 605485).
Remarks: Found in bottomland forest. Some years could be considered abundant migrant. *Records:* Ad ♂, near S.I.U. Airport, Jackson Co, Apr 5, 1966 (William George); ♀, Springfield, Nov 25, 1973 (K. Bohlen, HDB). *High counts:* 24, Kane Co (SBC), May 6, 1972; 60 killed at TV tower, Piatt Co, Sep 27, 1972 (Seets); 58, Jo Daviess Co (SBC), May 10, 1975.

PLOCEIDAE: Weaver Finches.

House Sparrow *(Passer domesticus)*

Status: Introduced. Now an abundant permanent resident.
Documentation: Specimen(s) — ♂, 2 miles south of Farmingdale, Sangamon Co, Mar 20, 1972 (ISM 605139).
Remarks: Found near human habitation. Successfully introduced at Brooklyn, New York, from England in 1852; established in Illinois by 1886.

European Tree Sparrow *(Passer montanus)*

Status: Introduced. Now an uncommon permanent resident in west-central part of state.
Documentation: Specimen(s) — ♂, 1 mile west of Orleans, Morgan Co, Oct 16, 1971 (ISM 605640).
Remarks: Prefers hedgerows and brush piles; does not inhabit urban areas to the extent as does the House Sparrow. Introduced at St. Louis, Missouri, in 1870. *Records:* 2, Lake Petersburg, Menard Co, Jan 16, 1972 (PW, HDB); 1 banded and photographed, 3 miles west of Macomb, McDonough Co, Oct 17, 1972 (E.C. Franks); 1, Evanston, Mar 27, 1976 (M. Mlodinow, LB, GR); *High counts:* 110, Pere Marquette St Pk (CBC), Dec 26, 1971 (AB26:376); 200, near Meredosia Lake, Morgan Co, Mar 4, 1972 (HDB); 120, Crane Lake (CBC), Dec 15, 1973 (AB28:380).

ICTERIDAE: Blackbirds.

Bobolink *(Dolichonyx oryzivorus)*

Late April — Late May
Early September — Early October

Status: Common migrant and summer resident in north. Fairly common migrant in central and south. Occasional summer resident in central.
Documentation: Specimen(s) — ♀, east of Springfield, Sep 2, 1972 (ISM 605268).
Remarks: Prefers fallow fields in spring; found mainly in marshy areas in fall. Fall migration is difficult to detect at times, but birds can frequently be heard flying overhead. *Summer records:* Nested, Sibley, Ford Co, July 8, 1955

Robertson-AFN9:382); 33 (Route 16, BBS), Kendall Co and LaSalle Co, June 21, 1975 (M.T. Gossmann-U.S. Fish & Wildlife Service, 1976, p. 668). *1 winter record:* 1, Crab Orchard NWR, Dec 6, 1953 (S & P, 1955, p. 51). *High counts:* 571, Jersey Co (SBC), May 6, 1972; 34 killed at TV tower, Sangamon Co, Sep 2, 1972 (HDB).

Eastern Meadowlark *(Sturnella magna)*

Late February — Mid-November

Status: Common migrant and summer resident. Common winter resident in south. Uncommon winter resident in north and central.
Documentation: Specimen(s) — 1, 4 miles east of Arcola, Douglas Co, Oct 15, 1971 (ISM 604900).
Remarks: Found in fallow fields, farmland and along roadsides. *High counts:* 97, Beverly (CBC), Dec 22, 1973 (AB28:377); 464, St. Clair Co (SBC), May 4, 1974; 591, near Olney (CBC), Dec 27, 1975 (AFN12:175).

Western Meadowlark *(Sturnella neglecta)*

Late February — Mid-November

Status: Fairly common summer resident in north and central; more numerous in western half of state. Uncommon winter resident throughout state.
Documentation: Specimen(s) — ♂, 5 miles north of Dakota, Stephenson Co, Apr 21, 1968 (NIU 2552).
Remarks: Prefers more open situations and less vegetation than Eastern Meadowlark. Outnumbers Eastern Meadowlarks in northwestern part of state. Status somewhat unclear because of likeness to Eastern Meadowlark. *Records:* Nested, Sibley, Ford Co, Aug 4, 1955 (Robertson-AFN9:382); nest, Whiteside Co, May 23, 1959 (Prentice-IAB115:11); 1, Carbondale, Jackson Co, Nov 8, 1970 (VK). *High counts:* 80, Rockford, Jan 1, 1970 (AFN24:314); 82, Kendall Co (SBC), May 6, 1972; 59 (Route 2, BBS), Ogle Co and Carroll Co, June 8, 1975 (LJ-U.S. Fish & Wildlife Service, 1976, p. 669).

Yellow-headed Blackbird *(Xanthocephalus xanthocephalus)*

Mid-April — Early October

Status: Locally uncommon migrant and summer resident in north. Rare migrant in remainder of state.
Documentation: Specimen(s) — ♂, Antioch, Lake Co, May 13, 1962 (NIU 758).
Remarks: Found in marshes, feed lots, and pastures. Colonies in north seem to be declining. *Summer records:* 12 pairs, north of Thomson, Carroll Co, June 14, 1959 (Shaws-IAB115:11); nest, Lake Co, June 29, 1963 (RR); young, Barrington, Lake Co, Aug 7, 1965 (RR); *Other records:* ♀, Pere Marquette St Pk, Dec 30, 1956 (Chanoit, Kirby-AFN11:170); several, Moline, Rock Island Co, May 2-31, 1968 (EF-AFN22:533); ♂, Pere Marquette St Pk, Apr 24, 1971 (HDB, PW); 1, Marshall Co, Apr 23, 1972 (VH-AB26:768); 2 Randolph Co, May 6, 1972 (Morrison-AB26:768); 1, Grand Tower, Jackson Co, May 14, 1972 (Baumgarter-AB26:768); ♀, near Cuba, Oct 6, 1973 (HDB, RS); 5 ♀, Jacksonville, May 3, 1974 (WO). *High counts:* 36, DeKalb Co (SBC), May 6, 1972; 19, Cook Co (SBC), May 10, 1975; 61, Lake Co (SBC), May 10, 1975.

Red-winged Blackbird *(Agelaius phoeniceus)*

Early March — Late October

Status: Abundant migrant and summer resident. Common winter resident in south and uncommon winter resident in central and north.

Documentation: Specimen(s) — ♂, 1 mile west of Rosedale, Jersey Co, Jan 15, 1972 (ISM 605088).

Remarks: Found in many habitats but favors swamps, marshes, roadside ditches, and clover fields. *High counts:* 1,000,000, Crab Orchard NWR (CBC), Dec 27, 1956 (AFN11:168); 19,000, Pere Marquette St Pk (CBC), Dec 30, 1956 (AFN11:170); 50,000, near Fairmont City, Madison Co, winter, 1969 (Wrischnik-IAB153:19); 375,000, Horsehsoe Lake (CBC), Dec 30, 1974 (AB29:414).

Orchard Oriole *(Icterus spurius)*

Late April — Late August

Status: Common migrant and summer resident in south. Uncommon migrant and summer resident in central. Occasional migrant and summer resident in north.

Documentation: Specimen(s) — Ad ♂, 2 miles north of Cobden, Union Co, Apr 21, 1966 (SIU A-2140).

Remarks: Inhabits rather open wooded situations; prefers orchards and willow-lined streams. *Records:* 2, Rockford, May 14, 1961 (LJ-AFN15:416); 1, McGraw Wildlife Area, May 12, 1968 (Dillon, 1971); Ad ♂ photographed, near Cobden, Union Co, Dec 16, 1975 (T. Merriman). *High counts:* 13, Coles Co (SBC), May 6, 1972.

Northern Oriole *(Icterus galbula)*

Late April — Mid-September

Status: Common migrant and summer resident. Very rare winter resident.

Documentation: Specimen(s) — ♂, near Bluffs, Scott Co, Sep 2, 1972 (ISM 605527).

Remarks: Found in woodland and trees along watercourses, ponds, and lakes. *Winter records:* 1 banded and photographed, Sterling, Jan 20, 1960 (Shaws-AFN14:313); 1, Moline, Rock Island Co, Jan 10, 1962 (Ely, PCP-AFN16:335); 1 injured and caught, Morton Arboretum, Dec 19, 1971 (AB26:375); Im ♂ at feeders, Salem, Marion Co, and Carbondale, Jackson Co, winter, 1972-73 (W. Jones, VK-AB27:625); Im ♂ at feeder, Shelbyville, Shelby Co, Jan 29, 1975 (RS, HDB). *High counts:* 85, Monroe Co (SBC), May 6, 1972; 105, Pike Co (SBC), May 5, 1973; 119, Cook Co (SBC), May 10, 1975.

Subspecies: The western Bullock's Oriole, *I. g. bullockii*, has been observed: 2 ♂, Horseshoe Lake, Alexander Co, May 8, 1965 (W. Southern). No specimen exists for state.

Rusty Blackbird *(Euphagus carolinus)*

Late Feburary — Late April
Mid-October — Mid-December

Status: Common migrant. Uncommon winter resident in central and south. Occasional winter resident in north.

Documentation: Specimen(s) — ♂, Wilkinson's Swamp, DeKalb Co, Oct 30, 1960 (NIU 755).

Remarks: Found in swamps and along woodland edge; at times can be found feeding in shallow water. *High counts:* 431, Mermet Lake Area (CBC), Dec 21, 1965 (AFN20:263); 615, Pere Marquette St Pk (CBC), Dec 26, 1965 (AFN20:265); 5,000 (in roost), Springfield (CBC), Dec 21, 1975 (AB30:437).

Brewer's Blackbird *(Euphagus cyanocephalus)*

Mid-March —Late April
Late October — Early December

Status: Uncommon and erratic migrant. Local uncommon summer resident in north. Rare winter resident.

Documentation: Specimen(s) — ♀, Carbondale, Jackson Co, Oct 28, 1940 (SIU A-66).

Remarks: Found in wet pastures and feed lots. A western species that is extending its range. Some plumages very close to that of Rusty Blackbird; great care should be taken in identification. Nesting has occurred near Zion, Lake Co, and Northfield, Cook Co, and probably other unknown areas in northern Illinois. *Summer records:* 2 pair seen carrying food, Waukegan, Aug 4, 1963 (CC); pairs, Waukegan and Skokie, summer, 1975 (CC, LB-AB29:982). *High counts:* 52, Pere Marquette St Pk, Dec 27, 1958 (AFN13:188); 20, Chandlerville, Cass Co, Dec 4, 1971 (HDB).

Great-tailed Grackle *(Quiscalus mexicanus)*

Status: Very rare vagrant.

Documentation: Specimen — ♀, north side sewage plant, Jacksonville, Oct 7, 1974 (ISM 605929).

Remarks: 1 record. First observed Oct 5, 1974 (Randall, 1975). Subspecies was determined to be *C. m. prosopidicola.*

Common Grackle *(Quiscalus quiscula)*

Late February — Late November

Status: Abundant migrant and summer resident. Common winter resident in south. Uncommon winter resident in north and central.

Documentation: Specimen(s) -- ♂, Springfield, Mar 23, 1973 (ISM 605659).

Remarks: Becoming ubiquitous, occurring in almost all habitats. During migration huge flocks occur, sometimes strung out for miles. *High counts:* 750,000, Crab Orchard NWR (CBC), Dec 27, 1956 (AFN11:168); 100,000, near Fairmont City, Madison Co, winter, 1969 (Wrischnik-IAB153:19); 75,000, Horsehsoe Lake (CBC), Dec 30, 1974 (AB29:414).

Brown-headed Cowbird *(Molothrus ater)*

Late February — Late November

Status: Common migrant and summer resident. Common winter resident in south. Uncommon winter resident in north and central.

Documentation: Specimen(s) — ♂, 1 mile west of Rosedale, Jersey Co, Jan 15, 1972 (ISM 605073).

Remarks: A parasitic nester. Has become more common as the country has opened up. Prefers open areas, but since cowbirds are raised by some woodland species, they also occur in woodlands. In winter, feedlots are a favorite area. *High counts:* 50,000, Crab Orchard NWR (CBC), Dec 31, 1958 (AFN13:187): 401, Pere Marquette St Pk (CBC), Dec 23, 1972 (AB27:374); 22, Chicago (CBC), Dec 29, 1973 (AB28:379); 20,000, Horsehsoe Lake (CBC), Dec 30, 1974 (AB29:414).

THRAUPIDAE: Tanagers.

Western Tanager *(Piranga ludoviciana)*

Status: Very rare vagrant.

Documentation: Photographic — ♂, Crabtree Nature Center, Cook Co, May 8, 1964 (Charles Westcott-on file ISM).

Remarks: There are other records of this western species but all lack sufficient details. *Records:* 1, near Rockford, May 5, 1916 (Nature Study Society of Rockford, 1917-18); 1, 5 miles northwest of Carbondale, Jackson Co, May 14, 1948 (S & P, 1955, p. 53); ♂ and ♀, Cook County Forest Preserve, July 7, 1955 (Thompson, 1955); ♂, Chesterfield, Macoupin Co, Aug 23, 1968 (Lehman, JEC-AFN23:65); 1, Glenview, Cook Co, May 4, 1969 (Spitzen-IAB151:15).

Scarlet Tanager *(Piranga olivacea)*

Late April — Early October

Status: Common migrant and uncommon summer resident.

Documentation: Specimen(s) — ♂, Decatur, Macon Co, Sep 21, 1975 (ISM 606282).

Remarks: Found in wooded areas. Prefers bottomland more than the Summer Tanager but does occur in upland forest. *Records:* 1, Barrington, Oct 19, 1968 (RR-AFN23:65); 2, Decatur, Nov 5, 1974 (RS); 1, Springfield, Apr 20, 1976 (HDB). *High counts:* 11 killed at TV tower, Sangamon Co, Sep 16-17, 1958 (Parmalee & Parmalee, 1959); 25, Vermilion Co (SBC), May 6, 1972; 24, Union Co (SBC), May 4, 1974; 48, Whiteside Co (SBC), May 10, 1975.

Summer Tanager *(Piranga rubra)*

Late April — Early September

Status: Common migrant and summer resident in south. Uncommon migrant and uncommon local summer resident in central. Occasional vagrant in north.

Documentation: Specimen(s) — ♂, Carbondale, Jackson Co, May 10, 1973 (ISM 605684).

Remarks: Found in upland woods. Records for north are probably over-migrants. *Records:* 1, Lake Forest, Lake Co, May 14, 1957 (Clow-AFN11:409); 1, Amboy, Lee Co, May 30, 1959 (PCP-AFN13:434); ♂ collected, Wheaton, DuPage Co, May 12, 1960 (NIU); ♂, Chicago, May 13, 1972 (CC-AB26:768); ♂, near Decatur, Apr 19, 1975 (RS); ♀, Springfield, Sep 25, 1975 (VK); 2, 1½ miles north of Cobden, Union Co, Oct 11, 1975 (William George). *High counts:* 19, Massac Co (SBC), May 5, 1973; 15, Jersey Co (SBC), May 10, 1975.

119

FRINGILLIDAE: Grosbeaks, Finches, Sparrows and Buntings.

Cardinal *(Cardinalis cardinalis)*

Status: Common permanent resident.
Documentation: Specimen(s) — ♂, 1 mile south of Eldred, Greene Co, Jan 15, 1972 (ISM 605140).
Remarks: This, the State Bird, is a familiar sight in residential areas and woodland. Numerically increases southward. *High counts:* 365, near Olney (CBC), Dec 28, 1957 (AFN12:175); 224, Clark Co (SBC), May 5, 1973; 439, Chicago North Shore (CBC), Dec 28, 1974 (AB29:410); 716, Crab Orchard NWR (CBC), Dec 28, 1974 (AB29:411).

Rose-breasted Grosbeak *(Pheucticus ludovicianus)*

Late April — Early October

Status: Common migrant. Common summer resident in north and central. Rare summer resident in only upper portion of southern region.
Documentation: Specimen(s) — ♂, east of Springfield, Sep 29, 1972 (ISM 605420).
Remarks: Usually found in wooded areas. Some winter records not adequately documented; however, there are 3 acceptable records: ♂, Moline, Rock Island Co, Dec 11, 1961 (Park-IAB121:4); 1 photographed, Westville, Vermilion Co, Jan 2-19, 1975 (Campbell-AB29:699); 1, Winnetka, Cook Co, Nov 1975 - Mar 1976 (AB30:428). *High counts:* 122, Cook Co, and 122, McHenry Co (SBC), May 6, 1972.

Black-headed Grosbeak *(Pheucticus melanocephalus)*

Status: Very rare vagrant.
Documentation: Photographic — ♂ at feeder, Carbondale, Jackson Co, mid-February - Mar 23, 1972 (Kleen, 1972).
Remarks: 5 records. A western species. *Other records:* ♂ photographed at feeder, Rockford, Jan 17, 1965 (J. Sullivan, WS); ♂, Carpenter Park, Springfield, Nov 24, 1973 (HDB); ♂, Wilmette, May 21, 1974 (AB28:809); Im ♂, Salem, Marion Co, Jan 29 - Mar 24, 1976 (Horsman, BP).

Blue Grosbeak *(Guiraca caerulea)*

Mid-May — Early September

Status: Uncommon migrant and summer resident in south and western part of central. Rare migrant and summer resident in remainder of central. Rare vagrant in north.
Documentation: Specimen — ♂, 1 mile southeast of Dongola, Union Co, May 22, 1976 (ISU 1700).
Remarks: Found along roadside, usually in short shrubs. Very local in distribution. *Records:* 1, Quincy, May 22, 1955 (TEM-AFN9:335); 1, Jackson Co, June 6, 1955 (Brewer, Hardy-AFN9:382); 1, Jackson Park, Chicago, May 18, 1964 (Baldwin-IAB130:18); nest, near Henry, Marshall Co, July 5, 1965 (Miller); ♂ injured (later died), Chicago, Apr 5, 1969 (H.T. Dean-AFN23:597);

Ad feeding young, Salem, Marion Co, Aug 13 & 14, 1971 (Jones-AB25:865); ♂ and juvenile, Mason State Forest, July 19, 1973 (HDB); 3, Jersey Co (SBC), May 4, 1974; 9 pairs, Mason Co, summer, 1974 (HDB); 1, Bluff Springs, Cass Co, Aug 4, 1974 (PW, RQR); 2, Charleston, Coles Co, Sep 28, 1974 (LBH-AB29:67); ♀, Decatur, Oct 11, 1974 (RS); 1, near Chandlerville, Cass Co, Apr 24, 1976 (RS, WO, HDB). *High count:* 18, Massac Co (SBC), May 6, 1972.

Indigo Bunting *(Passerina cyanea)*

Late April — Mid-October

Status: Abundant migrant and summer resident. Very rare winter resident in south and central.
Documentation: Specimen(s) — ♂, Germantown, Woodford Co, May 15, 1972 (ISM 605610).
Remarks: Found along roadsides and forest edge. *Winter records:* 1, near Pere Marquette St Pk, Dec 30, 1950 - Jan 1, 1951 (Bremser, Link-AFN5:134); 1 banded, Union County Refuge, Dec 31, 1972 - Jan 24, 1973 (Kleen, 1973); 2, Pike Co, Dec 21, 1974 (RQR, HDB). *High counts:* 158, St. Clair Co (SBC), May 6, 1972; 144, Crawford Co (SBC), May 4, 1974; 362, Pope Co (SBC), May 10, 1975; 145 (Route 46, BBS), Cumberland Co and Jasper Co, June 1, 1975 (M.C. Frazier-U.S. Fish & Wildlife Service, 1976, p. 676).

Lazuli Bunting *(Passerina amoena)*

Status: Very rare vagrant.
Documentation: Photographic — Im ♂ at feeder, Elgin, Kane Co, Dec 17-21, 1973 (RM, LB-on file ISM).
Remarks: 1 record. Another record of this western species is reported as seen near Pere Marquette St Pk in 1950, but no date or description is available (Link-AFN5:134).

[Painted Bunting *(Passerina ciris)*]

Status: Hypothetical.
Remarks: 3 reports with little or no details: ♀, along roadside in Wabash Co, June 10, 1871 (Ridgway, 1889); 1 (sex not given) Decatur, May 25, 1963 (Rauch and Richl-IAB129:6); ♂, north side of Chicago, Oct 1, 1967 (Schulze-IAB148:19); Could occur as an over-migrant, or might be escaped cage birds.

Dickcissel *(Spiza americana)*

Late April — Late August

Status: Abundant migrant and summer resident in central and south. Fairly common migrant and summer resident in north. Very rare winter resident.
Documentation: Specimen(s) — ♂, Beverly, Adams Co, Aug 19, 1972 (ISM 605662).
Remarks: Found in open areas, especially clover fields and roadside bushes; perches on telephone wires and fences. In early fall seems to disappear but can usually be found sulking in weedy fields. *Winter records:* 1 collected,

Olney, Dec 26, 1955 (Shaw-IAB97:11); 1, Princeton, Bureau Co, Dec 30, 1961 (AFN24:313); 1, Shelby Co, Dec 23, 1965 (HDB); 1, Adams Co, Nov 16, 1971 (JF-AB26:73); 1 banded, Charleston, Coles Co, Dec 8, and later observed, Dec 23, 1974 (LBH-AB29:68); 1, Horsehsoe Lake, Alexander Co, Jan 3, 1976 (WO, PW, HDB). *Other records:* 3, Evanston, Oct 15, 1974 (LB, GR). *High count:* 296, St. Clair Co (SBC), May 6, 1972.

Evening Grosbeak *(Hesperiphona vespertina)*

Mid-October — Mid-April

Status: Uncommon and irregular migrant and winter resident in north and central. Rare migrant and winter resident in south.

Documentation: Specimen(s) — ♂, Quincy, Adams Co, Feb 27, 1973 (ISM 605758).

Remarks: A large winter finch. Most frequently seen at bird feeders; can also be found in river bottoms where it is especially fond of box elder trees. Some winter, but most occur during migration to and from the coast. *Records:* 1, Grand Detour, Ogle Co, Apr 8, 1959 (LJ-AFN13:376); 1, Decatur, May 11, 1962 (TN-AFN16:420); 2, Grafton, Jersey Co, Oct 31, 1965 (SV); 1, Vienna, Johnson Co, Nov 29, 1968 (RM-AFN23:65); 8, Olney, Richland Co, Dec 23, 1968 (AFN23:294); 1, Charleston, Coles Co, May 10, 1969 (LBH-AFN23:597); 4, Union Co (CBC), Dec 31, 1972 (AB27:376); 1, Carterville, Williamson Co, May 9, 1973 (MH-AB27:780). *High counts:* 65, Oregon (CBC), Jan 5, 1969 (IAB149:27); 60, Chautauqua NWR, Dec 23, 1975 (AB30:427); 58, Crab Orchard NWR (CBC), Jan 4, 1976 (AB30:429).

Purple Finch *(Carpodacus purpureus)*

Mid-September — Early May

Status: Common migrant. Common winter resident in south, uncommon winter resident in north and central. [Formerly very rare summer resident in north.]

Documentation: Specimen(s) — ♀, Quincy, Jan 20, 1973 (ISM 605627).

Remarks: Found in river bottoms, where sycamore trees are favored, and in other woodland associations; comes readily to feeders. *2 old breeding records:* Set of eggs, Polo, Ogle Co (Cook, 1888); 1 egg, Waukegan, May 13, 1875 (Cory, 1909). *Other records:* 1, Shirland, Winnebago Co, Aug 26, 1972 (LJ-AB27:70); 1, Peoria, May 27, 1973 (Humphries-AB27:780); 1, near Decatur, Sep 7, 1974 (RP); 1, Wauconda, Lake Co, Aug 22, 1976 (LB). *High count:* 200, Rockford, Sep 30, 1957 (LJ-AFN12:35).

House Finch *(Carpodacus mexicanus)*

Status: Very rare vagrant.

Documentation: Photographic — ♂ at feeder, Glenview, Cook Co, Oct 1973 - Mar 1, 1974 (LB-on file ISM).

Remarks: 3 records. Probably from introduced East Coast population which is rapidly expanding. *Other records:* ♀ at feeder photographed, Mt. Vernon, mid-Nov 1971 - late Dec 1971 (Hannah-IAB160:20-21); ♀, Lincoln Park, Chicago, Oct 1, 1972 (CC-AB27:70).

Pine Grosbeak *(Pinicola enucleator)*

Late November — Early March

Status: Rare irregular winter resident in north. Very rare winter resident in central and south.

Documentation: Specimen(s) — ♂, DeKalb Co, Jan 31, 1972 (NIU 3063).

Remarks: Usually found in coniferous areas; has been found many times feeding on high-bush cranberry, hemlock, and ash. One of largest invasions occurred in early 1972 but was confined mainly to north. *Records:* 1, Quincy, Dec 4, 1956 (TEM-AFN11:270); 1, Rockton, Winnebago Co, Nov 24, 1957 (LJ-AFN12:35); 2, Morton Arboretum, Nov 28, 1957 (Campbell-AFN12:35); 8, Skokie, Cook Co, Feb 23, 1958 (Lehmann-AFN12:284); 1, St. Joseph, Champaign Co, Apr 7, 1962 (PN-AFN16:420); 1, Chicago, Dec 2, 1963 (CC-AFN18:360); 3, Pere Marquette St Pk, Dec 20, 1969 (Weber-AFN24:313); 2, Crab Orchard NWR, Dec 30, 1972 (G. Cooper-AB27:369). *High counts:* 25, Rockford, Mar 19, 1972 (WS-AB26:613); 30, Chicago, Jan 30 - Mar 4, 1972 (AB26:613).

[European Goldfinch *(Carduelis carduelis)*]

Status: Hypothetical. Probable escapes.

Remarks: Several old records plus 2 recent records. However, since there is no known colony now existent and wild birds from Europe seem a remote possibility, these birds should be considered escapes. *Records:* 1 with several hundred American Goldfinches, Quincy, Oct 26, 1957 (TEM-AFN12:36); ♂ photographed (by PW), Wilmette, Jan 31, 1971 (RR-AB25:585).

Hoary Redpoll *(Carduelis hornemanni)*

Late November — Early March

Status: Very rare winter resident in north.

Documentation: Specimen(s) — Ad ♀, Cook Co, Mar 1845 (USNM 83394).

Remarks: Great care should be taken in identification since it closely resembles the common Redpoll. *Few recent records:* 1, Evanston, Cook Co, Oct & Nov 3, 1968 (JG, Ware, Campbell-AFN23:65); 1, Glenview, Cook Co, Mar 2, 1969 (Palmquist-AFN23:488); 1, Barrington, Dec 18, 1969 (CW-AFN24:510); 1, Rockford, Mar 5, 1972 (LB, VK, GR-AB26:613).

Common Redpoll *(Carduelis flammea)*

Early November — Early March

Status: Uncommon and irregular migrant and winter resident in north. Occasional irregular migrant and winter resident in central. Very rare winter resident in south.

Documentation: Specimen(s) — ♂, 2 miles north of Nutwood, Jersey Co, Feb 26, 1972 (ISM 605107).

Remarks: Found in open weedy areas and in white birch, and conifer stands. Last big erruption year was 1971-72. *Records:* ♀ collected, near Glenwood, Cook Co, May 10, 1956 (Levy, 1963); 7, Springfield, Dec 22, 1957 (AFN12:178); 1, Peoria, Apr 12, 1966 (AFN20:515); 6, Olney, Richland Co,

Dec 27, 1969 (AFN24:306); 145, Morton Arboretum (CBC), Dec 21, 1969 (AFN24:311); 34, Urbana, Dec 28, 1969 (Roth, Clemans-AFN24:315); 96, Chicago (CBC), Dec 26, 1971 (AB26:370); 250, Rockford, Jan 25, 1972 (Shaws); 1, Beall Woods St Pk, Wabash Co, Feb 5, 1972 (R. Dolphin); 25, near Meredosia, Morgan Co, Feb 19, 1972 (PW); 4, Charleston, Coles Co, Feb 23 - Mar 16, 1972 (LBH-AB26:613); 62, Rockford, Mar 18, 1972 (HDB); 7, Kane Co (SBC), May 6, 1972; 30, Chicago area, Nov 15, 1975 (RS, HDB); 12, Jacksonville, Morgan Co, Nov 16, 1975 (WO).

Pine Siskin *(Carduelis pinus)*

Early October — Early May

Status: Fairly common but erratic migrant and winter resident. Very rare summer resident in central.
Documentation: Specimen(s) — ♂, Quincy, Jan 13, 1973 (ISM 605623).
Remarks: Usually found in conifer areas; also found in certain deciduous trees like sweetgum and white birch. At times occurs in large flocks. Seems to be a population that passes on migration about every year and some that stay for winter. Some winters does not occur at all, or in very limited numbers, such as 1974-75. *Breeding record:* Nest with young, I.S.U., Normal, McLean Co, May 29, 1973 (RS-AB27:780); *Other records:* 2, Chandlerville, Cass Co, May 20, 1972 (HDB); 41, Kane Co (SBC), May 6, 1972. *High counts:* 598, Morton Arboretum (CBC), Dec 19, 1971 (AB26:375); 500, Illinois Beach St Pk, Oct 25, 1975 (GR, LC).

American Goldfinch *(Carduelis tristis)*

Early May — Mid-November

Status: Common migrant and summer resident. Common winter resident.
Documentation: Specimen(s) — ♀, near Fort Chartres, Randolph Co, July 26, 1971 (ISM 604830).
Remarks: Found in open country, woodland edge and shrub areas. Although common at all seasons, definite migration does occur. *High counts:* Several hundred, Quincy, Oct 26, 1957 (TEM-AFN12:36); 500, near Schapville (CBC), Jan 1, 1964 (AFN18:221); 556, Chicago (CBC), Dec 26, 1971 (AB26:370); 600, Chillicothe (CBC), Jan 2, 1972 (AB26:371); 473, McLean Co (SBC), May 6, 1972; 446, Pike Co (SBC), May 5, 1973; 150, Crane Lake, Mason Co, Dec 15, 1973 (JF, HDB).

Red Crossbill *(Loxia curvirostra)*

Late October — Late April

Status: Fairly common but irregular winter resident in north and central. Rare winter resident in south. Rare summer resident in north and central.
Documentation: Specimen(s) — ♀, Bath, Mason Co, Aug 26, 1972 (ISM 605247).
Remarks: Associated with conifers. Seems to feed on a wider range of conifers than does the White-winged Crossbill. *Summer records:* Nest (failed due to House Sparrows, Forsythe, 1973), I.S.U., Normal, McLean Co, Apr 21, 1973

(RS, DBi-AB27:780); 5, Decatur, June 2, 1973 (FI-AB27:780); 10, Springfield, Aug 9, 1972 (HDB). *High counts:* 53, Crane Lake (CBC), Dec 16, 1972 (AB27:369); 31, Urbana (CBC), Dec 16, 1972 (AB27:377); 66, Barrington (CBC), Dec 27, 1972 (AB27:365); 35, Crab Orchard NWR, Mar 10, 1973 (VK-AB27:625); 11, McHenry Co (SBC), May 5, 1973; 100, Illinois Beach St Pk, Oct 25, 1975 (GR, LC).

White-winged Crossbill *(Loxia leucoptera)*

Late November — Late March

Status: Uncommon and irregular winter resident in north. Occasional winter resident in central. Very rare winter resident in south.
Documentation: Specimen(s) — ♂, 2 miles south of Bath, Mason Co, Feb 11, 1966 (ISM 603923).
Remarks: ·Favors Norway spruce and hemlock. Does not usually associate with Red Crossbill but at times may feed in same trees. *Records:* 47, Morton Arboretum (CBC), Dec 26, 1965 (AFN20:264); 5, near Cobden, Union Co, Feb 7, 1966 (George, 1968); 25, Winnebago Co, Jan 23, 1972 (AB26:613); 75, Rockford, Feb 11, 1972 (WS); ♀, Springfield, Apr 7, 1972 (HDB); 1, Barrington, May 30, 1973 (LB-AB27:781); 1, Illinois Beach St Pk, Sep 29, 1973 (CC-AB28:62); 1, Charleston, Coles Co, Apr 10, 1974 (LBH-AB28:810); 15, Cook Co (SBC), May 4, 1974; 1, Winnetka, Cook Co, May 15, 1974 (RR-AB28:810); 6, Union County State Forest, Jan 2, 1976 (Biggers).

Green-tailed Towhee *(Pipilo chlorurus)*

Status: Very rare vagrant.
Documentation: Sight record with acceptable details — 1, Lincoln Park, Chicago, June 1, 1954 (Eiseman and McQuate, 1954).
Remarks: 5 records. Normally a southwestern species. *Other records:* 1, Bushnell, McDonough Co, Dec 8, 1952 - Mar 9, 1953 (S & P, 1955, p. 55); 1 with White-crowned Sparrows, north of Murphysboro, Jackson Co, Apr 17, 1953 (Brewer-AFN7:276); 1, Rockford, Jan 20 - Feb 9, 1960 (Colehour-AFN14:313); 1 at feeder, Havana, Mason Co, Dec 1968 (Bellrose-AFN23:296).

Rufous-sided Towhee *(Pipilo erythrophthalmus)*

Late March — Late October

Status: Common migrant and summer resident. Fairly common winter resident in south. Uncommon winter resident in north and central.
Documentation: Specimen(s) — ♀, Springfield, Apr 22, 1974 (ISM 605907).
Remarks: Found on forest edge. *Records:* 3, Beverly (CBC), Dec 22, 1972 (AB27:366). 1, Barrington (CBC), Dec 27, 1972 (AB27:365). *High counts:* 31, near Olney (CBC), Dec 26, 1963 (AFN18:221); 42, Coles Co (SBC), May 6, 1972; 79, Vermilion Co (SBC), May 4, 1974; 84, Will Co (SBC), May 10, 1975; 44, Horsehsoe Lake (CBC), Jan 3, 1976 (AB30:432).
Subspecies: The Spotted Towhee *(P. e. arcticus)* is a rare migrant and winter resident. *Records:* 1, Murphysboro, Jackson Co, Dec 27, 1954 (Brewer, Hardy-AFN9:262); 1, Morton Arboretum, Dec 31, 1961 (AFN16:211);

♂ banded and photographed, Harrison, Winnebago Co, Dec 26, 1961 (LJ-AFN16:335); 1 banded and photographed, Tinley Park Forest Preserve, Cook Co, Oct 18, 1964 (KB-IAB132:11); 2 near Stonington, Christian Co, Feb 22, 1971 (HDB); 1 near Browning, Schuyler Co, Dec 15, 1973 (PW-AB28:380).

Lark Bunting *(Calamospiza melanocorys)*

Early September — Early May

Status: Rare vagrant.
Documentation: Photographic — ♂, near Chillicothe, Peoria Co, May 5, 1968 (Ralph Scott-on file ISM).
Remarks: 9 records. A western species. Should be looked for in feedlots with House Sparrows, at feeders, and in open areas along fences. *Other records:* 1, Rockford, Mar 18, 1949 (S & P, 1955, p. 56); 1, Lake Calumet, Sep 4, 1949 (S & P, 1955, p. 55); 1, Evanston, Sep 27, 1969 (Evanston Bird Club-IAB153:16); ♂, Flora, Clay Co, Feb 27, 1971 (VK-AB25:587); ♂, Marion Co, May 1, 1971 (Jones, Horsman-AB25:753); ♂, Northwestern University, Cook Co, May 16, 1971 (VK, CC-AB25:753); ♂ photographed (on file ISM), Olympia Fields, Cook Co, Mar 17, 1974 (Aura Duke); 1, Chicago, Apr 11, 1974 (M. Hogg-AB28:810).

Savannah Sparrow *(Passerculus sandwichensis)*

Mid-March — Mid-May
Early September — Mid-November

Status: Common migrant. Fairly common summer resident in north and rare summer resident in central. Uncommon winter resident in south. Rare winter resident in central and north.
Documentation: Specimen(s) — ♂, near Carbondale, Jackson Co, Nov 11, 1971 (ISM 605481).
Remarks: Inhabits grassland. In winter likes grassy corn stubble. *Summer records:* 1, Eureka, Woodford Co, summered, 1967 (Guth-AFN21:578); 1 carrying food, Chandlerville, Cass Co, June 23, 1974 (HDB); 1, Cass Co, July 26, 1975 (RP-AB29:982); 24 (Route 2, BBS), Ogle Co and Carroll Co, June 8, 1975 (LJ-U.S. Fish & Wildlife Service, 1976, p. 678). *Winter records:* 1, Gardner, Grundy Co, Dec 28, 1969 (CC); 3, Pere Marquette St Pk (CBC), Dec 26, 1971 (AB26:376); 38, Horseshoe Lake (CBC), Jan 3, 1976 (AB30:432). *High counts:* 50, Cook Co (SBC), May 6, 1972; 72, Sangamon Co, May 8, 1976 (HDB).

Sharp-tailed Sparrow *(Ammospiza caudacuta)*

Early May — Late May
Mid-September — Late October

Status: Uncommon migrant. [Formerly very rare summer resident in north?]
Documentation: Specimen(s) — ♀, Orion, Rock Island Co, Oct 6, 1959 (PM 549.1.1).
Remarks: Inhabits wet grassy areas and lakeshores with grasses and cattails. More numerous in fall than spring and arrives much later in spring than most

sparrows. Breeding now uncertain; old record of nest and eggs taken (no date) near Lake Calumet (Woodruff, 1907). *Records:* 2, Waukegan, Oct 1, 1967 (CC); 1, Sangchris St Pk, May 13, 1971 (HDB); 1, Powderhorn Lake, Cook Co, May 16, 1971 (B. Tweit, CC, LB-AB25:753); 1, Goose Lake Prairie, June 6, 1971 (LB, CC-AB25:865); 1, near Havana, Aug 24, 1974 (RS, HDB); 1, Illinois Beach St Pk, Nov 2, 1975 (CC). *High count:* 10, Evanston, Sep 20, 1975 (LB).

LeConte's Sparrow *(Ammospiza leconteii)*

Mid-March — Late April
Early October — Mid-November

Status: Uncommon migrant. Occasional winter resident in south. Rare winter resident in central and north. [Formerly summer resident in north and possibly central.]
Documentation: Specimen(s) — ♂, 1 mile south of Glenwood, Cook Co, Jan 16, 1954 (Levy, 1963).
Remarks: Inhabits various grasses and fallow fields. *Last breeding record:* Nest with 3 eggs, Evergreen Park, Cook Co, May 30, 1932 (Hammond, 1943). *Winter records:* 1, near Browns, Edwards Co, Dec 27, 1956, and 1, near Royalton, Franklin Co, Jan 8, 1957 (Graber, 1957); 1 collected, Quail Research Area, Jackson Co, Feb 6, 1957 (SIU); 1, Mason Co, Nov 28, 1970 (HDB); 1, Christian Co, Dec 5, 1970 (HDB); 1, Beverly, Adams Co, Dec 23, 1971 (JF-AB26:368); 4 banded from flock of 12, near Carbondale, Jackson Co, Jan 10, 1972 (VK, DH-AB26:613); 1, Dundee, Kane Co, Jan 5, 1975 (Dillon, RM-AB29:699). *Other records:* 1, Chicago, May 14, 1975 (LB-AB29:862). *High counts:* 11 in one field, Mason Co, Nov 8, 1975 (RS, HDB).

Henslow's Sparrow *(Ammodramus henslowii)*

Mid-April — Mid-October

Status: Occasional migrant. Very local summer resident in north and central. Very rare winter resident in south.
Documentation: Specimen(s) — ♂, Beach, Lake Co (Illinois Beach St Pk), Nov 12, 1927 (Stevenson & Brodkorb, 1933).
Remarks: A secretive sparrow. Inhabits tall grassland and fallow fields. No recent valid winter records. *Summer records:* Nests every year in vicinity of Beverly, Adams Co (JF); and at Goose Lake Prairie (DBi); some noted in Jo Daviess Co, between July 26 - Aug 4, 1961 (Peaslee-IAB122:18). *Other records:* 1, Navy pier, Chicago, Apr 12, 1957 (Eisemen & Shank, 1962); 1, Mark Twain NWR, Oct 18, 1964 (RA); 1, Evanston, Apr 26, 1969 (CC); 2, Evanston, May 1, 1971 (LB, CC-IAB159:13); 1, Argenta at TV tower, night of Oct 28-29, 1972 (INHS); 1, Decatur, Oct 13, 1974 (RS); 1, Liberty, Adams Co, Apr 15, 1976 (JF-AB30:850).

Grasshopper Sparrow *(Ammodramus savannarum)*

Mid-April — Early October

Status: Common migrant and summer resident. Very rare winter resident in central and south.

Documentation: Specimen(s) — ♂, Creve Coeur, Tazewell Co, Apr 29, 1972 (ISM 605569).

Remarks: Found in pastures and fallow fields. *Winter records:* ♂ collected, Champaign, Jan 9, 1932 (Brodkorb, 1934); 1 banded, Carbondale, Jackson Co, Jan 10, 1972 (VK, DH-AB26:613); 1, Quincy, Nov 1, 1963 (TEM). *High counts:* 31, Mason Co (SBC), May 5, 1973; 26, Lawrence Co (SBC), May 10, 1975.

[Baird's Sparrow *(Ammodramus bairdii)*]

Status: Hypothetical.

Remarks: A species of the great plains. Specimen needed to confirm this species in state. Several old sight records with no details and 2 (1 observer) recent sight records; both at Evanston, Apr 4-12, 1968 (RR) and Oct 15, 1975 (GR).

Vesper Sparrow *(Pooecetes gramineus)*

Late March — Late October

Status: Common migrant. Common summer resident in north. Uncommon summer resident in central and south. Rare winter resident.

Documentation: Specimen(s) — ♂, Victor Twp, DeKalb Co, June 5, 1966 (NIU 2236).

Remarks: Found along fence rows and in fallow and plowed fields. *Winter records:* 1, Waukegan, Jan 1, 1961 (AFN15:215); 1, Winnebago Co, Jan 29, 1972 (WS-AB26:613); 1 photographed, Barrington, Dec 27, 1972 (RM-AB27:365). *High counts:* 41, DeKalb Co (SBC), May 4, 1974; 25 (Route 15, BBS), Kankakee Co and Livingston Co, June 27, 1975 (J.W. Olson-U.S. Fish & Wildlife Service, 1976, p. 680).

Lark Sparrow *(Chondestes grammacus)*

Mid-April — Mid-September

Status: Uncommon migrant. Locally common summer resident in western half of state. Rare migrant and summer resident in eastern half of state.

Documentation: Specimen — ♀, 2 miles west of Manito, Mason Co, Aug 1, 1974 (ISM 605926).

Remarks: Found in sand prairie areas of state where it inhabits hedgerows, woodland edge, weedy fields and pastures. One of most common breeding species in sand areas of Mason, Cass, Tazewell, and Henderson counties. Winter records are unsatisfactory. *Records:* Pair with fledged young, near Pinckneyville, Perry Co, June 1956 (George, 1968); nest, Athens, Menard Co, June 21, 1958 (TN); nest, northwest Winnebago Co, Aug 1959 (LJ-AFN13:434); nest with 4 young, Charleston, Coles Co, May 30, 1969 (LBH); small colony, Custer Park, Will Co, summer, 1973 (LB); nest, near Oregon, Ogle Co, May 14, 1965 (Wade); nest, Decatur, May 1971 (TN). *High count:* 107, Mason Co (SBC), May 5, 1973.

Bachman's Sparrow *(Aimophila aestivalis)*

Early April — Late September

Status: Rare migrant and summer resident in south. Very rare vagrant in central and north. [May have formerly nested in central and north].
Documentation: Specimen(s) — ♂, near Champaign, Apr 2, 1932 (Brodkorb, 1934).
Remarks; Inhabits brushy hillsides. (For an excellent description of habitat, see Mengel, 1965). Records for central and north may represent over-migrants. Seems to be declining in Illinois; was known in north and central from 1920's to 1950's but now can seldom be found in south. *Records:* 1, Crab Orchard NWR, Apr 29, 1972 (VK, Biggers-AB26:768); 1, Ferne Clyffe St Pk, Johnson Co, Apr 29, 1972 (RR, JG-AB26:768); 1, Pope Co, summer, 1974 (Grabers); 2, Jackson Co, Sep 7, 1975 (BP).

Black-throated Sparrow *(Amphispiza bilineata)*

Status: Very rare vagrant.
Documentation: Photographic — 1, near Rockton, Winnebago Co, May 4, 1960 (Ralph Morse-on file ISM).
Remarks: 3 records. Southwestern species. *Other records:* Im, Lincoln Park, Chicago, Sep 11-13, 1948 (Nork, CC-AFN3:19); 1, Chicago, spring, 1961 (Montaque-AFN15:416).

Dark-eyed Junco *(Junco hyemalis)*

Late September — Late April

Status: Abundant migrant and winter resident.
Documentation: Specimen(s) — ♂, Dickson Mounds, Fulton Co, Jan 18, 1973 (ISM 605522).
Remarks: Found along woodland edge and a variety of other habitats. *Records:* Ad collected, 1 mile from Ohio River, near Elizabethtown, Hardin Co, June 9, 1881 (Forbes, 1881); 11, Kane Co (SBC), May 6, 1972; 21, McHenry Co (SBC), May 5, 1973; 1, Sangamon Co, June 5, 1974 (VK-AB28:810). *High counts:* 1,218, Barrington (CBC), Dec 29, 1971 (AB26:368); 1,167, Morton Arboretum (CBC), Dec 16, 1973 (AB28:383); 1,642, Chillicothe (CBC), Dec 30, 1973 (AB28:380); 1,832, Crab Orchard NWR (CBC), Dec 28, 1974 (AB29:411).
Subspecies: Besides the regular wintering subspecies *(J. h. hyemalis), J. h. shufeldti* and *J. h. montanus* (Oregon Juncos) occur as rare migrants and winter resident, and both have been collected. The subspecies *J. h. aikeni* (White-winged Junco) is hypothetical in state. *2 unverified records:* 1, Rockford, Apr 2-4, 1913 (Nature Study Society of Rockford, 1917-18); 1, Rockford, Dec 24, 1950 (Seal, Sheagren-AFN5:135).

Gray-headed Junco *(Junco caniceps)*

Status: Very rare vagrant.
Documentation: Photographic — 1, Springfield, Feb 9-26, 1974 (HDB, 1974).
Remarks: 2 records. A Rocky Mountain species. *Other record:* 1 banded, Blue Island, Cook Co, May 8, 1965 (KB).

Tree Sparrow *(Spizella arborea)*

Early November — Mid-April

Status: Common migrant and winter resident.
Documentation: Specimen(s) — ♂, Beverly, Adams Co, Dec 23, 1971 (ISM 605035).
Remarks: Prefers weedy fields and other open areas. Occasionally appears in large flocks, but most often occurs in groups of 10-30; at times flocks with other fringillids. *Records:* 1, Evanston, Oct 7, 1972 (LB); 9, Lake Co (SBC), May 10, 1975; 1, Winnegabo Co, Oct 17, 1975 (LJ). *High counts:* 926, Rockford (CBC), Dec 26, 1955 (AFN10:166); 2,006, western Mercer Co (CBC), Dec 30, 1962 (AFN17:206); 2,000, Barrington (CBC), Dec 20, 1970 (AB25:349); 1,407, Pere Marquette St Pk (CBC), Dec 29, 1973 (AB28:385); 700, Mason Co, Feb 23, 1974 (VK, HDB).

Chipping Sparrow *(Spizella passerina)*

Early April — Late October

Status: Common migrant and summer resident. Very rare winter resident.
Documentation: Specimen(s) — Im ♀, east of Springfield, Oct 24, 1971 (ISM 604910).
Remarks: Found in orchards, pastures, and residential areas. Seems to be population decline in last half century (Graber & Graber, 1963). Present winter records are sketchy; future records should be made with great care. *Records:* 3 at feeders, Lake Co, Dec 23, 1961 (RR-AFN16:211); 1, Morton Arboretum, Dec 26, 1966 (AFN21:255); 1, Pere Marquette St Pk, Dec 26, 1970 (Shaefer, Nelson-AB25:358); 1, near Olney, Dec 26, 1973 (Silva-AB28:377). *High counts:* 69, Coles Co (SBC), May 6, 1972; 114, Jersey Co (SBC), May 5, 1973.

Clay-colored Sparrow *(Spizella pallida)*

Late April — Late May
Mid-September — Mid-October

Status: Occasional migrant. Rare summer resident (breeding?) in north.
Documentation: Specimen(s) — ♀, 2 miles north of McLean, McLean Co, Apr 25, 1975 (ISU 1425).
Remarks: Found in open brushy areas and hedgerows. Evidence for breeding in state is slight. In fall closely resembles immature Chipping Sparrow and care should be taken in identification. *Summer records:* 2 ♂ singing, Lake Co, July 1972 (GR, LB, CC-AB26:867). *Other records:* 3, Chicago, May 11, 1959 (Fetter-AFN13:376); 1, Evanston, Oct 15, 1966 (CC); 1, Pere Marquette St Pk , Apr 27, 1971 (SV-AB25:753); 1, Evanston, Oct 2, 1971 (LB, GR, JG-AB26:73); 6, Cook Co (SBC), May 6, 1972; 1, Morgan Co, May 6, 1973 (P. Gibson, WO-AB27:781); 1, Normal, McLean Co, Apr 22, 1974 (DBi-AB28:810); 6, Evanston, Sep 25, 1974 (RR-AB29:68); 1, Fulton Co, May 18, 1975 (RS-AB29:862).

Field Sparrow *(Spizella pusilla)*

Late March — Late October

Status: Common migrant and summer resident. Common winter resident in south. Uncommon winter resident in central and occasional winter resident in north.
Documentation: Specimen(s) — ♀, Carbondale, Jackson Co, Jan 7, 1973 (ISM 605487).
Remarks: Found in open brushy areas and along forest edge. *Records:* 66, Mermet Lake Area, Dec 21, 1965 (AFN20:263); 2 at feeder, near Elgin, Dec 27, 1973 (PW, VK); 61, Pere Marquette St Pk (CBC), Dec 29, 1973 (AB28:385). *High counts:* 149, McLean Co (SBC), May 5, 1973; 225, Will Co (SBC), May 4, 1974; 249, Crab Orchard NWR (CBC), Jan 4, 1976 (AB30:429).

Harris' Sparrow *(Zonotrichia querula)*

Late March — Mid-May
Late September — Early December

Status: Uncommon fall migrant in the western half of state and occasional fall migrant in the eastern half of state. Rare spring migrant and winter resident.
Documentation: Specimen(s) — ♀, 2 miles north of Cobden, Union Co, Mar 18, 1967 (SIU A-1677).
Remarks: Found in bushy areas, especially in multiflora rose hedge where it occurs with White-crowned Sparrow. *Records:* 1 banded, Rockford, Jan 1, 1960 (AFN14:205); 1, Deer Grove, Cook Co, Jan 31, 1965 (Campbell-AFN19:385); 1, Jackson Co, May 8, 1971 (VK-AB25:753); 2, Beverly, Adams Co, Dec 23, 1971 (JF-AB26:368); 2 banded, Union Co, Jan 8, 1972 (VK-AB26:613); 1, McLean Co (SBC), May 5, 1973. *High count:* 35-50, Bushnell, Nov 5, 1956 (LH-AFN11:30).

White-crowned Sparrow *(Zonotrichia leucophrys)*

Late April — Mid-May
Late September — Early December

Status: Fairly common migrant. Fairly common winter resident in south. Uncommon winter resident in central. Occasional winter resident in north.
Documentation: Specimen(s) — ♀, Evanston, May 17, 1973 (ISM 605664).
Remarks: Found in hedgerows, especially multiflora rose, weedy areas, and woods edge. Numbers wintering vary from year to year. *High counts:* 110, near Olney (CBC), Dec 27, 1969 (AFN24:306); 103, Decatur (CBC), Dec 26, 1971 (AB26:372); 800, Cook Co (SBC), May 6, 1972; 292, Crab Orchard NWR (CBC), Dec 1973 (AB28:380).
Subspecies: The northwestern race, *Z. l. gambelii,* has been collected in Illinois. Probably occurs every year, but few observes attempt to identify beyond species level. *Records:* 1 banded, Chicago, May 6, 1956 (KB-AFN10:338); 1 banded, Chicago, Oct 7, 1968 (KB-IAB149:12); 2, Fulton Co, Oct 11, 1971 (GR, LB-AB26:73); 1, near Beverly, Adams Co (CBC), Dec 21, 1974 (RQR, HDB).

Golden-crowned Sparrow *(Zonotrichia atricapilla)*

Status: Very rare vagrant in north.
Documentation: Specimen — Im ♂, Waukegan, Nov 28, 1935 (CAS 8175).
Remarks: 2 records. West coast species. *Other record:* 1 observed, Lincoln Park, Apr 29, 1942 (Clark & Nice, 1950).

White-throated Sparrow *(Zonotrichia albicollis)*

Mid-April — Mid-May
Late September — Mid-November

Status: Abundant migrant. Common winter resident in south. Uncommon winter resident in central and north.
Documentation: Specimen(s) — ♂, east of Springfield, Oct 12, 1972 (ISM 605309).
Remarks: Found in woods, woodland edge, thickets and weed patches. Usually occurs in large flocks during peak migration. *Records:* 531, Mermet Lake area, Dec 21, 1965 (AFN20:263); 1,000, Chicago, Apr 30, 1966 (CC, CW); 10, Chicago, Dec 23, 1972 (RR-AB27:368); 176, Crab Orchard NWR, Dec 30, 1972 (Bush-AB27:369); 84, Pere Marquette St Pk (CBC), Dec 29, 1973 (AB28:385); 328, Will Co (SBC), May 4, 1974.

Fox Sparrow *(Passerella iliaca)*

Mid-March — Mid-April
Early October — Late November

Status: Common migrant. Fairly common winter resident in south. Occasional winter resident in central and north.
Documentation: Specimen(s) — ♂, 3 miles south of Springfield, Oct 20, 1972 (ISM 605328).
Remarks: Found in brushy, weedy areas and woodland edge. *Records:* 13, Crane Lake area, Mason Co, Dec 18, 1971 (AB26:372); 14, Pere Marquette St Pk (CBC), Dec 26, 1971 (AB26:376); 2, Waukegan, Jan 1, 1972 (AB26:379); 2, Chicago, Dec 23, 1972 (RR-AB27:368); 4, Morton Arboretum, Dec 16, 1973 (AB28:383); 1, Springfield, Sep 27, 1975 (VK); 1, Lake Co (SBC), May 10, 1975. *High counts:* 22, Crab Orchard NWR, Jan 4, 1976 (AB30:429); 52, Sangamon Co, Mar 14, 1976 (HDB).

Lincoln's Sparrow *(Melospiza lincolnii)*

Late April — Late May
Mid-September — Early November

Status: Fairly common migrant. Occasional winter resident in south. Rare winter resident in north and central. [Formerly rare summer resident in north].
Documentation: Specimen(s) — ♂, 2 miles northwest of Easton, Mason Co, Oct 23, 1971 (ISM 604906).
Remarks: Found in weedy areas, wet bushy areas, and woodland. Old breeding records are from Cook Co (Woodruff, 1907) and Lake Co (S & P, 1955, p. 58). *Winter records:* 1, Great Lakes Naval Training Center, Lake Co, Dec 13, 1970 (LB, GR-AB25:587); 1, Pomona, Jackson Co, Feb 5, 1971

(VK-AB25:587); 1, Beverly, Adams Co, Dec 23, 1971 (Funks-AB26:368); 2, Crane Lake, Mason Co, Dec 18, 1971 (PW-AB26:372); 1, Morton Arboretum, Dec 19, 1971 (AB26:375); 1, Chautauqua NWR, Dec 31, 1971 (HDB); 1, Barrington, Dec 23, 1974 (RM-AB29:699). *High count:* 71, Cook Co (SBC), May 10, 1975.

Swamp Sparrow *(Melospiza georgiana)*

Late September — Mid-May

Status: Common migrant. Uncommon summer resident in north. Common winter resident in central and south. Uncommon winter resident in north.
Documentation: Specimen(s) — ♂, near Bluffs, Scott Co, Oct 7, 1972 (ISM 605874).
Remarks: Found in marshy areas and weed patches. *Records:* Nest, Lake Co, May 31, 1964 (MacMillan). *High counts:* 66, Chillicothe (CBC), Dec 29, 1968 (AFN23:296); 52, Lake Co (SBC), May 6, 1972; 188, Crane Lake (CBC), Dec 15, 1973 (AB28:381); 429, Pere Marquette St Pk, Dec 29, 1973 (AB28:385); 52, Morton Arboretum, Dec 16, 1973 (AB28:383); 194, Cook Co (SBC), May 10, 1975.

Song Sparrow *(Melospiza melodia)*

Mid-March — Early November

Status: Common migrant. Common summer resident in north and central. Fairly common summer resident in south. Common winter resident in south and central. Fairly common winter resident in north.
Documentation: Specimen(s) — ♂, 5 miles south of Timewell, Brown Co, Nov 10, 1971 (ISM 604948).
Remarks: Usually found in semiopen areas, especially along creeks, ditches, weed patches, and log piles. Breeding range may be expanding south. Migration pattern is poorly worked out in state; some individuals may be permanent residents. *High counts:* 79, Chicago (CBC), Dec 28, 1963 (AFN18:222); 312, Beverly (CBC), Dec 22, 1973 (AB28:377); 320, Pere Marquette St Pk (CBC), Dec 29, 1973 (AB28:385); 411, Will Co (SBC), May 4, 1974.

[McCown's Longspur *(Calcarius mccownii)*]

Status: Hypothetical.
Remarks: Coale (1877) states that 3 ♂ were obtained from a market (in Chicago?) which were supposedly shot at Urbana, but it is also believed that these specimens could have come from elsewhere. Other unverified records from Morton Arboretum (AFN15:213) and Rockford, which list 3 dates: Oct 15, Jan 7, and May 25, no years (Nature Study Society of Rockford, 1917-18).

Lapland Longspur *(Calcarius lapponicus)*

Mid-October — Mid-April

Status: Common but erratic migrant. Uncommon winter resident.
Documentation: Specimen(s) — ♂, Clinton Twp, DeKalb Co, May 13, 1967 (NIU 2462).

Remarks: Inhabits open areas. Likes short grassy fields as well as stubble and plowed fields. During snows, comes up to roads to feed with Horned Larks. At times occurs in large flocks. *Records:* 1, Lincoln Park, Chicago, Sep 14, 1968 (CC); 2, Evanston, Sep 19, 1975 (LB). *High counts:* 546, Rockford (CBC), Dec 26, 1955 (AFN10:166); 1,500, Urbana (CBC), Dec 29, 1956 (AFN11:171); 175, Morton Arboretum (CBC), Dec 26, 1965 (AFN20:264); 307, Decatur (CBC), Jan 2, 1967 (AFN21:253); 58, Barrington, Dec 27, 1967 (PD-AFN22:266); 535, DeKalb (CBC), Jan 2, 1972 (AB26:373); 200 near Sicily, Christian Co, Nov 18, 1973 (HDB); 150, Kane Co (SBC), May 4, 1974; 60, McHenry Co (SBC), May 4, 1974; 200, Olive Branch, Alexander Co, Jan 28, 1975 (RS, HDB).

Smith's Longspur *(Calcarius pictus)*

Mid-March — Early May
Mid-October — Mid-November

Status: Common spring migrant. Rare fall migrant in central. Occasional migrant in north. Rare migrant in south.

Documentation: Specimen(s) — ♀, near Sicily, Christian Co, Apr 16, 1972 (ISM 605148).

Remarks: Found in short grass, fallow and stubble fields; seldom comes to road as does Lapland Longspur. Probably more common in north and should be found in south more than records suggest. Observers tend to neglect field habitats. Winter records are questionable since winter-plumage longspurs are difficult to separate and no documentations of winter sightings are available. *Records:* 14, Joy, Mercer Co, mid-Oct 1958 (Green, RT-AFN13:37); 1, Urbana, Nov 10, 1963 (PN-AFN18:43); 1, Chicago, Apr 30, 1966 (CC, CW-AFN20:515); ♂, Lake Calumet, Apr 26, 1969 (CC-AFN23:597); 2, Valmeyer, Randolph Co, Nov 14, 1971 (Stricklings-AB26:73); several, Lawrence Co, Mar 30 & 31, 1974 (P. Roush-AB28:649); 2 collected, 3 miles northeast of Paw Paw, Lee Co, Apr 15, 1976 (Southern); 9, Sangamon Co, May 4, 1974 (HDB). *High counts:* 50, Moweaqua, Shelby Co, Apr 12, 1970 (HDB); 200, New City, Sangamon Co, Mar 28, 1971 (HDB); 500, near Meredosia, Morgan Co, Mar 31, 1972 (LB-AB26:613).

[Chestnut-collared Longspur *(Calcarius ornatus)*]

Status: Hypothetical.

Remarks: No specimens or other sufficient documentation. Could occur rarely during migration, and following records are probably correct. *Sight records, with little or no details:* Several, Cook Co, Apr 24, 1910 (Coale, 1910); 5, DuPage Co, Apr 20, 1912 (Eifrig, 1913); 1, Washington Park, Chicago, Apr 18, 1923 (S & P, 1955, p. 58); 2, Mattoon, Coles Co, Dec 31, 1968 (Stutesman-AFN23:298); 20, Shelbyville, Shelby Co, Dec 30, 1968 (Stutesman-AFN23:301).

Snow Bunting *(Plectrophenax nivalis)*

Late October — Late March

Status: Fairly common migrant and winter resident in north. Occasional migrant and winter resident in central. Very rare winter resident in south.
Documentation: Specimen(s) — ♂, 5 miles west of DeKalb, DeKalb Co, Mar 13, 1960 (NIU 1814).
Remarks: Found most frequently along roadsides and lake edges; also occurs in fields and other open, windswept areas. Should be found more in south since it is considered a casual winter visitant in Kentucky (Mengel, 1965). Usually found during snow periods but may be due to coming up to roads for feeding areas. *Records:* 40-50, Urbana, Feb 9, 1955 (Marvel, Robertson-AFN9:262); 4, Decatur, Dec 30, 1962 (AFN17:203); 1, Shelbyville Reservior, Shelby Co, Dec 27, 1967 (AFN22:274); 1, Chautauqua NWR, Dec 11, 1971 (HDB, JF); 1, Lawrence Co, Dec 23, 1973 and 1, Jan 6, 1974 (P. Roush-AB28:648); 6, Rend Lake, Nov 8, 1975 (BP, R. Hays); 1, Union Co, Jan 2, 1976 (PW, WO, B. Adams). *High counts:* 123, Barrington (CBC), Jan 1, 1969 (AFN23:243); 500, Sterling, Whiteside Co, Jan 9, 1971 (Shaws-IAB158:24); 780, DeKalb, Jan 2, 1972 (AB26:373); 600, Union, McHenry Co, Apr 6, 1975 (RR-AB29:862).

LITERATURE CITED

Allen, J.A.

    1881   Ridgway's Revised Catalogue of the Birds of Illinois. *Bull. of the Nuttall Ornithological Club*, 6:171-172.

American Ornithologists' Union

    1957   *Check-List of North American Birds.* Fifth Edition. Baltimore, Maryland. American Ornithologists' Union.

    1973   Thirty-second Supplement to the American Ornithologists' Union Check-List of North American Birds. *Auk*, 90:411-419.

    1976   Thirty-third Supplement to the American Ornithologists' Union Check-List of North American Birds. *Auk*, 93:875-879.

Audubon, John James

    1831   *Ornithological Biography.* Edinburg, Adam and Charles Black. Vol. I.

Balding, Terry

    1964   Ancient Murrelet Taken in Illinois. *Auk*, 81:443.

Barnes, R.M.

    1935   Bird Banding Wholesale. *Oologist*, 52:45.

Bartsch, Paul

    1922   An Inland Record for the Man-o'-War Bird. *Auk*, 39:249-250.

Bellrose, Frank

    1939   Prairie Falcon in Central Illinois. *Auk*, 56:75-76.

    1944   Bald Eagles Nesting in Illinois. *Auk*, 61:467-468.

Bennett, Esther

    1952   *Checklist of Birds of Southern Illinois.* Mimeographed at Southern Illinois University. Carbondale.

    1957   Nesting Birds of the Shoreline and Islands of Crab Orchard Lake, Illinois. *Trans. of the Illinois State Acad. of Science*, 50:259-264.

Binford, Laurence

    1957   *Illinois Bird Specimens in the University of Michigan Museum of Zoology.* Unpublished manuscript. 61 pp.

    1958   Marbled Godwit, Red Phalarope, and Northern Phalarope at Chicago. *The Audubon Bulletin*, 107:5-6.

Birkenholz, Dale

1958   Notes on a Wintering Flock of Long-eared Owls. *Trans. of Illinois State Acad. of Science*, 51:83-86.

Blackwelder, E.

1899   A Note on Kirtland's Warbler. *Auk*, 16:359-360.

Bohlen, H. David

1971   First Record in Illinois of Audubon Warbler *(Dendroica Auduboni-Townsend). The Audubon Bulletin*, 158:26.

1974   A Gray-headed Junco in Illinois. *Illinois Audubon Bulletin*, 169:13.

1975a   Ash-throated Flycatcher in Illinois. Summary of Records East of the Mississippi River. *Auk*, 92:165-166.

1975b   An Arctic Loon at Springfield, Illinois. *Illinois Audubon Bulletin*, 173:17-18.

Bohlen, H. David and Richard Sandburg

1975   Sight Record of the Sharp-tailed Sandpiper in Illinois. *Illinois Audubon Bulletin*, 172:4-5.

Brewer, Richard

1963   Ecological and Reproductive Relationships of Black-capped and Carolina Chickadees. *Auk*, 80:9-47.

Briggs, Shirley

1969   Some Notes on an Early Iowa Record and Paul Bartsch. *Iowa Bird Life*, 39:85-87.

Brodkorb, Pierce

1934   Notes from Central Illinois. *Auk*, 51:41.

Brooks, William

1965   Effect of Weather on Autumn Shorebird Migration in East-Central Illinois. *The Wilson Bulletin*, 77:45-54.

Bull, John

1974   *Birds of New York State.* Garden City, New York, Doubleday, Natural History Press.

Burr, Brooks M. and David M. Current

1974   The 1972-1973 Goshawk Invasion in Illinois. *Trans. of the Illinois State Acad. of Science*, 67:175-179.

1975   Status of the Gyrfalcon in Illinois. *The Wilson Bulletin*, 87:280-281.

Burr, Brooks M. and Steve D. Ogle

1973 A Large Hawk Flight at East Peoria. *Illinois Audubon Bulletin*, 165:41.

Bursewicz, John

1958 Record of Scissor-tailed Flycatcher. *The Audubon Bulletin*, 107:9.

Butler, Amos W.

1897 The Birds of Indiana. *Indiana Dept. Geology and Natural Resources*, 22nd Annual Report. Indianapolis.

Cahn, Alvin R.

1930 Additions to the Easter Birds of Little Egypt. *The Wilson Bulletin*, 42:214-215.

Clark, Charles T. and Margaret M. Nice

1950 William Dreuth's Study of Bird Migration in Lincoln Park, Chicago. *Chicago Acad. of Science Special Publ.*, No. 8.

Clemans, Alexa and George Kulesza

1973-74 Swallow-tailed Kite. *Champaign County Audubon Society Newsletter*, No. 9:4.

Coale, Henry K.

1877 McCown's Longspur in Illinois. *Bulletin of the Nuttall Ornithological Club*, 2:52.

1910 A New Bird for Illinois. *Auk*, 27:75.

1910 The Chestnut-collared Longspur in Illinois. *Auk*, 27:341-342.

1911 Clark's Nutcracker in Illinois. *Auk*, 28:266.

1912 Birds of Lake County. Chapter XIV of *A History of Lake County, Illinois*, by John J. Halsey. Published by Roy S. Bates.

1914 Richardson's Owl in Northeastern Illinois. *Auk*, 31:536.

1919 Magpie in Northeastern Illinois. *Auk*, 36:113-114.

1924 *Tyrannus verticalis*, A New Bird for Illinois. *Auk*, 41:603.

1925 Violet-green Swallow in Illinois. *Auk*, 42:137-138.

Cook, Wells W.

1888 Report on Bird Migration in the Mississippi Valley in the Years 1884 and 1885. *U.S. Dept. Agriculture Division of Economic Ornithology and Mammalogy*, Bulletin 2.

Cooke, May T.

1941   Returns from Banded Birds: Recoveries of Some Banded Birds of Prey. *Bird-Banding*, 12:157.

Cory, Charles B.

1909   The Birds of Illinois and Wisconsin. *Field Mus. Nat. Hist. (Zool. Ser.)*, Vol. 9. Pub. 131.

Deane, Ruthven

1903   Richardson's Owl in Illinois. *Auk*, 20:305.

1905   Additional Record of the European Widgeon. *Auk*, 22:76.

Dickinson, J.E.

1897   Notes from Northern Illinois. *The Wilson Bulletin*, 9:17-18.

Dillon, S. Tenison

1971   Additional Avian Species Seen at McGraw Wildlife Foundation. *The Audubon Bulletin*, 159:18-20.

1973   Continued Avian Census at McGraw Wildlife Foundation, Dundee. *Illinois Audubon Bulletin*, 165:42-43.

DuMont, Philip A.

1935   An Old Record of the Brown-headed Nuthatch in Iowa and Illinois. *The Wilson Bulletin*, 47:240.

Dwight, Jonathan, Jr.

1925   The Gulls of the World. *Amer. Mus. of Nat. Hist.*, Vol. 52, Art. 3, pp. 63-401.

Eifrig, Charles W.G.

1913   Notes on Some of the Rarer Birds of the Prairie Part of the Chicago Area. *Auk*, 30:236-240.

1915   Cory's Least Bittern in Illinois. *Auk*, 32:98-99.

Eiseman, Ralph M.

1957   An Additional Holboell's Grebe Specimen from Illinois. *The Audubon Bulletin*, 101:1.

Eiseman, Ralph M. and Nelda McQuate

1954   Green-tailed Towhee in Illinois. *The Audubon Bulletin*, 92:4.

Eiseman, Ralph M. and Max C. Shank

1962   Birds of the Chicago Navy Pier Area. *The Audubon Bulletin*, 122:1-11.

Ekblaw, George E.

1917   "Rantoul" and "Rantoul-Winter Record." *The Audubon Bulletin*, Spring, 1917:52, 54.

Farris, Allen L.

1970   Distribution and Abundance of the Gray Partridge in Illinois. *Trans. of the Illinois State Acad. of Science*, 63:240-245.

Forbes, Stephen A.

1881   The Snowbird in Southern Illinois in June. *Bulletin of the Nuttall Ornithological Club*, 6:180.

Ford, Edward R.

1932   The Season: Chicago Region. *Bird-Lore*, 34:344-345.

1956   Birds of the Chicago Region. *Chicago Acad. of Science, Special Publ.*, No. 12.

Ford, Edward R., Colin C. Sanborn, and C. Blair Coursen

1934   Birds of the Chicago Region. *Chicago Acad. of Science*, 5:17-80.

Forsythe, Carol J.

1973   Red Crossbill on a Very Busy Campus. *Illinois Audubon Bulletin*, 166:31-32.

Gault, Benjamin T.

1894   Kirtland's Warbler in Northeastern Illinois. *Auk*, 11:258.

1910   The Brown Pelican in Illinois. *Auk*, 27:75.

1922   *Checklist of the Birds of Illinois.* Chicago. Illinois Audubon Society.

George, William G.

1968   The Association of Invading White-winged Crossbills with a Southern Tree. *The Wilson Bulletin*, 80:496-497.

1968   *Checklist of Birds of Southern Illinois, 1968.* Mimeographed at Southern Illinois University, Carbondale.

1969   The Current Status of Certain Bird Species in Southern Illinois. *The Audubon Bulletin*, 150:12-15.

1972   Breeding Status of the Purple Gallinule, Brown Creeper, and Swainson's Warbler in Illinois. *The Wilson Bulletin*, 84:208-210.

Graber, Jean W. and Richard R. Graber

1965   Occurrence of Scissor-tailed Flycatcher in Illinois. *The Audubon Bulletin*, 136:5-7.

1973   Nesting Distribution of the Veery in Illinois. *Illinois Audubon Bulletin*, 164:50-52.

Graber, Richard R.

1957   Sprague's Pipit and LeConte's Sparrow in Illinois. *The Audubon Bulletin*, 102:5-7.

1968   Nocturnal Migration in Illinois, Different Points of View. *The Wilson Bulletin*, 80:36-71.

Graber, Richard R. and Jean W. Graber

1963   A Comparative Study of Bird Populations in Illinois, 1906-1909 and 1956-1958. *Illinois Nat. Hist. Survey Bulletin*, Vol. 28, Art. 3.

Graber, Richard R., Jean W. Graber, and Ethelyn L. Kirk

1971   Illinois Birds: Turdidae. *Illinois Nat. Hist. Survey Biological Notes*, No. 75.

1973   Illinois Birds: Laniidae. *Illinois Nat. Hist. Survey Biological Notes*, No. 83.

1974   Illinois Birds: Tyrannidae. *Illinois Nat. Hist. Survey Biological Notes*, No. 86.

Gregory, Stephen S.

1923   Western Grebe in Illinois. *Auk*, 40:526.

1948   Ferruginous Roughleg in Cook County, Illinois. *Auk*, 65:317.

Griscom, Ludlow

1922   Problems of Field Identification. *Auk*, 39:31-41.

Hahn, Paul

1963   *Where is that Vanished Bird?* Toronto, University of Toronto Press.

Hammond, E.K.

1943   Unusual Breeding Records from the Chicago Region. *Auk*, 60:599-600.

Hanson, Harold C. and Charles W. Kossack

1963   The Mourning Dove in Illinois. *Illinois Dept. of Conservation Technical Bulletin*, No. 2.

Hasbrouck, E.M.

1944a   Apparent Status of the European Widgeon in North America. *Auk*, 61:93-104.

1944b   The Status of Barrow's Goldeneye in the Eastern U.S. *Auk*, 61:544-554.

Helmeyer, Charles E. and Boardman Conover

1948   Catalogue of the Birds of the Americas. *Field Mus. of Nat. Hist. (Zool. Ser.)*, Vol. 13, Part 1, No. 3, p. 196.

Hine, Ashley

1924   Lewis's Woodpecker Visits Chicago. *Auk*, 41:156-157.

Holder, R.H.

1861   Birds of Illinois. *Trans. Illinois State Agriculture Society for 1859-60*, Vol. IV, pp. 605-613.

Hull, Edwin D.

1913   The Swallow-tailed Kite in DeWitt County, Illinois. *Auk*, 30:112.

Hurter, Julius

1881   The Harlequin Duck and the Glossy and Wood Ibises in Southern Illinois. *Bulletin of the Nuttall Ornithological Club*, 6:124.

Hyde, A. Sidney

1927   Rock Wren in Illinois. *Auk*, 44:111-112.

Illinois Audubon Society

1916-72   *The Audubon Bulletin*, Nos. 1-163.

1973-76   *Illinois Audubon Bulletin*, Nos. 164-177.

Kennicott, Robert

1855   Catalogue of Animals Observed in Cook County, Illinois. *Trans. Illinois State Agriculture Society for 1853-55*, Vol. I, pp. 580-591.

Kleen, Vernon M.

1972   Black-headed Grosbeaks in Illinois. *The Audubon Bulletin*, 163:20-21.

1972-74   *Illinois Statewide Spring Bird Counts*. Mimeographed. Springfield, Illinois. Department of Conservation.

1973   A Winter Record for the Indigo Bunting in Illinois. *Illinois Audubon Bulletin*, 166:30-31.

Lambert, Earl L.

1930   A Burrowing Owl Record for Hancock County, Illinois. *The Wilson Bulletin*, 42:213.

Larson, Gary E.

1973   The Monk Parakeet in Illinois: New Views of Alarm. *Illinois Audubon Bulletin*, 166:29-30.

Levy, Seymour H.

1963   LeConte's Sparrow Wintering in Northern Illinois. *The Wilson Bulletin*, 75:204.

1963   Late Spring Record of the Common Redpoll in Northern Illinois. *The Wilson Bulletin*, 75:205.

Loucks, William E.

1892   *Birds of Peoria and Tazewell Counties, Illinois.* Unpublished Manuscript in Peoria Library.

Matthews, Paul

1969   An Anhinga in Marion County. *The Audubon Bulletin*, 149:16.

Mayfield, Harold

1960   The Kirtland's Warbler. *Cranbrook Institute of Science Bulletin*, No. 40.

Mengel, Robert M.

1965   *The Birds of Kentucky.* Ornithological Monographs No. 3. The American Ornithologists' Union. Lawrence, Kansas. The Allen Press.

Mills, Harlow B. and Frank C. Bellrose

1959   Whooping Crane in the Mid-West. *Auk*, 76:234-235.

Mills, Harlow B., William C. Starrett, and Frank C. Bellrose

1966   Man's Effect on the Fish and Wildlife of the Illinois River. *Illinois Nat. Hist. Survey, Biological Notes*, No. 57.

Montgomery, Robert A. and James Rice

1967   Observation of Brant in Southern Illinois. *The Wilson Bulletin*, 79:242.

Moyer, John W.

1931   Black-bellied and Fulvous Tree Duck in Illinois. *Auk*, 48:258.

Musselman, T.E.

1916-17   Unusual Birds Along the Mississippi River near Quincy. *The Audubon Bulletin*, Winter, pp. 39-40.

1921   A History of the Birds of Illinois. *Journal of the Illinois State Hist. Soc.*, 14:1-73.

1937   Young Black Rail Banded in Illinois. *Auk*, 54:204.

1948   Hawk Owl in Illinois. *Auk*, 65:456.

1950   Three Brown Pelicans in Illinois. *Auk*, 67:233.

1951   Saw Whet Owl, *Aegolius a. acadicus*, Nesting in Illinois. *Auk*, 68:378-379.

1968   Chuck-wills-widow and Wood Ibis in Central Illinois. *The Wilson Bulletin*, 80:230.

National Audubon Society

1945-46   *The Season.*

1947-70   *Audubon Field Notes.* Vols. 1-24.

1971-72   *American Birds.* Vols. 25-30.

Nature Study Society of Rockford

1917-18   Birds of Rockford and Vicinity. *The Nature Study Society of Rockford Bulletin*, No. 4.

Nelson, Edward W.

1876   Birds of Northeastern Illinois. *Bulletin of the Essex Institute*, 8:89-155.

1877   Notes Upon Birds Observed in Southern Illinois Between July 17 and September 4, 1875. *Bulletin of the Essex Institute*, 9:31-65.

Nisbet, Ian C.

1970   Autumn Migration of the Blackpoll Warbler: Evidence for Long Flight Provided by Regional Survey. *Bird Banding*, 41:207-240.

Packard, Gary C.

1958   Yellow Rail at Champaign. *The Audubon Bulletin*, 107:8.

Parmalee, Paul W.

1958   Remains of Rare and Extinct Birds from Illinois Indian Sites. *Auk*, 75:169-176.

Parmalee, Paul W. and Barbara G. Parmalee

1959   Mortality of Birds at a Television Tower in Central Illinois. *The Audubon Bulletin*, 111:1-4.

Parmalee, Paul W. and Gregory Perino

1970   A Prehistoric Archaeological Record of the Roseate Spoonbill in Illinois. *Trans. of the Illinois State Acad. of Science*, 63:254-258.

Petersen, Peter C.

1972   Brown Pelican in Muscatine County. *Iowa Bird Life*, 42:51.

Pitelka, Frank A.

1940   Nashville Warbler Breeding in Illinois. *Auk*, 57:115-116.

Pough, Richard H.

1957   *Audubon Western Bird Guide.* Plate 12.

Pratten, Henry

1855   Catalogue of the Birds of Illinois. *Trans. Illinois State Agriculture Society for 1853-55*, Vol. I, pp. 598-609.

Princen, L.H.

1968   Unusual Bird Sightings in Central Illinois During 1967. *Proceedings of the Peoria Acad. of Science*, 1:46-49.

1969   Unusual Bird Sightings in Central Illinois During 1968. *Proceedings of the Peoria Acad. of Science*, 2:20-23.

1970   Unusual Bird Sightings in Central Illinois During 1969. *Proceedings of the Peoria Acad. of Science*, 3:24-27.

1972   Unusual Bird Sightings in Central Illinois During 1971. *Proceedings of the Peoria Acad. of Science*, 5:39-44.

1974   Unusual Bird Sightings in Central Illinois during 1973. *Proceedings of the Peoria Acad. of Science*, 7:26-30.

Quindry, L.

1929   Notes from Champaign County, Illinois. *Auk*, 46:556.

Randall, Robert Q.

1975   First State Record Great-tailed Grackle. *Illinois Audubon Bulletin*, 172:3.

Ridgway, Robert

1874   Catalogue of the Birds Ascertained to Occur in Illinois. *Annals of the Lyceum of Natural History, New York*, 10:364-394.

1880   On Six Species of Birds New to the Fauna of Illinois with Notes on Other Rare Illinois Birds. *Bulletin of the Nuttall Ornithological Club*, 5:30-32.

1881   A Revised Catalogue of the Birds Ascertained to Occur in Illinois. *Illinois State Laboratory of Natural History Bulletin*, No. 4, pp. 163-208. Bloomington.

1889-95   *The Ornithology of Illinois.* Springfield. Illinois Natural History Survey. Vol. 1, 1889; Vol. 2, 1895.

Roth, Roland R.

1967   *An Analysis of Avian Succession on Upland Sites in Illinois.* Master's Thesis.

Russell, Robert P., Jr.

1967   Is Your Latest Sighting on the Hypothetical List? *The Audubon Bulletin*, 144:11-15.

Sanborn, Colin C.

1922   The Season: Chicago Region. *Bird-Lore*, Vol. 24, pp. 45-46.

1930   Recent Notes from the Chicago Area. *Auk*, 47:268-269.

Schnell, Gary D.

1967   Frequency Distribution of Rough-legged Hawk. *The Audubon Bulletin*, 143:13-14.

Schorger, A.W.

1964   The Trumpeter Swan as a Breeding Bird in Minnesota, Wisconsin, Illinois, and Indiana. *The Wilson Bulletin*, 76:331-338.

Smart, Glen

1960   Ross' Goose Taken at Horseshoe Lake, Illinois. *The Wilson Bulletin*, 72:288-289.

Smith, E.T.

1941   The Seasons. *Audubon Magazine*, July-August, p. 393.

Smith, Harry R. and Paul W. Parmalee

1955   A Distributional Check List of the Birds of Illinois. *Illinois State Museum Popular Science Series*, Vol. IV.

Smith, Philo W., Jr.

1888   Nesting of the Nashville Warbler in Fulton County, Illinois. *Bay State Oologist*, 1:44.

Stevenson, James and Pierce Brodkorb

1933   Bird Notes from the Chicago Region. *Auk*, 50:371-373.

Stoddard, H.L.

1917   The Roseate Tern *(Sterna dougalli)* on Lake Michigan. *Auk*, 34:86.

Swink, Floyd

No date   *Birds of the Morton Arboretum.* Lisle, Illinois, The Morton Arboretum.

Thompson, Milton

1955   Notes on Unusual Birds. *The Audubon Bulletin*, 95:15.

U.S. Fish and Wildlife Service

1973   *Breeding Bird Survey, 1973.*

1976   *Breeding Bird Survey, 1975.*

Verner, Jared

1975   Pintails Nest Again at Goose Lake Prairie. *Illinois Audubon Bulletin*, 173:15.

Waldbauer, G.P. and J. Hays

1964   Breeding of the Purple Gallinule in Illinois. *Auk*, 81:227.

Walley, H.D.

1966   The Carolina Parakeet in Illinois. *The Wilson Bulletin*, 78:231-232.

Wasson, I.B.

1956   Close View of Black Swift. *The Audubon Bulletin*, 99:5.

Widmann, Otto

1907   A Preliminary Catalog of the Birds of Missouri. *Trans. of the Acad. of Science of St. Louis*, 17.

1909   A Second Record for the Fulvous Tree Duck Taken in Missouri. *Auk*, 26:304.

Wilds, Stephen D.

1972-73   Waterfowl Harvest on Keokuk Pool, Mississippi River 1969 and 1970. *Proc. Iowa Acad. of Science*, 79:79-84.

Woodruff, Frank M.

1896   The Raven in Illinois. *Auk*, 13:83-84.

1907   The Birds of the Chicago Area. *The Chicago Acad. of Science Bulletin*, No. 6.

Wyman, L.E.

1915   Richardson's Owl in Illinois. *Auk*, 32:101.

INDEX TO COMMON NAMES

Notes

Notes